Copper Coins and the Emperor's Wallet

Brill's Series on Modern East Asia in a Global Historical Perspective

VOLUME 9

The titles published in this series are listed at *brill.com/meah*

Copper Coins and the Emperor's Wallet

The Role of Currency in Ming China

By

Sui-Wai Cheung

BRILL

LEIDEN | BOSTON

Cover image: "The Chenghua emperor and a son at the Lantern Festival." The painting shows the Chenghua emperor (r. 1465–1487) celebrating the Lantern Festival with palace women and eunuchs in the first lunar month. Next to the emperor, a young prince points out something to his father. The child in this painting may have been the future emperor, Zhu Youtang. Credit: National Museum of China.

Library of Congress Cataloging-in-Publication Data

Names: Cheung, Sui-wai, 1961- author.
Title: Copper coins and the emperor's wallet : the role of currency in ming China / Sui-Wai Cheung.
Description: Boston, Massachusetts : Brill, 2024. | Series: Brill's series on modern east asia in a global historical perspective, 2212-1730 ; volume 9 | Includes bibliographical references and index.
Identifiers: LCCN 2023037660 (print) | LCCN 2023037661 (ebook) | ISBN 9789004687523 (hardback) | ISBN 9789004687530 (ebook)
Subjects: LCSH: Money–China. | China–Economic conditions.
Classification: LCC HG1285 .C46623 2024 (print) | LCC HG1285 (ebook) | DDC 332.4/951–dc23/eng/20230925
LC record available at https://lccn.loc.gov/2023037660
LC ebook record available at https://lccn.loc.gov/2023037661

Typeface for the Latin, Greek, and Cyrillic scripts: "Brill". See and download: brill.com/brill-typeface.

ISSN 2212-1730
ISBN 978-90-04-68752-3 (hardback)
ISBN 978-90-04-68753-0 (e-book)

This book is printed on acid-free paper and produced in a sustainable manner.

For Yin-shan and Laura

Contents

Acknowledgements

The author acknowledges with thanks the Faculty of Arts, The Chinese University of Hong Kong, for funding the research.

Figures, Tables, and Maps

Figures

Tables

Maps

Ming Dynasty Emperors

Personal name	Reign title and period	Temple name
Zhu Yuanzhang	Hongwu (1368–98)	Taizu
Zhu Yunwen	Jianwen (1399–1402)	Huidi
Zhu Di	Yongle (1403–1424)	Taizong, Chengzu
Zhu Gaochi	Hongxi (1424–1425)	Renzong
Zhu Zhanji	Xuande (1426–1435)	Xuanzong
Zhu Qizhen	Zhengtong (1436–1449)	Yingzong
Zhu Qiyu	Jingtai (1450–56)	Daizong, Jingdi
Zhu Qizhen	Tianshun (1457–1464)	Yingzong
Zhu Jianshen	Chenghua (1465–1487)	Xianzong
Zhu Youtang	Hongzhi (1488–1505)	Xiaozong
Zhu Houzhao	Zhengde (1505–1521)	Wuzong
Zhu Houcong	Jiajing (1521–1566)	Shizong
Zhu Zaihou	Longqing (1567–1572)	Muzong
Zhu Yijun	Wanli (1573–1620)	Shenzong
Zhu Changluo	Taichang (1620)	Guangzong
Zhu Youxiao	Tianqi (1621–1627)	Xizong
Zhu Youjian	Chongzhen (1628–1644)	Sizong

Ming Weights and Measures

Length

1 *chi* (foot) = 12.3 inches
10 *chi* = 1 *zhang* = 123 inches
180 *zhang* = 1 *li* = 22,140 inches (0.35 miles)

Area

1 *mu* = 0.14 acre
100 *mu* = 1 *qing* = 14 acres

Weight

1 *qian* = 0.13 ounce
10 *qian* = 1 *liang* (tael) =1.3 ounces
16 *liang* = 1 *jin* (catty) = 20.8 ounces (1.3 pounds)
100 catties = 1 *dan* = 130 pounds

Volume

1 *shi* = 107.4 liters
(*Note*: Though *shi* was a measure of volume, it was equal to 1 *dan* in weight.)

Sources: Edward L. Farmer, *Early Ming Government: The Evolution of Dual Capitals* (Cambridge: Harvard University Press, 1976), 2 (table 2: Terms of Measure); Ray Huang, *Taxation and Government Finance in Sixteenth-Century Ming China* (Cambridge: Cambridge University Press, 1974), xiv (Ming Weights and Measures); Frederick W. Mote and Denis Twitchett, ed., *The Cambridge History of China*, vol. 7: *The Ming Dynasty 1368–1644, Part 1* (Cambridge: Cambridge University Press, 2008), xxi (Ming Weights and Measures).

Currency and Taxation in Ming China, 1368–1644

In ancient China, the word for money was *quan* (fountain), because the ancient Chinese believed that money should flow like water in a fountain. They also believed that the profit from making coins was unlimited, like a fountain bringing forth endless water, because the product was worth more than it cost to make. This Chinese concept of state wealth was shared by all its dynastic governments.

As the ideal currency was durable in form and stable in supply, China, like other countries in the world, made their money out of metal. Early in the first century BCE, the Chinese historian Sima Qian wrote that gold, silver, and copper had been used as money as early as the first Chinese dynasty, the Xia dynasty (ca. 2070–1600 BCE).[1] Sima Qian also noted that Emperor Wudi (r. 141–87 BCE, Han dynasty), in whose court he served, had increased his wealth by issuing copper coins, leather money, and silver coins. The leather money was made from the skins of rare white deer, which were raised by the emperor himself in the imperial pasture. Each piece of deerskin was worth 400,000 copper coins.[2] The emperor also issued three grades of silver coins,[3] which were nearly as rare in Chinese history as the white deerskin money. (Ancient China had no rich silver mines, hence it was likely that Emperor Wudi made these coins from silver items that he already had in the palace.) Silver had long been used as a currency in China, but it circulated in the form of bullion and ingots.

The first metal used for casting coins in China was copper. Because raw copper was too soft to inscribe, the ancient Chinese made their copper coins out of bronze, an alloy of copper and tin. Before Ying Zheng unified China in 221 BCE, it was divided into several states, each with its own distinctive bronze

1 Sima Qian wrote *Shiji* [*Records of the Grand Historian*] (104 BCE, repr. Beijing: Zhonghua shuju, 1963), a monumental history of ancient China. See Peng Xinwei, *Zhongguo huobishi* (1958, repr. Shanghai: Shanghai renmin chubanshe, 1988), 64.

2 At the time, it was traditional for feudal lords to visit the emperor and give him a large piece of jade as a gift. Emperor Wudi required that every lord use a piece of this white deerskin as a mat for the jade. See Sima Qian, *Shiji*, 1426–27.

3 The silver coins were made of an alloy of silver and tin. The highest grade, inscribed with a dragon, was worth 3,000 copper cash; the second grade, inscribed with a horse, was worth 500 copper cash; and the lowest grade, inscribed with a tortoise, was worth 300 copper cash. See Sima Qian, *Shiji*, 1427.

 | DOI:10.1163/9789004687530_002

FIGURE 1 Strings of copper coins. Left: This famous painting, called *Qingming shanghe tu* [*Along the River during the Qingming Festival*], n.d., by Zhang Zeduan (1085–1145), depicts ordinary people in Kaifeng, capital of the Northern Song dynasty, on their Qingming Festival Day. Right: **A:** A father and son examine a street vendor's toys or snacks, which usually cost only a few coins each. **B:** In front of a food stall, two waiters carry strings of copper coins to pay a deliveryman standing next to his cart.
CREDIT: LEFT: PALACE MUSEUM, BEIJING. RIGHT: DESIGN & CULTURAL STUDIES WORKSHOP, SHIU-LAN (JULLY) HUANG AND WEI-CHAO CHANG, ALONG THE RIVER DURING THE QINGMING FESTIVAL (TAIPEI: COSMOS CLASSICS, 2016), 165–66.

coins, which were spade shaped in eastern China, knife shaped in central and southern China, and round in western China. They all had a small hole in the center (which could be round or square), so that they could be strung together and carried to market. (See Figure 1.) When Ying Zheng founded the Qin dynasty (221–207 BCE), he tried to impose a single standard for coins, but he was only able to regulate their shape; as a result, the round coin with a square hole became the common form for copper coins, not only during the Qin but throughout imperial China's long history, but their weights varied widely.[4] Peng

4 Each Qin coin was supposed to weigh 12 *zhu*, but, as historians have discovered, no two Qin coins weighed the same—at least none that have been unearthed by archeologists so far. One historian weighed 8 Qin coins and found that their average weight was 16 grams (each *zhu* weighed 0.75 gram); but another historian weighed 64 coins, to find that their average weight was only 10 grams (so each *zhu* weighed 0.625 gram). See Peng Xinwei, *Zhongguo huobi shi*, 83n6.

Xinwei, the pioneering historian who wrote the *Monetary History of China,* noted that copper cash was also the first state currency in unified China.[5]

Given that the ancient Chinese perceived the manufacture of money as *quan*, an endlessly flowing fountain of wealth, the question was: who should profit from it? Who should have the right to cast coins? In 81 BCE, a grand debate over this question was held among sixty senior officials in the imperial court of the Western Han dynasty and later recorded in the *Yantie lun* [*Discourses on Salt and Iron*]. Although all the officials agreed that making copper coins could generate profit, they argued over whether the throne or the public—common people, merchants, gentry, feudal lords, and so on—should have the monopoly on coin manufacture. One side thought that the throne should not compete for this profit with the people (*min*), whereas the other side warned that if the people made this profit, they would become rich enough to challenge the throne. The latter group won the support of Emperor Zhaodi (r. 87–74 BCE).[6] Thus casting coins was seen as an important source of wealth, and this wealth belonged to the throne.

This book examines the institutional history of copper coins—coins minted by the state—throughout the Ming. The archival sources on Ming coinage were imperial edicts and decrees, which focused on the coins' circulation in the capitals Nanjing and (especially) Beijing, where the imperial mints were located. For most of the dynasty, many of the copper coins in circulation in the provinces were from previous dynasties or made by counterfeiters. In addition to exploring how these various kinds of coins affected one another in the market, we look at how copper coins interacted with and were affected by paper notes and silver ingots, the other forms of state currency during the Ming. All three types of currency would come to be accepted in tax payments, but at the beginning, the founding emperor, Zhu Yuanzhang, set up a taxation system that consisted mostly of in-kind (goods) and labor services. Households were registered by occupation and taxed accordingly, in order to support different levels of government with labor services, grain, other kinds of food, weapons, timber, cloth, stationery, and so on. These resources—or this lack of resources when the system foundered—also had an effect on Ming currency.

5 Peng Xinwei, *Zhongguo huobi shi*, 78.

6 A contemporary official named Huan Kuan recorded and printed this debate under the title *Yantie lun* [*Discourses on Salt and Iron*]. See Wang Liqi, *Yantie lunjiaozhu* (Beijing: Zhonghua shuju, 1992), especially 56–58. *Yan tielun* was reprinted at least twice in the Ming (1501 and 1554). The Institute for Advanced Studies on Asia Library at Tokyo University holds both editions.

Zhu, the son of impoverished tenant farmers, was determined to establish an agrarian empire, one in which state administration was supported by farmers, not merchants or nomadic herders, such as the Mongols from the steppes north of China, who had added China to their empire in 1279, founding the Yuan dynasty. Born in 1328 in a time of drought, famine, and peasant rebellions, Zhu Yuanzhang had lost most of his family to starvation by the time he was sixteen. To survive, he joined a Buddhist monastery, became a wandering beggar, and, as a young man, joined the Red Turbans, a rebel army that espoused Confucianism. He rose through the ranks to become its military leader and in 1368, at the age of forty, overthrew the Yuan (Mongol) dynasty, founding the Ming dynasty. He reigned as the Hongwu emperor for thirty years.[7]

As the founding emperor, Zhu was a conservative who wanted to return to ancient Chinese tradition as well as an isolationist.[8] He created a kind of state administration so different from that of the Yuan that historians now call it "the Hongwu model." Whereas the Yuan empire had been a multinational state in which the government was composed of diverse races and cultures, including Mongols, Han Chinese, Muslims, and people from the Middle East and Europe, Zhu Yuanzhang envisioned an empire only for Han Chinese. He recruited officials from the scholarly-elite of the Han Chinese and paid for state administration by taxing his subjects, requiring them to render labor service and in-kind taxes, rather than money. His vision for the empire and prejudice against commerce were summed up in his statement: "When producers are hard at work and consumers are few, abundance comes as a natural result."[9] Agricultural production was of primary importance: to protect Ming crops from Mongol incursion, he had the Great Wall along the northern frontier repaired and extended, creating a literal division between nomadic herders and farming cultures. Unlike the Yuan empire, which was expansionist in terms of territorial acquisition and external trade, Zhu restricted the Ming from expanding beyond the Great Wall and discouraged maritime trade,

7 For a good biography of Zhu Yuanzhang, see Wu Han, *Zhu Yuanzhang zhuan* (1965, repr. Tianjin: Baihua wenyi chubanshe, 2000).

8 Ray Huang commented on Zhu's embrace of Confucianism and neo-Confucianism, noting: "The reliance on doctrinal cohesion to maintain communal order exceeded the extent reached by any other dynasty in Chinese history." See Ray Huang, "The History of the Ming Dynasty and Today's World," *Chinese Studies in History* 19, no. 4 (1986): 5.

9 *Ming shilu*, Taizu (repr. Taipei: Academia Sinica, 1962), 3682, quoted in Huang, "The History of the Ming Dynasty," 14. See also R. Bin Wong, "Taxation and Good Governance in China, 1500–1914," in *The Rise of Fiscal States: A Global History, 1500–1914*, ed. Bartolomé Yun-Casalilla et al. (Cambridge: Cambridge University Press, 2012).

forbidding his subjects to go to sea, fraternize with foreigners visiting China, or buy foreign goods.[10]

After his death in 1398, maritime trade gradually revived, especially under the Yongle emperor in the early fifteenth century, when Admiral Zheng He made seven voyages as commander of the Treasure Fleet (*Baochuan*). As Chinese exports, such as silk and the distinctive cobalt-blue and white Ming porcelain, were in high demand in Japan and Southeast Asia, the thriving market gave Chinese subjects a way to (illegally) avoid their household registration and its tax obligations, shaking the financial foundations of the government. In the mid-fifteenth century, to save the empire, the Ming government abandoned the household registration system to levy a tax on land to be paid in silver. Ming China was still an agrarian empire, supported by its farmers and its land tax, but the government increasingly relied on silver, instead of rice, to pay its soldiers. In the following century, the increase in trade from the Portuguese, Spanish, and Dutch brought in even more silver from the Americas and Japan, as well as seeds and starters for new crops—such as maize and sweet potatoes—that were hardier than rice, increased agricultural output, and made famine less likely.

But, as the historian Ray Huang noted, throughout its history, China was beset by Mongol invasions, flooding from the Yellow River, and a capricious climate, which could bring flooding or drought or both during monsoons.[11] By 1628, when Zhu Youjian became the seventeenth Ming emperor, drought and unprecedented cold weather had caused successive years of crop failure from central to northern China. Peasants could not pay their land tax, and, without their silver, the Ming government could no longer pay the soldiers who defended the Great Wall along its northern frontier. Military leaders concentrated their limited defense at the Shanhai Pass, the northeastern segment of the Great Wall, to defend Beijing against the Manchus. But in northwestern China, unpaid soldiers mutinied, joined by starving peasants. In the third lunar

10 In 1395, four years before he died, Zhu even warned his descendant emperors against attacking fifteen Asian countries because the empire would reap no benefit from annexing them in terms of resources and people. They included Korea, Japan, Liuqiu (now Okinawa), Annam (now northern Vietnam), and Siam (now Thailand). See Wu Han, *Zhu Yuanzhang zhuan*, 163. In this sense, the Hongwu emperor was practical about foreign affairs.

11 Huang attributed China's early adoption of a centralized government to three factors: the need to mount a national (not just local) defense after Mongol tribes attacked the northern farmers, the need for a coordinated system of flood control throughout the length of the Yellow River, and the constant threat of droughts or floods from the unreliability of the monsoon rains. See Huang, "The History of the Ming Dynasty," 4–7.

month of 1644, these rebels, led by Li Zicheng, captured Beijing, and the last Ming emperor committed suicide. The Ming general at Shanhai Pass allowed Manchus into China, forming an alliance with them to retake Beijing in the hope of suppressing the rebellion. In the fifth month, a joint force of Manchus and Ming elite troops defeated Li Zicheng and captured Beijing, beginning the Qing dynasty.

Despite the founding emperor's aversion to relying on money to run his empire, at the beginning of the Ming two types of metal currency—silver and copper—had been circulating in the market for centuries. According to Gresham's law, "bad money drives out good money."[12] In other words, the use of two different metal currencies in a single market—or bimetallism—encouraged people to spend the bad money and hoard their good money until the bad money gradually disappeared from the market. Irving Fisher restated Gresham's law more accurately as "cheap money drives out dear money," arguing: "When anyone has the choice of paying his debts in either of two moneys, motives of economy will prompt him to use the cheaper."[13]

In late imperial China, copper coins were cheap money, and silver was dear money. But, contrary to Gresham's law, copper coins did *not* drive out silver. Fernand Braudel, writing about bimetallism in premodern Europe, stated that gold and silver were "hostile brothers."[14] But in late imperial China, silver bullion and copper coins circulated simultaneously. Economic historian Chen Chau-nan stated that this was because the silver-copper exchange ratio in China was so much higher than the gold-silver ratio in Europe, making silver and copper poor substitutes for each other.[15] Gresham's law did not apply to bimetallism in China because of the poor substitution between silver and copper, the dear and the cheap money, respectively. Instead, as we shall see, this law was in effect among many varieties of copper coins. If people were allowed to settle their debts with any kind of copper coin, they would hold on to the good coins and pay their debts with worn, low-weight, bent, defaced, or clipped ones.

---

12 Named for Sir Thomas Gresham, a financial agent for Queen Elizabeth I in 1558.

13 Irving Fisher, *The Purchasing Power of Money: Its Determination and Relation to Credit Interest and Crises* (New York: Macmillan, 1926), 113–14.

14 Fernand Braudel, *The Structures of Everyday Life: The Limits of the Possible* (Berkeley: University of California Press, 1992), 459.

15 Chen Chau-nan wrote that the value of copper to silver "was more than 100:1 in nineteenth-century China as compared to the gold/silver ratio of about 16:1 in Europe, [which] would also have contributed to the difficulty of substituting one currency for the other," in "Flexible Bimetallic Rates in China, 1650–1850: A Historical Example of Optimum Currency Areas," *Journal of Money, Credit and Banking* 7, no. 3 (1975): 361.

When the Ming emperors issued copper coins, they attempted to fix a ratio between copper coins and silver. Because it had more than one type of legal money, the state needed a ratio between them so that it could use one money to pay for the other. For administrative convenience, such as to pay salaries, a ruler would attempt to "fix" the exchange ratio. Chen Chau-nan noted that the exchange ratio between the two monies fluctuated freely, in spite of authorities' desperate attempts to set an official rate that would carry over in the market.[16] Considering that this was the case, Chen wondered why China did not simply abandon the dual monetary system and shift to a single silver standard, for the sake of convenience.[17]

On the one hand, it was true that local societies in Ming China always needed small change, that is, copper cash. When a villager went to the farmers' market, he might give one or two coins as alms to a beggar and then spend the rest at the market. (At this time, the daily wage of a worker in Beijing was 25–30 cash, and a piece of paper cost 1 copper cash; a piece of cake, 1 cash; 10 slices of betel nut, 2 cash; a catty of firewood, 2.5 cash; a duck, 6–7 cash; and a cat, 30–40 cash.)[18] But copper coins had been used for centuries, and many types of coins from earlier dynasties were still in circulation. There was no real danger of running out of copper cash. Why did Ming emperors continue to mint them, even when they lacked the resources to do so? And why did copper coins, small change, become the state currency at a time when copper coins were rarely used at all in Europe?

Here it must be noted that the Hongwu emperor did not use the few copper coins that he had minted or the paper notes that were also a state currency in state administration, at least not at first. He diminished their monetary function, paying his soldiers in rice, and gave his copper coins and paper money, along with other gifts such as silk cloth, to honored guests. He designed his state administration such that money played an insignificant role. Although he wanted this state of affairs to continue after his death, it proved impossible to maintain. But much of the fiscal and civil administration that provided the context for copper coin manufacture was set up—or set in motion—by the founding emperor.

The Hongwu emperor had a very clear idea of how his agrarian empire should be administered. He wanted a simple bureaucracy, supported by

16 Chen Chau-nan, "Bimetallism: Theory and Controversy in Perspective," *History of Political Economy* 4, no. 1 (1972): 101.

17 Chen, "Flexible Bimetallic Exchange Rates in China," 360.

18 The literature and scholarly writings of the time give us a rough idea of the purchasing power of a copper coin. See Peng Xinwei, *Zhongguo huobishi*, 692–93, 695, 727.

farmers. Ming China comprised about 1,100 counties, but each county had only one magistrate, appointed by the emperor, plus a few assistants who worked mostly on criminal cases. As we shall see in Chapter 1, instead of using local magistrates, the emperor appointed rural landlords through the *lijia* system (see Chapter 1) to collect and deliver the land tax—the rice that paid his soldiers and civil officials.

Zhu Yuanzhang's desire to avoid the uncertainty of relying on money had its own complications. Without money, it was impossible for all the resources from taxation (especially grain and labor) first to be gathered in the capital and then to be redistributed to their destinations. Ray Huang wrote that, to keep the in-kind taxes from piling up at service facilities, the revenue-gathering agencies delivered them directly to dispensing agencies, and "items of income and expenditure were matched up so as to cancel each other out."[19]

Adding to the problems of fiscal accountability, as Huang pointed out, the Ming government, acting from the capital without regard to differences across the empire, applied a uniform land tax across China despite vast regional variations in growing conditions, crops, markets, and even land tenure arrangements and units of measurement.[20] Huang wrote that the only way that local officials could compensate for these variations was to manipulate their data and revise or ignore government regulations, noting:

> This lack of exactitude in the fiscal machinery had numerous consequences. An outstanding example was that Ming officials customarily compensated for shortages in one item of state revenue with funds and materials derived from another. What we regard as the salt gabelle [the state salt monopoly] in Ming times actually contained portions of the land taxes. After the middle period the land taxes also became inseparable, if not totally indistinguishable, from several other sources of income. Government income and expenditures in Ming times can be compared to water channels in a swamp, in that they had constant tendency to diverge and re-converge.[21]

Nanjing, as the imperial capital and home of the Hongwu emperor, became the center of these shifting channels of income and expenditure.

---

19 Ray Huang, *Taxation and Government Finance in Sixteenth-Century Ming China* (Cambridge: Cambridge University Press, 1974), 5.

20 Huang, *Taxation and Government Finance*, 2.

21 Huang, *Taxation and Government Finance*, 3.

The emperor became the final authority in fiscal (and all other areas of) administration, but in the early Ming, as in earlier dynasties, a high official known as the chief councilor was the head of the office of the Secretariat and the working head of the government. The chief councilor acted as a prime minister, considering all aspects of state affairs and then deciding how to proceed. Zhu Yuangzhang appointed Hu Weiyong, one of his early supporters, as the chief councilor to help him keep track of all the details of running an empire. Hu read all the petitions and documents submitted by the six government ministries (see below) and then selected the important ones to discuss with the emperor. Because this also gave Hu the option of keeping the emperor from knowing about the real issues, Zhu Yuanzhang fired Hu and abolished the institution of the Secretariat, determined to lead the government himself.

The historian Charles O. Hucker noted that the Secretariat not only administered the empire "effectively" but had been "a significant potential check on the absolutism of the emperor" and argued that this was the real reason that the Hongwu emperor abolished the Secretariat and had Hu executed in 1380.[22] Although several accusations were made against Hu, including that he had conspired with the Japanese to assassinate the emperor, historians have generally agreed with Hucker that there was not enough evidence against Hu to prove such a claim. At any rate, Zhu abolished the Secretariat and even cautioned his descendants against reviving it because of doing so could expose them to the risk of being accused of treason. Zhu envisioned the throne as the head of the government.[23] This meant that the emperor had to attend to *all* administrative details, even the most inconsequential. Huang noted: "In one eight-day period Hung-wu [Hongwu] is said to have received 1,660 memorials in which 3,391 issues were discussed."[24] Huang also wrote that the emperor must have believed that these details were important, because the practice of collecting in-kind taxes heightened the risk that tax goods would accumulate, "over-burdening the service facilities, the weakest section of the whole fiscal establishment."[25]

But by abolishing the Secretariat, and in effect becoming his own prime minister, Zhu took on a mountain of paperwork. Before the end of his reign, he was calling for secretarial help from the Hanlin Academy, a loosely organized group of litterateurs who drafted and edited the more ceremonious imperial

22 Charles O. Hucker, *The Traditional Chinese State in Ming Times (1368–1644)* (Tucson: University of Arizona Press, 1961), 53.

23 See also Wu Han, *Zhu Yuanzhang zhuan*, 175–78.

24 Huang, *Taxation and Government Finance,* 5.

25 Huang, *Taxation and Government Finance.*

pronouncements as well as imperially sponsored historical and other works.[26] The Hongwu emperor treated these scholars as his private secretaries.

After Zhu abolished the Secretariat, he turned over civil administration to the six government ministries, which were named for their responsibilities as follows: the Ministry of Personnel, the Ministry of Revenue, the Ministry of Rites, the Ministry of War, the Ministry of Punishment, and the Ministry of Works. Although these ministries were the official civil administration, they acted independently of one another, and none of their ministers had the power to make policy, only to suggest them and attempt to carry them out. But real power rested with the emperor.

The supreme authority of the emperor became a weakness in Ming fiscal administration. The Hongwu emperor tried to remain apprised of every trifling administrative detail, but many later emperors did not; they found it more convenient to delegate increasing responsibility to their "secretaries" from the Hanlin Academy. The result was that this group served as a buffer between the emperor and the six government ministries. During the Yongle reign (1402–1424), the emperor's reliance on secretarial aides from the Hanlin Academy as well as his palace eunuchs became more routine, and by the time of the Xuande reign (1425–1435), the practice had produced an important new institution, the Grand Secretariat (*Nei'ge*).[27] The Grand Secretariat consisted of three or four grand secretaries. They were usually low-ranking officials who were also appointed as ministers or vice ministers in the six ministries only for the purpose of prestige. The Secretariat gradually developed collegial procedures for handling routine matters under the leadership of an informally designated senior grand secretary.[28] As Hucker pointed out, this gave a senior grand secretary nearly the same power as a prime minister.[29]

Although the Grand Secretariat may have been a check on the emperor, the institution had weaker foundations than the grand councilors in the early Ming.

---

26 Charles O. Hucker, *A Dictionary of Official Titles in Imperial China* (1985, repr. Taipei: Southern Materials Center, 1988), 223.

27 The Xuande emperor established the Inner Court Study (*Neishutang*), where four Hanlin scholars taught 200–300 young eunuchs. Some of these eunuchs later became the emperor's secretaries, were in touch with court officials, and became influential at court. See Shih-shan Henry Tsai, *The Eunuchs in the Ming Dynasty* (Albany: State University of New York, 1996), 13.

28 Hucker, *A Dictionary of Official Titles*, 72–73.

29 "The way was open, consequently, for a senior Grand Secretary to attain to almost the same level of authority as that enjoyed formerly by a prime minister. The Grand Secretary even came to be referred to commonly as 'the administration.'" See Hucker, *The Traditional Chinese State,* 54.

The grand secretaries attended and counseled the emperor, remonstrated with him, screened documents submitted to him by all government agencies, and drafted the imperial rescripts in which decisions were promulgated. Of necessity, they worked closely with the palace eunuchs, who very often controlled all access to the throne. Moreover, their career trajectories commonly led them onto the Grand Secretariat through a succession of posts as academicians engaged in editing and compiling, rather than through demanding administrative posts. For these reasons, officialdom in general, known as the Outer Court, did not find it easy to accept grand secretaries as its leaders and spokesmen. Instead, officials commonly associated grand secretaries with the Inner Court of palace women, eunuchs, and imperial kinsmen and in-laws. In their role as coordinating go-betweens, grand secretaries often found themselves distrusted and reviled by irascible emperors, on the one hand, and indignant officials opposed to a government run by imperial whim, on the other.[30] As we shall see, Ming fiscal administration was hampered even further by the blurred and shifting line between the public purse and the emperor's wallet.

Following this introduction, the book consists of four chapters that describe different phases in the currency and taxation system during the Ming dynasty and a conclusion that answers questions raised by Chen, other economic historians, and me, as well as disproving theories proposed by others. As discussed in these chapters, Western economic theories on state money in general and Ming China in particular did not always apply to the Ming coinage system. The vibrant global trade as well as in China's domestic market economy in the sixteenth century attract great scholarly interest, yet the research literature lacks a thorough study on the institutional history of copper coins in the Ming, which is crucial for understanding the silver-copper dual money system in late imperial China. This book fills this gap in the scholarship on China's monetary and fiscal past.

As the first in-depth study of Ming state coinage, this book also looks at some of the political and social factors that affected the coinage system in each reign period and shows how ideas about the coinage system and whom it should benefit changed over the course of the Ming as emperors, ministries, and provincial governments vied for a portion of the "fountain of wealth" from the coinage system.

Chapter 1 chronicles the history of paper money, called the "precious note," as a state currency, from its use as a gift to the changes in its function and its place in the market from 1368 to 1435. Under the Hongwu emperor, the

30 Hucker, *A Dictionary of Official Titles*, 73.

government collected taxes in kind and in labor services through household registration, allowing Zhu Yuanzhang to run his empire without money. Not until the final decade of the fourteenth century did he begin to use his state currency to pay the salaries of provincial officials. As "precious notes" flooded the market and depreciated in value, the Hongwu emperor tried to forbid the use of copper coins and silver. By the time of the Yongle reign, officials understood that if the government wanted its paper money to circulate, it had to allow people to use the "precious note" to pay taxes.

Chapter 2 shows that, during the fifteenth century, when the ban on tributary missions was lifted, foreign trade flourished, and market activities were revived. Taking advantage of this, the Ministry of Revenue was the first government institution to convert in-kind taxes into payment in silver. In 1465 the Chenghua emperor gave copper coins official recognition as well, when they were accepted for certain tax payments and government fees. This marked the beginning of their role in Ming government finance but not the end of the state's quarrel with their use in the market.

Chapter 3 examines how the emperors from 1465 to 1566 ran their palaces as the rise in commercial activities further eroded the Hongwu model of in-kind taxes and labor services. By the time of the Hongzhi emperor (1488–1505), when many households as well as individuals had avoided registration to live as "free workers," the Department of Imperial Banquets, which provided food for the palace as well as for state banquets, began to run out of money. The Hongzhi emperor repeatedly ordered the Ministry of Revenue to lend it silver, but the loans attracted criticism by officials. In 1503, in a desperate attempt to pay his operating expenses, the Hongzhi emperor reopened the imperial mint, hoping to make a profit from casting coins but lacked enough money to buy the raw copper. For the first time, copper coins were made out of brass, instead of bronze.

Chapter 4 discusses changes in monetary policy from 1567 to 1644, which covers the reign of the Longqing, Wanli, Taichang, Tianqi, and Chongzhen emperors. Although the coinage system failed to replace in-kind taxes for provisioning the emperor's table, government officials still believed that minting a coin, which was worth more in silver than it cost to produce, could provide unlimited wealth if only it were better managed, and they intended to take a share of the profit in order to benefit "the people." Shortly after the death of the Jiajing emperor in 1566, provincial governments took over control of the manufacture of copper coin from the throne. From 1567 to 1644, during the reign of the last five Ming emperors, bureaucratic institutions tried to generate revenue from their own mints.

The conclusion answers Chen Chau-nan's question as to why Ming administration did not abandon copper and switch to silver, takes another look at why bimetallism created "hostile brothers" in Europe but not in China, and debunks economic historian Richard von Glahn's theory that a silver economy replaced a copper coin economy. Moreover, we illustrate the differences between European theories and Chinese ideas about money and the value of their coins.

By studying the institutional history of copper coins—when, how, by whom, with what, and why they were made—and how copper cash interacted with and was affected by the other types of currency (paper notes and silver) used throughout the Ming dynasty, we show that the goal of the Ming coinage system was not to strengthen the overall economy but, rather, to create a new source of income, especially after the breakdown of the household registration system, when the emperor needed another income stream in order to maintain his domain in Beijing. But despite the emperor's hopes, copper coins never played a major role in palace finance. By the final years of the Ming dynasty, their major function was for paying construction workers to build palace halls and emperors' tombs.

This book looks below the shifting surface of the story of copper coinage in Ming China. It reveals how the imperial coffers were financed, how emperors and statesmen, as well as common people, perceived and used the copper coins at their disposal and exposes the impecunious reality of the Sons of Heaven.

CHAPTER 1

How Precious was a Precious Note? State Currency in the Early Ming, 1368–1435

1 The Value of Paper

The first paper money in China can be traced to the eleventh century, when merchants invented the *jiaozi* (exchange bills) for the annual silk fair in Yizhou, Sichuan Province. The fair attracted silk merchants from all over China, who found that the large quantity of copper coins they needed for the fair made them heavy and unwieldy to carry. Paper *jiaozi* were easier to manage than strings (or wagonloads) of copper coins and progressed from IOUs signed by reputable merchants to promissory notes from merchant banks.[1] In 1023, taking advantage of the situation, the Song government established a currency bureau and monopolized the issuance of *jiaozi*, making it the official Song currency, along with copper coins. In 1024, the Song court issued its first official paper note.[2]

In 1127 after the Song government lost control over northern China to the Jurchen-ruled Jin dynasty, China was divided into two opposing regimes, but both issued paper money to pay administrative and, especially, military expenses. In the early thirteenth century, the Mongols rose in the north, conquering the Jin in 1234. In 1271, Kublai Khan established the Yuan dynasty, financing his war against the Southern Song dynasty with paper money. A few years later, Marco Polo traveled to China, later claiming to have served at the court of Kublai Khan. Polo left an impressive account of the circulation of paper money there:

---

1 To foster interregional trade at their silk fair, local merchants set up a bank in Yizhou with branches in other major cities. For a 3 percent charge, a traveling merchant could deposit coins in a branch bank and retrieve them in Yizhou, or vice versa. This was a new form of money, which soon attracted the attention of the Song court. In 1024, using the excuse that the merchant banks were vulnerable to bankruptcy, the imperial court took over the issue of *jiaozi* and called it *guan jiaozi* (official *jiaozi*). See Peng Xinwei, *Zhongguo huobi shi*, 431.

2 See William N. Goetzmann and Elisabeth Koll, "Paying in Paper: A Government Voucher from the Southern Song," in *The Origins of Value: The Financial Innovations That Created Modern Capital Markets*, ed. William N. Goetzmann and K. Geert Rouwenhorst (New York: Oxford University Press, 2005), 93. See also Yang Lien-sheng, *Money and Credit in China, a Short History* (Cambridge: Harvard University, 1952), 53.

 | DOI:10.1163/9789004687530_003

> This paper currency is circulated in every part of the Great Khan's dominions; nor dare any person, at the peril of his life, refuse to accept it. All his subjects receive it without hesitation, because, wherever their business may call them, they can dispose of it in the purchase of any merchandise they may require, such as pearls, jewels, gold, or silver. With it, in short, every article may be procured.[3]

By 1375, when the Hongwu emperor and founder of the Ming dynasty issued its own paper money, paper currency had been circulating in China for almost 350 years.[4]

With its use of paper notes, China seemed to take the global lead in developing nominal money—that is, money with little or no value of its own. At the time, many European countries still used only using metal currency. As the historian Richard von Glahn stated,

> For those who imagine the evolution of monetary systems as a linear progression from primitive commodity monies to gold and silver coinage and finally to purely nominal currencies like paper money, the early appearance of paper money in China in the eleventh century appears to be a glaring anomaly.[5]

Von Glahn explained this by noting the wide differences in economic thought between China and the West. Until early modern times, Western economic thought was dominated by the Aristotelian tradition—the belief that the value of money came from its exchange value as a commodity. Thus monetary standards in the West were based on precious metals, namely silver and gold. He wrote: "Such a conception had little tolerance for fiat currencies." In contrast, classical Chinese monetary theory emphasized the duty of a ruler "to overcome the vicissitudes of dearth and plenty and to provide for the material needs of his subjects." This gave ample endorsement to the use of fiat currencies, such as paper money, to achieve that goal.[6]

Alfred Mitchell-Innes, a British politician and economist in the early twentieth century, saw all forms of money as tokens, whose weight or material was

---

3 *The Travels of Marco Polo*, ed. Milton Rugoff (New York: New American Library, 1986), 125.

4 Richard von Glahn presented a good summary of the development of paper money from Song to Ming dynasties, in his "The Origins of Paper Money," in Goetzmann and Rouwenhorst, ed., *The Origins of Value*, 65–89.

5 Von Glahn, "The Origins of Paper Money," 66.

6 Von Glahn, "The Origins of Paper Money," 66.

unimportant.[7] What was significant was the name or distinguishing mark of the issuer, which would not guarantee a metallic standard but did guarantee that the issuer would accept this particular token to pay a tax debt. In other words, Mitchell-Innes regarded currency in terms of its use as credit.[8] Whether a ruler cast a coin or printed paper money, he created a token that could be used in the market and to pay taxes.

In this chapter, I discuss another use of paper money in China: money as an imperial gift. According to Mitchell-Innes, a major purpose of money was for paying taxes. But when the Hongwu emperor issued paper money, he did not intend to receive it back in taxes. He presented it as a gift to honored guests. Not until 1393 did the gifting function of the state currency end.

In addition to using paper money as a gift instead of for tax payment, the Hongwu emperor showed an aversion to reliance on money for administering his empire. After the Hongwu emperor began to issue money (copper coins and then paper notes), he did not use it for state administration. As a rebel leader, Zhu Yuanzhang cast coins to pay his soldiers,[9] but as the Hongwu emperor, he paid his soldiers in grain.

Initially Zhu even experimented with having farmers deliver their tax grain directly to the soldiers for whom it was intended. In 1388, he had 5,000 civilian households in Yingtian Prefecture in South Zhili Province deliver their tax grain to the 5,000 soldiers in the Jingwu Guard—a "lateral transfer" aimed at relieving the burden on service facilities. Ray Huang noted: "Although this fantastic procedure was later discontinued, the principle of disbursing tax revenues without first consolidating the payments persisted and became a general practice under the Ming."[10] This added to the fiscal obfuscation that plagued the empire.

Throughout most of the founding emperor's reign, taxes were paid in labor services or in kind and determined by household registration. Household

7 The opinions of Alfred Mitchell-Innes came from two articles published in the 1910s: "What Is Money?," *Banking Law Journal* (May 1913): 377–408; idem, "The Credit Theory of Money," *Banking Law Journal* (December 1913–January 1914): 151–68. These articles were reprinted as chapters in L. Randall Wray, ed., *Credit and State Theories of Money: The Contributions of A. Mitchell Innes* (Cheltenham, UK: Edward Elgar, 2004), 14–49 and 50–78, respectively.

8 See Wray, *Credit and State Theories of Money*, 20, 42.

9 Peng Xinwei, *Zhongguo huobi shi*, 637. In addition to Zhu, many other warlords, such as Han Lin'er, Zhang Shicheng, Xu Shouhui, and Chen Youliang, built mints to pay their soldiers. See Zhu Pengshou, *Anle kangpingshi suibi* (Beijing: Zhonghua shuju, 1982), 252.

10 Huang wrote that this practice continued into the Qing, until the late 1800s. See Huang, *Taxation and Governmental Finance*, 45.

registration was fundamental to running the Ming state and the reason that the Hongwu emperor could manage his empire without money.

2 Managing an Empire without Money

2.1 *Household Registration for Goods and Services*

Household registration as a tool for taxation and social control dated back to ancient China.[11] In the early Ming dynasty, household registration was a way of categorizing households by occupation and geographic location in order to levy in-kind taxes and labor services. Many of these goods and services were used to support local government and military garrisons, so it was important to keep the local households as stable as possible, which was accomplished by making the household occupation hereditary and its location permanent.[12]

The main household categories were: civilians (landowner-farmers), artisans and craftsmen, merchants, salt farmers, and the military. In addition, there were other, minor occupational categories, such as Buddhist monks and Daoist priests. Because the state found it unreasonable to ask monks and priests for labor services, it instead restricted their numbers. Being a scholar or a scholar-official was another important occupation, considered the first of the four traditional occupations in Confucianism,[13] but it was not a household category. Except in cases in which military victories were rewarded with an official position, the only way to become a scholar-official was to pass the imperial examinations—which required students to write essays requiring applicants to employ a word-perfect knowledge of the *Four Books* and *Five Classics* of ancient China (the Confucian classics, written before 300 BCE) to solve government problems. The exams were designed to be difficult to ensure that officials earned their place in the state bureaucracy on the basis of merit,

11 To make household registration effective, Shang Yang, the prime minister of the Qin state during the Warring States period (276–221 BCE), institutionalized penalties for those who escaped it. His measures helped the Qin state become powerful, and, a century later, under the rule of Ying Zheng, the Qin unified China. Jason Young, *China's Hukou System: Markets, Migrants and Institutional Change* (London: Palgrave Macmillan, 2013), 30–31.

12 Although Ming law did not state outright that people were forbidden to relocate, everyone was registered in a particular household by locale as well as occupation. Because household members had to offer their labor services in person and locally, it was nearly impossible for them to move out of their villages without becoming tax evaders.

13 According to classical Confucian tradition, the four main occupations were, in order of importance: scholars and scholar-officials, landowners-farmers, artisans, and merchants.

rather than inherited power or wealth.[14] Scholar-officials were exempt from a portion of their land taxes and labor services.[15]

To make it easier for the government to collect labor services and in-kind taxes and to keep that tax base stable, the head of a household was registered in a particular occupation at a specific geographic location, and his sons and other descendants were supposed to follow him in that occupation and remain in that place. Just as every generation in the household worked in the same occupation, a household was expected to engage in only one occupation. In reality, there was plenty of crossover between occupations, and many people had two or more jobs. For example, military men who became officials after they were promoted following a battlefield victory might become landowners as well. Farmers took on a role as merchants when they sold their crops In the local marketplace, as did artisans who sold their wares. Depending on the growing season and the weather, farmers traveled to the city to work as artisan-laborers, and artisans took seasonal work on the farms. Some artisans who were recruited to live in the capital turned their city dwellings into shops and became merchants as well; and merchants could also become farmers or act as agents for scholar-officials who wanted to engage in commerce.

Other than the fact that people held more than one occupation or juggled seasonal occupations, the household registration system also involved a certain amount of attrition. If a farmer or artisan went bankrupt, or if he preferred to live and work as a "free worker"—that is, someone unregistered in any household and hidden from the labor-service taxation system—he could perform heavy labor, for instance, as a sailor or boat hauler on the Grand Canal. A farmer-landowner could also escape household registration by becoming a tenant farmer. If he did not want to pay land taxes in kind or contribute labor services, the landowner could donate his land to a temple or sell it to a scholar-official's household. In that case, he was listed in the tax record as a tenant, slave, servant, or adoptive son, whichever was appropriate for the

14 The imperial examinations were civil service exams at three levels: prefectural, provincial, and imperial. Passing the last two ensured scholars of official positions. The exams were grueling and required years of study in most cases, although wealthy people were allowed to buy junior official positions or degrees at any time; and when the country was in crisis, the state even sold high positions and degrees. Also, the cost of hiring a tutor and taking years to study for the exams usually meant that only sons in wealthier households could afford to do so.

15 In the early Ming, officials had to pay in-kind taxes on land that they owned, but in 1521 they were exempted from land taxes according to their rank. See Wu Han, "Zailun shenquan," in *Wu Han shixue lunzhu xuanji* (1948, repr. Beijing: Renmin chubanshe, 1986), 2: 593–95.

temple or official's household. These two kinds of households—the temple and the scholar-official's household—were largely exempt from labor services, and they had the legal capacity to make such an arrangement. As a result, both parties benefited (which may have been one reason that government income from labor service decreased over the course of the Ming).

Younger generations in hereditary occupations such as artisans and salt farmers might escape their household registration to work at jobs that they preferred, although they had few legitimate ways to achieve that. They could perform heavy labor as unregistered workers. If they were willing to be outcasts and had some talent, they could become traveling entertainers—musicians, dancers, jugglers, or actors. There were always musicians and singers performing popular music in villages, during festivals, and in restaurants, teahouses, and brothels. But this was low-status work.

Because household registration applied to people who were permanently settled in villages and cities, people who lived in remote, inaccessible areas or lacked a fixed abode could avoid registration. Aboriginal people who lived deep in the hills were unregistered, as were boat people, who lived on the water. Beggars were mostly homeless as well as impoverished, and traveling musicians and entertainers were nomadic, following the festivals and thus difficult to find. Although there were some highly trained musicians and entertainers who performed for the emperor, they lived in the palace, were registered in artisan households, and had more status than traveling entertainers. But they were relatively few in number.

To obtain labor services from subjects without a fixed abode, the state could conscript them into the military. At the founding of the Ming, the Hongwu emperor sent officials to every province "to catch and place those landless people into military households." At that time, Mongol tribes in the north and northwest posed the most serious threat to the Ming state,[16] whereas, at the end of the Ming, the danger came from Jurchens in the northeast. But throughout the dynasty, "the military establishment was at all times the largest personnel component of the Ming government."[17] Unsurprisingly, the military also had the highest attrition rate of any occupation. In many cases, soldiers simply deserted and became, if not beggars or bandits, then unregistered or free workers, tenant farmers, sailors, boat haulers on the Grand Canal, and so forth.

Young men living in the border regions, where there were large garrisons, tended to join those garrisons to earn a cash income, as, by the mid-Ming, so

16 In 1450 Oirats captured the Zhengtong emperor, but afterward their power gradually waned.

17 Hucker, *Traditional and Governmental Finance*, 17.

many soldiers had deserted that the state had to recruit them from the market and pay them in cash, instead of the grain and salt that soldiers registered in a military household received. The Ministry of Revenue set up the Taicang Treasury in 1442 to send silver to the garrisons, especially those in border regions, to pay their soldiers. Because a soldier's salary was meager (less than a tael of silver), their commanders exchanged the Taicang silver for copper coins according to the market exchange rates to pay the soldiers.[18]

In addition to fighting battles to maintain or expand the empire,[19] soldiers were posted in the capital to protect the emperor or serve as transport soldiers for the tax grain (or grain tribute). Later, during the reign of the Yongle emperor, naval soldiers sailed on the treasure ships, which were more concerned with diplomacy and trade than warfare, but engaged in battles with pirates and in other countries to ensure access to trading ports. But throughout the Ming, the requirement that soldiers risk their lives for low pay and low status created little incentive for serving in the military.

2.2 *Moving the Capital South*

To manage the empire without money, the state needed to find the workers and materials to carry out the emperor's projects, and one of the Hongwu emperor's first projects was to move the capital from Dadu (Beijing) in the north to the Yangzi valley in the south. In 1356, leading a rebel force against the Yuan dynasty, he had captured Jiqing *lu*, a large administrative district on the southern bank of the Yangzi River, made it the base of his rebel force, and changed its name to Yingtian Prefecture to legitimize his rebellion. ("Yingtian" means "responsive to heaven," and, according to Confucian tradition, an emperor ruled with the mandate of heaven.) Zhu called his new capital Nanjing (Southern Capital). This was the first time that a city south of the Yangzi had been the capital of unified China.

Yingtian Prefecture was protected to the north by the Yangzi River, which offered a good defense against invasion by nomadic tribes. The area was rich in agricultural farmland, which produced a majority of the food for the imperial

18 The Ministry of Revenue melted down silver to make standardized ingots that weighed about 50 taels each and sent them to generals in border garrisons to pay their soldiers. Because melting down the ingots to pay a soldier's low salary was inconvenient and costly, the generals exchanged the ingots for copper cash.

19 For instance, during the reign of the Yongle emperor, Chinese troops invaded and occupied Annam, the northern part of modern-day Vietnam. In addition, the emperor commanded his armies against the Mongols in outer Mongolia (outside Ming China) on five different occasions. See Hok-lam Chan, "The Chien-wen, Yung-lo, Hung-hsi, and Hsuan-te Reigns, 1399–1435," in Mote and Twitchett, ed., *The Cambridge History of China*, 226–31.

families, officials, and soldiers in the capital. Although Zhu had considered relocating the capital to Yangzhou, a first-rate commercial city on the Yangzi, it had less agricultural production and was on its northern bank, without the river for defense. Additionally, as Frederick Mote noted, after having crossed the Yangzi, an army would find it far easier to move from Yingtian than from Yangzhou, because the northern district of Yangzhou comprised low-lying swamps and crisscrossing water channels—which would hinder rapid mobilization of the army—whereas the land north of Yingtian was dry.[20]

As Map 1 shows, Nanjing was protected by three city walls in the Ming. The outermost wall was not built until 1390. In the early Ming dynasty, the new capital was protected by only two concentric city walls. The inner wall surrounded the square-shaped Imperial City including the palace and its gardens. The palace housed the emperor, the empress, the emperor's concubines, their children, and the eunuchs and female servants, or palace women, who served them. In the early Ming, thousands of women lived and worked in the palace, providing various services, including cooking.[21] Palace women seem to have been selected for imperial service when very young, from respectable families that want to curry favor with that court. Palace women were expected to be pleasing in appearance and manner. They lived in seclusion from the outside world unless they were given as imperial gifts to favored personages or until they were pensioned off in old age.[22]

Outside the palace but within the walls of the Imperial City was the Imperial Ancestral Temple, the Altar of Soil and Grain, inner treasuries, and eunuch quarters. The Capital City comprised everything within the outermost wall.[23] This means the six ministries (personnel, revenue, rites, war, punishment,

---

20 Frederick W. Mote, "The Transformation of Nanking, 1350–1400," in *The City in Late Imperial China*, ed. G. William Skinner (Taipei: Southern Materials Center, 1977), 122.

21 The number of palace women is unclear, but the number at the end of the dynasty was estimated at 9,000. See Frederick W. Mote, "Yuan and Ming," in *Food in Chinese Culture: Anthropology and Historical Perspectives*, ed. Kwang-chih Chang (New Haven: Yale University Press, 1977), 213.

22 In the early years of the dynasty, palace women were organized into six bureaus specializing in various aspects of palace maintenance (ceremonial, food, housekeeping, silk manufacturing, etc.); but for an unknown reason, eunuchs gradually assumed their duties, and after the 1420s their presence dwindled to just the Apparel Bureau. See Hucker, *The Traditional Chinese State*, 10–11.

23 The perimeter of this wall was about 59 *li* (some sources give figures of 61 or 96 *li*). A *li* is about one-third of a mile. The wall had 13 city gates, and it was from 20 to 60 feet high. The foundations were made of granite and the walls of large bricks. See Edward L. Farmer, *Early Ming Government: The Evolution of Dual Capitals* (Cambridge: Harvard University Press, 1976), 56.

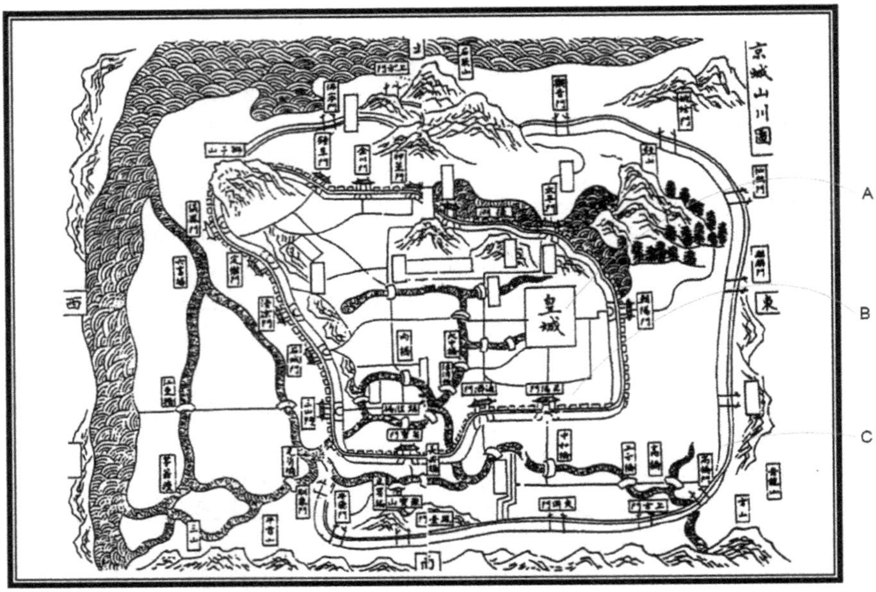

MAP 1 Nanjing. **A.** *Huangcheng* (Imperial city), where the palace was located. **B.** *Ducheng* (Capital city) was encompassed by a wall built in 1373. **C.** The outer wall was built in 1390.
SOURCE: *HONGWU JINGCHENG TUZHI*, PREFACE (1395, REPR. NANJING: NANJING CHUBANSHE, 2006), 15

and works), barracks, and local government offices (for Yingtian Prefecture, Shangyuan County, Jiangning County, etc.). The new capital was heavily garrisoned; the Hongwu emperor initially stationed forty-eight military units there, which later increased to fifty-two.[24] To accommodate so many soldiers, the government built quarters for them in the northern and northeastern districts of the Capital City. Every soldier was given a house measuring about 190 square feet.[25]

24 According to Yu Zhijia, 37 of the 52 units were stationed within the city walls. These military units should have comprised 5,600 soldiers each, but in reality, as soldiers died or deserted, few units could maintain this size. In 1371, the chief general carried out an inspection and reported a total of 207,800 soldiers stationed in Nanjing and its environs. Yu Zhijia, "Mingdai liangjing jiandu yu weisuo junhu qianxi zhi guanxi," *Zhongyang yanjiuyuan lishi yuyan yanjiusuo jikan* 64, no. 1 (1993): 138–41; see also *Mingshi* (1739, repr. Beijing: Zhonghua shuju, 1974), 2176, 2193.

25 Yu Zhijia, "Mingdai liangjing jiandu," 141, 150. Each house was 15 Chinese feet long and 12 Chinese feet wide according to the source. Using the conversion rate of 1 Chinese foot to 12.3 inches (see "Ming Weights and Measures"), the house would have been 189 square feet (15.4 × 12.3 feet).

Along with buildings and walls, a capital city needed people. Many of the local inhabitants of Shangyuan and Jiangning Counties had been forcibly moved out to make room for the capital. In 1373, these original inhabitants were encouraged to return, in part to fulfill their obligatory labor services.[26] The Ming government built houses for them within the city walls. In return, the city dwellers were registered by household into geographic taxation districts such as urban wards (*fang*). Later, it became clear that still more workers were needed to maintain the city. The emperor wanted to "fill out the population of the capital," but Nanjing was too small to accommodate more people. This was likely the reason that the emperor constructed the third, outermost wall in 1390. This new wall had a sprawling perimeter of 120 to 180 *li* (about 42 to 63 miles)[27] and 15 city gates.[28] Those who lived within this outer wall were also grouped into *fang* for labor services.[29]

The *Ming shilu* [*Veritable Records of the Ming Dynasty*] recorded massive forced migration from other provinces to Nanjing during the Hongwu reign—numbering 5,300 households in 1391, followed by 20,000 households in 1395, and 14,241 households in 1397—increasing the capital's population by nearly 40,000 households.[30] If each household consisted of only 3 members (husband, wife, and one child), the additional population totaled a further 120,000 people, all registered as artisans. The early seventeenth-century scholar Gu Qiyuan noted that the emperor had moved a total of 45,000 "wealthy households" to the capital since 1380.[31] These households worked under eunuch agencies in the palace.[32] In other words, the Hongwu emperor was concerned not only with the size but also the composition of the capital's population. The artisan category included everyone from potters and brickmakers to architects and shipwrights, papermakers and printers, cooks, carpenters, blacksmiths,

26 In this case, household registration made it difficult for people to avoid being moved back into their previous locale.

27 See "Ming Weights and Measures."

28 Farmer, *Early Ming Government*, 56.

29 See Gu Qiyuan, *Kezuo zhuiyu* (1618, repr. Beijing: Zhonghua shuju, 1987), 58.

30 See Han Dacheng, *Mingdai chengshi yanjiu* (Beijing: Zhongguo renmei daxue chubanshe, 1991), 48–49. Frederick Mote wrote that the Hongwu emperor moved about 79,000 households to Nanking (in "The Transformation of Nanking," 145). However, Han Dacheng examined the wording of Gu Qiyuan's essay, and argued that his figure of 45,000 households did not a result from a single migration in 1380 but, rather, that *since* 1380, during the Hongwu reign the total number of households that had been moved to Nanjing was about 45,000.

31 The emperor may have selected wealthy households because they could pay the cost of moving to Nanjing themselves.

32 Gu Qiyuan, *Kezuo zhuiyu*, 64.

weavers and dyers, and so on. Silk farmers, who raised silkworms and harvested their silk, also fell into the artisan category; initially, sericulture was women's work. In return for housing, artisans provided the labor that was crucial for maintaining the capital.

Unfortunately, no historical records specifically describe the people relocated to the capital. Some of them probably were landowners (because landowners were among the wealthiest people in China) who, after they had paid their way to the capital, received basic training from skilled artisans. There was usually a headman for each kind of work. These headmen may have been artisans in the previous dynasty who remained in the area. They worked under the eunuchs from the agencies that organized and oversaw artisans' labor. It seems likely that much of the artisan work performed by the new inhabitants was unskilled; the headmen or eunuchs who trained these people, however, were skilled workers. What we do know is that twenty-four eunuch agencies served the throne, each of which was in charge of the labor services of several artisan households.[33]

2.3 *Eunuchs: the Emperor's Servants and Gatekeepers*

Eunuchs were indispensable in the daily operation and maintenance of the palace. Some eunuchs lived with the harem, for whom they served as guardians, servants, or youthful companions of the empress and the emperor's wives and concubines.[34] Eunuchs were considered safe as guardians because their emasculation ensured that any children born to the emperor's harem would be his own offspring.[35] Eunuchs were also considered safe as civil servants in the palace because they could not have sons that might try to take the throne and start their own dynasties.[36]

Within the palace, eunuchs were responsible for the imperial seals, keys, and books as well as headgear, footwear, and ceremonial and everyday clothing. They guarded the inner treasury, the palace granary, and the palace gates;

33 For more details about the 24 eunuch agencies, see Ding Yi, *Mingdai tewu zhengzhi* (Shanghai: Shanghai shudian, 2011), 17–20.

34 Although many eunuchs were young boys seized in battle with the border tribes or sent as tribute by neighboring countries, some Chinese men chose emasculation as their only way to gain entry to a better life, particularly in later reigns under emperors who were better-disposed toward them than the Hongwu emperor. See Tsai, *The Eunuchs in the Ming Dynasty*, 17–19.

35 Eunuchs and palace maids were the only people who worked regularly in the palace where the imperial concubines lived.

36 Wang Chunyu and Du Wanyan, *Mingchao Huanguan* (Beijing: Shangwu yinshuguan, 2016), 3.

prepared the daily meals; made the wine, vinegar, dried fruit, noodles, and so on; and took care of the horses in the imperial stables. They were in charge of medicine and surgery; incense supplies and offerings to the ancestors in the imperial temple; construction and repair of ponds, gates, and buildings; and gathering of copper, iron, and tin. They also took care of the crown prince and his clothing, seals, books, meals, and medicine.[37] (See Table 1 for the full list of eunuch agencies and their duties in the palace.)

As denizens of the palace and servants of the emperor, eunuchs were privy to imperial secrets and aware of the human failings of the Son of Heaven; in this role, they could either protect or exploit an emperor. Although stories of scheming and corrupt eunuchs versus high-minded scholar-officials recur throughout Chinese history, the scholar-officials wrote most of this history. But there were also eunuchs such as Admiral Zheng He, who garnered the respect of his contemporary scholar-officials, as well as many other eunuchs who were neither corrupt nor self-serving but loyal servants of an emperor whose aims ran counter to those of the officials. As Ray Huang pointed out, the eunuchs acted on behalf of the emperor and the scholar-officials for the bureaucracy, and the conflict between them was political.[38]

In addition to serving in the palace, eunuchs also served in the civil service to manage maritime customs, oversee local administration in the provinces and military garrisons, and even keep an eye on the generals on the emperor's behalf. But in the early years of the Ming, the court eunuchs' influence was limited by the founding emperor's contempt for them. In instructions to the minister of rites, the Hongwu emperor wrote:

> Not one or two of these people out of thousands are good. Those who are evil frequently number thousands. If they are employed as ears or eyes, then the ears and eyes are covered. If they are employed as the heart and bowels, then the heart and bowels will be sick. The way to control them is to make them fear the laws and not permit them to have merit. If they fear the laws, then they will be attentive to their conduct. If they have merit, then they will be arrogant and lustful.[39]

37 Tsai, *The Eunuchs in the Ming Dynasty*, 30.

38 Ray Huang, *1587, A Year of No Significance: The Ming Dynasty in Decline* (New Haven: Yale University Press. 1981), 19–21.

39 The founding emperor gave this instruction in 1369, the second year of his reign. See *Ming shilu*, Taizu, 861, quoted in Tsai, *The Eunuchs in the Ming Dynasty*, 29.

Historian Shih-shan Henry Tsai noted that the founding emperor initially kept their numbers low (sixty eunuchs in the imperial household) and their salaries "skimpy and fixed." Eunuchs were not allowed to be literate or to communicate with officials, and they had to live in the palace. But as the imperial household grew, the Hongwu emperor needed more eunuchs to serve them; fifteen years after his accession, he recruited another 361 eunuchs for the harem and, in late 1383, another seventy-six for the Inner Court, including two literate eunuchs who were in charge of reframing palace events for the historical record.[40] Even though he obviously depended on his eunuchs, the Hongwu emperor continued to mistrust them;[41] in 1384 he had an iron plaque affixed to the front of the palace, which read: "Eunuchs are forbidden to interfere with government affairs. Those who attempt to do so will be subjected to capital punishment."[42] Their numbers and their influence increased exponentially later, under emperors who were better-disposed toward them,[43] and they became what Tsai characterized as a "third administrative hierarchy" within the government.[44]

2.4 *Labor Services and In-Kind Taxes*

Despite the forced migration, Nanjing needed more laborers. The households that had been relocated to work as artisans for the eunuch agencies served the emperor and the imperial families in the palace, but the government agencies in Nanjing also needed workers to build and repair their buildings and ships. An official record in 1393 stated that the empire had 232,000 registered laborers in 62 categories (e.g., carpenter, painter, blacksmith), and over half of them, or nearly 130,000 laborers, were employed by the Ministry of Works in Nanjing for one season every one, two, three, four, or five years. (The frequency of a subject's labor service was probably contingent on the need for a particular

40 Tsai, *The Eunuchs in the Ming Dynasty*, 29–30.

41 It is ironic that when the Hongwu emperor began "purging" the scholar-officials by the thousands, beginning with his own supporters, he used eunuchs to spy on his scholar-officials. Tsai, *The Eunuchs in the Ming Dynasty*, 98.

42 *Mingshi*, 7765, quoted in Tsai, *The Eunuchs in the Ming Dynasty*, 13.

43 By the reign of the Hongzhi emperor (1488–1505), about 30–40 of eunuchs were in each agency, making a total of 720–960 eunuchs serving in the palace. The Wanli emperor (1573–1620) recruited 6,000 new eunuchs in the first six years of his rule. In 1644, when Beijing was under attack by rebels, more than 70,000 eunuchs fled the palace, running for their lives. The historian Ding Yi believed that, including the eunuchs who served outside Beijing, in the final years of the Ming, the number of eunuchs totaled about 100,000. See Ding Yi, *Mingdai tewu zhengzhi*, 22–24.

44 Tsai called eunuchs "the necessary cement that held imperial institutions together and made China's polygamous society work" (*The Eunuchs in the Ming Dynasty*, 8–9).

kind of work and the worker's proximity to the capital.) The Ministry of Works provided these temporary state workers with living quarters in Nanjing.[45]

Providing food for this population was another concern. The Ministry of Works gave the provincial artisans subsidies for living expenses while they worked in Nanjing. In the early Ming, this totaled 0.6 *shi* (about 78 lbs.) of rice per month, or 1 *shi* per month if the artisan was married, along with firewood for fuel and heat.[46] In addition, the emperor had to feed about 200,000 soldiers and their families, who were stationed permanently in the capital and its environs.[47] If every soldier consisted of a family of three, the population of Nanjing increased by 600,000. Every month, Zhu paid soldiers 1 *shi* of rice and a small amount of salt apiece to support their families. Moreover, soldiers might receive winter uniforms or simply the cloth with which to make them.[48] To feed his soldiers in Nanjing, the emperor needed 2.4 million *shi* of rice a year. The emperor also paid his Nanjing officials in rice; about 5,500 officials received 50–900 *shi* annually according to their rank.[49] (See Table 1.) All the rice that went to the soldiers and officials in the capital came from the rice tribute, the land tax that farmers throughout the Yangzi valley paid to the emperor. As shown below, Zhu managed the massive grain tribute by dividing the fertile Yangzi provinces into several grain districts, with a civilian in each district as the grain chief (*liangzhang*), who was responsible for collecting and delivering the grain to the capital.[50]

2.5 *The Lijia*

Whereas the cities in the empire were divided into urban wards for household registration, rural areas used the *lijia* system, which was described by the historian Liang Fangzhong as "a semi-official organization for local self-government

45 Han Dacheng, *Mingdai chengshi yanjiu*, 50. See also *DaMing huidian*, in *Xuxiu siku quanshu* (1587, repr. Shanghai: Shanghai guji chubanshe, 1997), 792: 268–73.

46 The artisans who had been relocated permanently to Nanjing worked for the palace; there is no record that they received living subsidies from any palace institution. Their services were in return for the land in the capital city in which their houses were built.

47 *Mingshi*, 2176.

48 Huang, *Taxation and Government Finance*, 49, 65. Yu Zhijia noted that many soldiers, unless they were stationed in Nanjing, were underpaid, in *Mingdai junhu shixi zhidu* (Taipei: Xuesheng shuju, 1987), 63.

49 According to a 1392 report, 2,749 military officials worked in Nanjing (see *Ming junhu shixi zhidu*, Taizu, 3270). Assuming the number of civil officials working there was similar to this figure, the officials totaled about 5,500.

50 For more about the grain chiefs, see Liang Fangzhong, *Mingdai liangzhang zhidu* (1957, repr. Beijing: Zhonghua shuju, 2008).

TABLE 1 Annual salaries of Ming officials in 1371 and 1387 (in *shi*)

Rank/Year	1371	1387
1A	900	1,044
1B	750	888
2A	600	73
2B	500	576
3A	400	420
3B	300	312
4A	270	288
4B	240	252
5A	180	192
5B	160	168
6A	100	120
6B	90	96
7A	80	90
7B	75	84
8A	70	78
8B	65	72
9A	60	66
9B	50	60

SOURCE: *MING SHILU*, TAIZU (REPR. TAIPEI: ACADEMIA SINICA, 1962), 1182, 2778
Note: Ming officials received their salaries monthly, but here they are converted into annual salaries to facilitate analysis.

by the people [that] was also the unit for paying land tax and labor service. It was the main trunk of the whole labor service system."[51]

The rural *lijia* households were headed by farmer-landowners (also known as civilians, or *min*). Like the wards in the cities, the *lijia* was organized by geographic proximity, in this case through the *li*, which can be loosely translated as "village"; in this sense, however, "village" had an administrative function. It was modeled after a grouping of 110 neighboring rural households, with one adult male representing each household. This number was used as the template for

51 See Liang Fang-chung (Liang Fangzhong), *The Single-Whip Method of Taxation in China* (Cambridge: Harvard East Asian Monograph, 1956), 5.

dividing the *li* into *jia* (sections).[52] The adult male representatives from the ten wealthiest households became the *li* chiefs, who organized the in-kind tax payments and labor services. The remaining 100 households were divided into ten sections of ten men each (one from each household).

Every year, one *li* chief led one *jia* (nine householders plus one *jia* chief) to the county magistracy,[53] to live and work there for a year. During that year, they had to provide all the supplies and labor that the magistrate needed. Liu Zhiwei noted that county magistrates in the early Ming relied on the common people for food, including grain, meat, and vegetables; for clerical supplies, such as paper, pens, and ink; and household necessities such as charcoal, timber, candles, and oil. Whenever the magistrate left his office—for instance, to perform a religious ritual, preside over a county examination, give alms to famine victims, and host banquets for visiting officials—the *jia* had to provide the materials and labor. The *jia* also worked in the magistrate's office as underlings—clerks, jailers, servants, and so on.[54] The *li* chief and the men in that year's *jia* also had to act as police officers and tax collectors for the entire *li* to which they belonged. Because the Hongwu emperor sent only one man to run the county magistrate's office, the civilian householders in the *jia* were absolutely essential to the operation of the magistracy, but the magistrate's demands had no limits, which made this onerous labor service in the early Ming. After the year ended, the *li* chief and the ten householders were allowed to return to their village, to be replaced by another *li* chief and his *jia* the following year.

While one *jia* worked in the magistrate's office, the remaining nine *jia* (90 households) paid taxes in kind, which might include silk or poultry, but mainly grain. In addition to paying in-kind taxes, the remaining *jia* performed labor services, such as building dams, for different levels of the government.

In the fertile Yangzi valley, some *li* combined to form one large grain district, headed by a grain chief, who was invariably from a wealthy household. Every year, this grain chief, assisted by *li* chiefs, was responsible for transporting the tax grain from the villages to government granaries in nearby military garrisons or the imperial capital. As long as Nanjing remained the capital, grain transport was relatively easy. But in 1421, after the Yongle emperor moved the capital to Beijing in northern China, this labor service became more difficult.

---

52 The number of 110 households per *li* was only approximate, representing the government model. In reality, one *li* was usually the size of one village.

53 Liang, *The Single-Whip Method of Taxation*, 5.

54 Liu Zhiwei, *Zai guojia yu shehui zhijian: MingQing Guangdong lijia fuyi zhidu yanjiu* (Guangzhou: Zhongshan daxue chubanshe, 1997), 80–83, 125–26.

The grain chiefs had to pay the extra transportation costs (which was why wealthy households were appointed), with the result that relocating the capital led to bankruptcy for many grain chiefs.

The Hongwu emperor did not forbid the monetary tax outright, but it was levied mostly on commercial activities and only for small amounts of money. In 1391, for instance, the emperor expressed concern for traveling merchants who had difficulty storing their goods in Nanjing, and then had several government warehouses built on the bank of the Qinhuai River, just outside the southern gate. He rented the warehouses to merchants for the low price of 0.01 tael of silver per warehouse per month.[55] The emperor also permitted county officials to levy a monetary tax on local commercial activities such as land transfer and wine making; he encouraged them to use this petty cash to subsidize official religious ceremonies in their jurisdictions.[56] But these amounts were negligible. For instance, in every land transfer, the new owner had to bring the signed deed of sale to the county magistrate to be endorsed, which meant the magistrate verified the deed's validity, impressed a red seal on it, and noted the change of owner and taxpayer in his own records. For this administrative service, the magistrate could collect only 40 copper cash, which paid for the cost of the stationery.[57]

In short, the Hongwu emperor used in-kind taxes and labor services to run the capital in Nanjing as well as the Ming empire. This raises a question as to why he issued money at all?

3 From Copper to Rice to Precious Notes

Initially, the Hongwu emperor, who had paid his soldiers in copper cash when he was a rebel leader, issued copper coins as the state currency.[58] He established an imperial mint, the Baoyuan (Source of Treasure Bureau) Mint, in Nanjing and encouraged local governments to build mints in their own provinces. Making the coins was easy; the problem was acquiring enough raw copper to do so. The only rich copper mines in the early Ming were in Yunnan, a

55 *Ming shilu*, Taizu, 3139–40.

56 *DaMing huidian*, 789: 627–28.

57 *DaMing huidian*, 789:627.

58 The coin was called the "Hongwu *tongbao*," after Hongwu, the reign, and *tongbao* (lit., "circulating treasure"), which meant "coin." The unit of account was a *wen* (cash), with five official denominations: one, two, three, five, and ten; the most common in the marketplace was the one-cash coin, which weighed 1 *qian* (0.1 tael, or about 0.13 ounces. See "Ming Weights and Measures."

region still controlled by a Mongol prince. Thus the Baoyuan Mint in Nanjing had little raw copper for making coins, and most provinces were not eager to build their own mints. To ensure continuous operation of the Baoyuan Mint, the imperial government levied a copper tax on commoners in Nanjing.[59] The only way that many people could pay it was to hand over their housewares and farming tools made of copper to the government.[60] Needless to say, the copper tax was extremely unpopular.

To remedy the situation and "remove the harm from coinage," in 1375, the eighth year of the Hongwu reign, the emperor shut down the Baoyuan Mint and changed the state currency from copper coins to a paper money called the *baochao* (precious note). Made of mulberry bark paper, the *baochao* came in six denominations: 100, 200, 300, 400, 500, and 1,000, or the one *guan*. As seen on the one-*guan* note in Figure 2, the value of one *guan* was represented by 10 strings of copper coins, each of which consisted of 100 coins.[61] (See Figure 2.)

When paper money formally replaced copper coins as the state currency, the emperor did not ban the use of copper cash but the use of gold and silver in market exchanges.[62] He saw these two precious metals as the real competitors to his paper money. Copper coins were always needed in the market for small change, meaning less than the 100-cash note.

The precious note did not affect state administration initially, because it was used mostly for gifts, not salaries. Ming officials continued to receive their salaries in rice, which was particularly inconvenient for them. If they had no other cash income, they had to sell their rice to afford other food and daily necessities for their families. The following case dramatically illustrates their dilemma. In 1377, Minister Zeng Bingzheng from the office of transmission "acted against the will of the Hongwu emperor" and was ordered to leave his official position and Nanjing.[63] As an official, Zeng had received 400 *shi* a year, but this left him without the savings to pay for traveling back to Nanchang, his native prefecture in Jiangxi Province. To raise the money, he sold his four-year-old daughter. When the emperor heard about this, he was so incensed that he sent

59 From a catty of scrap copper, the mint was able to produce 13 to 15 one-cash coins. Xu Xueju, *Guochao dianhui* (1601, repr. Beijing: Beijing daxue chubanshe, 1993), 4743.

60 *Ming shilu*, Taizu, 1669.

61 *Ming shilu*, Taizu, 1669–70. In 1389, four smaller denominations were added: 20, 30, 40, and 50. See Peng Xinwei, *Zhongguo huobi shi*, 429.

62 *Ming shilu*, Taizu, 1670.

63 Zeng Bingzheng was serving in Nanjing as the minister of the Office of Transmission, a central government agency responsible for receiving, registering, and presenting all the memorials from the empire. See Hucker, *A Dictionary of Official Titles*, 553.

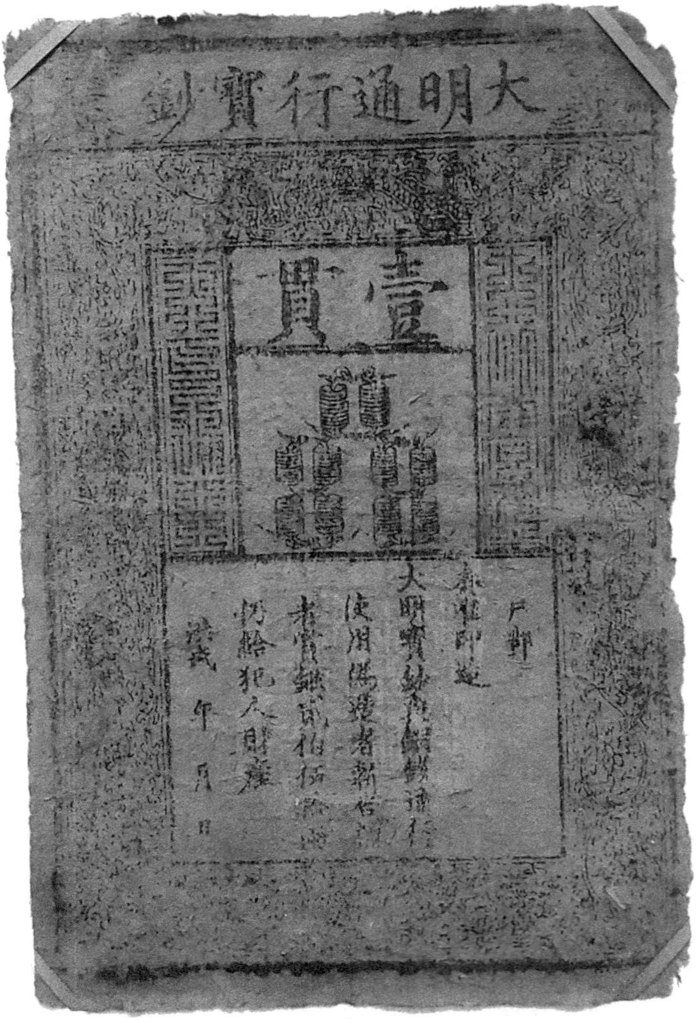

FIGURE 2 Paper money of the Ming. This is a one-*guan* note. The upper part is printed in Chinese characters that say “Great Ming Universally Circulated Precious Note” with a picture of 10 strings of copper coins (each string containing 100 coins). In the lower part, the text indicates the Ministry of Revenue as the issuing agency and an imperial order that this note should circulate at par with copper coins, that anyone who forged the note would be beheaded, and that the informer would be rewarded with the property of the forger plus 250 taels of silver. The text ends with the reign title of Hongwu, the dynastic founder. Note, however, that this paper money was not necessarily produced in the Hongwu period, because the third Ming emperor, Zhu Di, to legitimize his reign, ordered that “Hongwu” remain on the notes.

CREDIT: BRITISH MUSEUM

men to apprehend Zeng and castrate him.[64] (The source of this information did not explain why the emperor was angry. Although the practice of selling daughters in a lean year was not unusual, the emperor may have felt that, by doing so, Zeng had shown himself unworthy to be a parent. The emperor may also have felt that Zeng's behavior was aimed at making the emperor look stingy, because he paid Zeng so little that the man had to sell a child to afford the cost of travel.)

In addition to their low salaries, Ming officials had to put up with the extra cost and inconvenience of receiving their pay in rice. They had to pay transaction costs to convert their rice into cash at local markets. They had to pay the transportation costs of the rice from government granaries. Then, in Nanjing, for example, the price of their rice would have dropped significantly by the time that they were paid, because more than 200,000 soldiers and officials were selling their rice salaries at the same time to be able to afford other necessities.

But the Hongwu emperor refused to pay his officials in either paper notes or copper coins. In 1381, the Ming army launched an attack on Yunnan, which it occupied in 1384.[65] At this point, the emperor could have built a transportation line between the Yunnan copper mines and Nanjing. Although such an undertaking would have been expensive, it would have secured a continuous supply of raw copper for the imperial mint. But the emperor did not avail himself of the opportunity. Instead, he continued to issue paper money while managing his empire with a method that did not use money. In 1387, a decade after Zeng Bingzheng sold his daughter to pay for his travel expenses, the emperor finally revised the salary scale for officials. As seen in Table 1, the salary of an official rank of 3A (e.g., Zeng Bingzheng) increased from 400 *shi* of rice a year to 420.[66]

Unlike copper coins, paper money was lightweight and relatively cheap, both to make and to transport. In 1390 the *Ming shilu* had 69 entries for the emperor's gifts of paper currency, which totaled about 89 million *guan,* or 89 billion in copper cash.[67] A gift from the emperor of paper money functioned like cash coupons. It could be used to buy goods in the market but, as Ray Huang noted, its major function was as a gift—a special award to imperial princes and high-ranking officials, or as a return gift from the emperor to

64 *Mingshi*, 3987–88.

65 See Bin Yang, *Cowrie Shells and Cowrie Money: A Global History* (London: Routledge, 2019), 95.

66 *Ming shilu*, Taizu, 2778.

67 Of these 69 cases, 53 either specified the exact amounts or defined the nature of the grants clearly enough to permit calculation of the sums involved. Huang, *Taxation and Government Finance*, 69.

foreign missions.[68] In the first lunar month of 1394, several aboriginal chieftains and their entourages from the Yunnan, Sichuan, and Huguang Provinces, totaling 541 men, visited Nanjing and offered tribute to the emperor. In return for their loyalty, the emperor gave them 23,395 *guan* of paper money, along with 23 bolts of *jin* (silk brocade), 176 bolts of *wenqi* (a fine, thin silk), and 242 bolts of *juan* (a thick, stiff silk).[69] In the same month, after learning that Tang He, the duke of Xin, was dying, the emperor gave him 750 *guan* to pay for materials and labor for building his tomb.[70]

Thus paper money initially entered the market through the guests or friends of the emperor. The emperor gave the notes specific values but at first, except in the case of insignificant commercial taxes, did not receive them in tax revenue. Because paper money was needed to pay commercial taxes, it could be bought from money changers in markets, especially in big cities, by those who needed to pay the tax but had no other way to obtain paper money. After taxes were collected in currency, money changers opened currency exchange shops or "money shops" in or near the city in which the tax collecting offices were located. (Money shops had always operated in market towns, to exchange copper and silver and the various kinds of copper coins.)

The precious note was rarely used in market exchanges, although it might be used to buy land. Social historian Fu Yiling found eight deeds for land transfer in Huizhou Prefecture during the Hongwu reign, all involving precious notes except for one in 1373, which was paid in silver two years before paper money was issued.[71] But the use of paper money for land transfers in the Hongwu

---

68 Huang, *Taxation and Government Finance*, 69.

69 Silk was another important imperial gift. It was either collected as taxes in kind from provinces or manufactured in Nanjing. The highest-quality silk was brocade (*jin*), then *wenqi*, and finally *juan*. Only high-level officials could afford brocade; lower-level officials wore clothing made of *juan*. See Li Chiao-ping, *Tien-kung-kai-wu: Exploitation of the Work of Nature: Chinese Agriculture and Technology in the XVII Century* (Taipei: China Academy, 1980), 72.

70 *Ming shilu*, Taizu, 3373. A native of Fengyang, Tang He came from the same village as Zhu Yuanzhang. During Zhu's rise from rebel general to emperor, Tang was one of his closest associates and principal lieutenants. When Zhu established the Ming dynasty in 1368, he made Tang the marquis of Zhongshan, with an annual stipend of 1,500 *shi*. Ten years later, Zhu made Tang the duke of Xin, with an annual stipend of 3,000 *shi*. Following a court appearance on New Year's Day in 1390, Tang suffered a stroke, leading to the loss of his voice. The emperor allowed him to retire, and, thereafter, Tang made only rare public appearances. Tang died in 1395, one year after he received 750 *guan* of paper money from the emperor. See his biography in L. Carrington Goodrich and Chaoying Fang, ed., *Dictionary of Ming Biography 1368–1644* (New York: Columbia University Press, 1976), 1248–51.

71 Fu Yiling, "Mingdai qianqi Huizhou tudi maimai qiyue zhong de tonghuo," 1980, repr. in his *MingQing shehui jingji shi lunwen ji* (Beijing: Renmin chubanshe, 1982), 242–43.

period was a special case. A new landowner had to register his deed of sale with the country magistrate, therefore, the deed's content, including the type of currency used in the transaction, had to be strictly legal. Paper money was the legal state currency, unlike, for instance, the copper coins that had been minted privately or issued by earlier dynasties.

Because the demand for paper money was small but its supply was large, in 1393 the emperor converted the rice salary into paper money for officials in the provinces. The official conversion rate was 2.5 *guan* (equal to 2,500 cash, or 1,000 cash per *guan*) for 1 *shi* of rice.[72] But when the provincial official took his 2.5 *guan* to market, he could not buy 1 *shi* of rice with it. In 1394, when the emperor learned that the market worth of a *guan* had plummeted to a paltry 160 cash worth in Zhejiang, and similar devaluations had occurred in other southern provinces such as Fujian, Guangdong, and Guangxi, he became so enraged that he banned the circulation of copper coins. He even decreed that his subjects had to hand over all their copper coins to the government in exchange for precious notes within half a month, and anyone who held on to or used the coins would be punished.[73]

These measures proved as impractical as they were draconian. Although, five years earlier, the emperor had added smaller denominations of paper money, marketplaces still needed copper coins to handle small exchanges, worth less than 10 cash. That Ming sources had no record of officials' discussions or comments on these measures demonstrates a diplomatic silence. In the market, the imperial order was ignored. In 1397, one year before his death, the emperor was incensed to discover that merchants in Hangzhou still quoted the prices of their goods in gold or silver. Believing that this was the reason for the unpopularity of paper money there, he reinstated the ban on using gold and silver in exchanges.[74]

In 1398, the Hongwu emperor died at age seventy, having ruled the empire for thirty-one years.[75] Although his successors vowed to continue his model of state administration, this proved impossible as the role of state currency changed.

72 *DaMing huidian*, 789:684.

73 *Ming shilu*, Taizu, 3417.

74 *Ming shilu*, 3632.

75 There is no record of how he died, only that his physicians were punished and that 46 concubines were sacrificed at his funeral.

4 Civil War, a New Capital, and a Surfeit of Precious Notes

After the Hongwu emperor died, the question of succession sparked a civil war. By law, and in accordance with Confucian tradition, the firstborn legitimate son, Zhu Biao, would succeed the Hongwu emperor and, in fact, had been made crown prince in 1368. After Zhu Biao died in 1392, his eldest son, Zhu Yunwen, became the new crown prince, also in accordance with Confucian tradition (in which the throne always went to an eldest son). Thus in 1398 Zhu Yunwen, at age twenty-one, succeeded his grandfather, and in 1399 he took the reign title of Jianwen.

Wary of the military threat that his uncles posed, the young emperor first reduced their armies and then placed them under house arrest. But his uncle Zhu Di, the Prince of Yan and lord of Beiping (the name of Beijing in the early Ming), refused to leave Beiping and went to war with his nephew.

The Jianwen emperor had adopted his grandfather's attitude toward eunuchs, castigating them as untrustworthy and limiting their influence. In marked contrast, Zhu Di's closest adviser was the eunuch Ma Sanbao, a Yunnan native who had been taken prisoner as a boy when the Ming troops conquered Yunnan, then was castrated and given to the young Prince Zhu Di as a servant.[76] Ma Sanbao fought alongside Zhu Di on military campaigns against the Jianwen emperor. In 1402, acting on information from eunuchs in the palace, Zhu Di was able to avoid the heavily fortified cities, cross the Yangzi River, and take Nanjing peacefully. The nearly three-year civil war ended in the seventh month of 1402. Although the rebel army did not find the Jianwen emperor, the feudal lord from the north was crowned emperor and in 1403 began using Yongle as his reign title. Then, he changed Ma Sanbao's name to Zheng He and named him the "Senior Eunuch" (*Taijian*) in the palace.[77] Unlike the Hongwu emperor and the grandson who had modeled himself after him, Zhu Di "gave merit" to eunuchs.

The new emperor was eager to prove to his subjects that he was the true successor, despite the departure from Confucian tradition. As soon as he took Nanjing, Zhu Di denounced the Jianwen emperor for mismanaging the empire and annulled his entire reign, declaring that the Hongwu reign had lasted through 1402 even though the Hongwu emperor had died in 1398. As part of legitimizing his own reign, Zhu Di attempted to show that he would implement every policy that his father the Hongwu emperor had put in place,

76 Zhu Xie, *Zheng He* (Beijing: Sanlian shujian, 1956), 23–25. Many eunuchs were foreign—sent by Korea, Vietnam, and other tributary states as gifts to the emperor or taken in battle as slaves, as was the case with Ma Sanbao. Any enemy's son taken in battle was castrated, to prevent him from having sons and starting a rebellion to found a dynasty of his own.

77 Wang Chunyu and Du Wanyan, *Mingchao Huanguan*, 130; Zhao Lingyang, "Lun Mingdai zhi huanhuo," in his *Mingshi lunji* (Hong Kong: Shixue yanjiu hui, 1975), 1.

including that of issuing paper money. Zhu Di not only continued to issue precious notes but retained the same printing format. In the eleventh month of 1402, Xia Yuanji, the new minister of revenue, petitioned him to make a new printing block, because the old one had been worn down, and suggested that, at the same time, they could replace the character for Hongwu with that of Yongle. But Zhu Di insisted that the character for Hongwu appear on the new printing block, saying: "I follow all established laws stipulated by the Taizu [the temple name of Zhu Yuanzhang]. Hongwu should be printed [on the precious notes] forever."[78] In this way, he linked the legitimacy of his rule with his father's name on the state's paper currency.

4.1 *Moving the Capital to Beijing*

In fact, Zhu Di did not adhere to all his father's policies any more than he agreed with his every prejudice. As soon as he had usurped the throne, he decided to move the imperial capital from Nanjing to his own previous domain in Beiping Prefecture. In January 1403, he gave the city the status of northern capital, that is, Beijing, and sent Zhu Gaochi, his eldest son (who later became the Hongxi emperor), there, along with a ministry to oversee the branch offices of central administration.[79]

Moving the imperial capital to Beijing was an expensive and protracted undertaking. Although the city had been the capital during the Yuan dynasty, many of its buildings had to be renovated or rebuilt. Once again, as had happened in Nanjing thirty-some years earlier, a new emperor had to assemble building materials, laborers, and food for them, to build his capital. Adding to the difficulties, Beijing was located on the arid North China Plain, from which it was inconvenient to transport water and which was far from the fertile lower Yangzi valley.

The previous dynasty, the Yuan state, was the first unified empire to build a capital at Beijing and had relied mainly on coastal sea routes to transport their rice tribute from the Yangzi delta to the northern capital. But when the officials in charge of sea junks refused to transport the rice, the capital could not feed its Mongol soldiers. This was why Zhu Yuanzhang took the city without a battle: the Mongol soldiers had escaped or retreated before his army ever entered the city. Realizing he could not trust the sea route, Zhu had built his capital at Nanjing, in the lower Yangzi valley, where rice was plentiful.

The Yongle emperor decided to build canals linking his new capital to the Yangzi provinces, in order to bring the rice north to Beijing and feed imperial

---

78 *Ming shilu*, Taizong, 260.

79 The metropolitan prefecture was also renamed Shuntian (Obedient to Heaven) to match Nanjing, i.e., Yingtian (Responsive to Heaven). See Hok-lam Chan, *Legends of the Buildings of Old Peking* (Hong Kong: Chinese University Press, 2008), 98.

households, officials, and soldiers without using the sea route.[80] The Yuan government had built the Huitong Canal on the Shandong Peninsula; the Yongle emperor planned to enlarge it to accommodate more grain tribute junks, ensure that his soldiers were fed, and protect the capital.

4.2 *Precious Notes for Capital Officials*

But Nanjing was also low on food. Three years of civil war had depleted the city's grain reserve. To feed his troops, the Yongle emperor took grain from his officials. The Hongwu emperor had only used precious notes as gifts or to pay low-ranking officials in the provinces, but in 1403 the Yongle emperor began to pay all his officials in the capitals in paper money as well as rice (see Table 2). He used a formula based on rank, with the highest percentage of paper money to rice (60 percent) for the highest-ranking officials.[81] To compensate for their loss in rice, the emperor paid his officials paper money at the rate of 10 *guan* for every lost *shi* of rice. This meant that an official with a rank of 1A, who had had an annual salary of 1,044 *shi*, instead received only 418 *shi* plus 6,260 *guan* (626 × 10) in paper money to make up the deficit.

The new policy increased the production of paper money. Nanjing had about 5,500 officials. If the rank of 5A (whose annual salary was 115 *shi* and 770 *guan*) is used as the standard, the annual *baochao* payment would total about 4,235,000 *guan*. The same rate (10 *guan* in exchange for 1 *shi*) seemed to apply to provincial officials as well. As shown earlier, beginning in 1393, the Hongwu emperor paid provincial officials in paper money instead of rice at the rate of 2.5 *guan* per *shi*. The Yongle emperor's 1403 policy raised their income by once again paying a portion of their salaries in rice, with the amount of rice depending on their province and their rank. For the portion of their salaries that the emperor paid in paper money, he used the new rate of 10 *guan* per *shi*.[82] Although the rate change seems like an increase in salary, in terms of purchasing power (because of inflation) an official's salary in paper money may not have increased at all; any increase was due to being paid once again in rice.

Paying officials a portion of their salaries in paper money saved the grain reserve, but at the cost of morale. In that way, the policy harmed the entire

---

80 Previous dynasties, such as the Sui (581–618) and the Tang (618–907), had built great and unified empires based on their canal networks.

81 The emperor paid a percentage of officials' salaries in paper currency as follows: 60 percent for officials in ranks 1A to 2B, 50 percent for officials in ranks 3A to 4B, 40 percent for those in ranks 5A to 6B, and 20 percent for those in ranks 7A to 8B. The officials in ranks 9A and 9B were unaffected, probably because their salaries were already low; they continued to receive their full salary in rice.

82 *DaMing huidian*, 789:684.

TABLE 2 Annual salaries of Nanjing officials in 1387 and 1403 (in *shi* and *guan*)

Rank/Year	1387	1403
1A	1044 *shi*	418 *shi*; 6,260 *guan*
1B	888 *shi*	355 *shi*; 5,330 *guan*
2A	732 *shi*	293 *shi*; 4,390 *guan*
2B	576 *shi*	230 *shi*; 3,460 *guan*
3A	420 *shi*	210 *shi*; 2,100 *guan*
3B	312 *shi*	156 *shi*; 1,560 *guan*
4A	288 *shi*	144 *shi*; 1,560 *guan*
4B	252 *shi*	126 *shi*; 1,260 *guan*
5A	192 *shi*	115 *shi*; 770 *guan*
5B	168 *shi*	101 *shi*; 670 *guan*
6A	120 *shi*	72 *shi*; 480 *guan*
6B	96 *shi*	58 *shi*; 380 *guan*
7A	90 *shi*	72 *shi*; 180 *guan*
7B	84 *shi*	67 *shi*; 170 *guan*
8A	78 *shi*	62 *shi*; 160 *guan*
8B	72 *shi*	58 *shi*; 140 *guan*
9A	66 *shi*	66 *shi*; 0 *guan*
9B	60 *shi*	60 *shi*; 0 *guan*

SOURCE: *MING SHILU*, TAIZU, 1182, 2778; *DAMING HUIDIAN*, IN *XUXIU SIKU QUANSHU* (1587, REPR. SHANGHAI: SHANGHAI GUJI CHUBANSHE, 1997), 789:681

Notes: In 1403 the Yongle emperor converted a percentage of officials' rice salaries into paper currency at a rate of 10 *guan* for 1 *shi*, as follows: 60 percent for officials whose rank was from 1A to 2B; 50 percent for those with rank 3A to 4B; 40 percent for those with rank 5A to 6B; and 20 percent for those with rank 7A to 8B. The officials with ranks 9A and 9B were unaffected, probably due to their already-low salaries; they continued to receive their full salary in rice.

government, as it was composed of officials whose salaries had become linked to the market value of paper money, which was falling rapidly. In the fourth month of 1403, the Yongle emperor admitted that the circulation of paper money was poor. To force people to use the precious notes, he reinstated the ban on gold and silver in exchanges.[83] In the first month of 1404, he added that someone caught doing so would be exiled, along with his entire family.[84]

83 *Ming shilu*, Taizong, 346.
84 *Ming shilu*, 497.

Officials seemed to take this seriously enough to make some arrests. The *Ming shilu* noted that the emperor had pardoned a civilian in Huguang Province, who had been arrested and sentenced to exile in 1404 after paying for his father's funeral in silver. When the case was brought before the Ministry of Punishment in Nanjing for final review, the Yongle emperor instructed the ministry to pardon him. He stated that, unlike those who traded in silver for profit, this man had a good heart, showing filial piety to his dead father; the funeral was an urgent reason to use silver as money.[85] This was probably not the only case brought before the ministry; although the filial son was pardoned, there is no reason to suppose that other people caught using silver or gold as money were pardoned as well.

4.3 *Taking Precious Notes out of Circulation: the Salt Tax and Crime Restitution Fees*

What the emperor had not yet understood was that severe punishments would not halt the devaluation of paper money. In the seventh month of 1404, Chen Ying, a censor-in-chief,[86] submitted a memorial to the Yongle emperor, pointing out that the major problem with paper money was that there was too much of it. He said, "For years the paper money circulates poorly because the state has issued too many notes but without any measure to collect them back. [As a result,] goods become more valuable than paper money."[87] Although the word for inflation had not yet been devised, Chen Ying had observed and understood the relationship between the supply of money and the price of commodities.

Chen Ying was the first official to suggest that the government create channels for returning paper money to the state treasury and removing it from circulation. He saw a way to do this through the salt administration. Since the beginning of the Ming, the government had monopolized salt production as a way to supply grain to frontier garrisons, through a grain-for-salt exchange system. Salt traders bought and then delivered grain to military garrisons in return for salt licenses, which permitted them to obtain salt from salt fields. They could then sell the salt in designated districts.[88] Chen Ying proposed to expand the state's benefit with a consumption tax on salt, to be paid in paper

85 *Ming shilu*, 517–18.

86 The Censorate was a top-echelon agency of the Ming central government. A total of 110 investigating censors were the emperor's front-line surveillance agents, headed by two censors-in-chief, two vice censors-in-chief, and four assistant censors-in-chief. See Hucker, *A Dictionary of Official Titles*, 74.

87 *Ming shilu*, Taizong, 589.

88 Wing-kin Puk, *The Rise and Fall of a Public Debt Market in 16th-Century China: The Story of the Ming Salt Certificate* (Leiden: Brill, 2016), 22–23.

money. He estimated that the empire had 10 million civilian households and 2 million military households, with average households consisting of five people, about 60 million people in all. He recommended a salt consumption tax on these 60 million people paid monthly in quantities based on their age—one catty (1.3 lbs.) for a young person ten to fifteen years old, and two catties for an adult, that is, anyone over age fifteen. In return for every catty of state salt, people would pay one *guan* in tax. In this way, the state could collect 250 million *guan* in three months, which would take the inflated currency out of circulation. The imperial court supported Chen Ying's proposal but cut the tax in half, to one *guan* for an adult (two catties) and half a *guan* (500 copper cash) for a child (one catty).[89] In this way, the state took 125 million *guan* out of circulation in three months.[90]

But paper money continued to have low value in the market. In 1411, the emperor dispatched Censor Kuang Ye to Nanjing to investigate the situation. According to the *Ming shilu*, Kuang was so kindhearted that he arrested only two "market bullies"[91] and then returned to Beijing, where he told the emperor that the population of Nanjing held the emperor in such awe that no one else would dare to obstruct the circulation of paper money.[92] Although the Yongle emperor seemed reassured by this report, that same year he agreed to reduce the amount of paper money in official salaries to keep the precious notes out of circulation. As seen in Table 3, officials ranked from 1A to 6B benefited from this new policy.[93] By receiving more rice and less paper money, they were less affected by depreciation of the notes.

In 1413, the Yongle emperor announced a second measure to remove paper currency from circulation: crime restitution (*shuzui*). During the Hongwu period, paying a fine, instead of being punished for a crime, was more of a privilege than a policy. The practice allowed transgressors to mitigate their punishment by making contributions to the state, but only as special dispensation by the emperor; and it was up to the emperor to decide the form of their "contribution"—for example, whether it would be a gift of raw copper or the transport of rice to a frontier garrison. In 1413 the Yongle emperor institutionalized the practice so that some punishments could be reversed by payments in

89 *Ming shilu*, Taizong, 589–90.

90 For an introduction to the salt consumption tax, see Fujii Hiroshi, "Mingdai no toguchi shoshiohô ni tsuitnie," *Shakai keizai shigakkai* 13, no. 3 (1943).

91 The Chinese government used the term "local bullies" or "market bullies" for people who used their power and influence to commit crimes with impunity.

92 *Ming shilu*, Yingzong, 3503.

93 For example, in 1403, a 1A official received an annual salary of 418 *shi* of rice and 6,260 *guan* in precious notes. In 1411, his salary changed to 522 *shi* and 5,220 *guan*.

TABLE 3 Annual salaries of Nanjing officials in 1403 and 1411 (in *shi* and *guan*)

Rank/Year	1403	1411
1A	418 *shi*; 6,260 *guan*	522 *shi*; 5,220 *guan*
1B	355 *shi*; 5,330 *guan*	444 *shi*; 4,440 *guan*
2A	293 *shi*; 4,390 *guan*	366 *shi*; 3,660 *guan*
2B	230 *shi*; 3,460 *guan*	288 *shi*; 2,880 *guan*
3A	210 *shi*; 2,100 *guan*	210 *shi*; 2,100 *guan*
3B	156 *shi*; 1,560 *guan*	156 *shi*; 1,560 *guan*
4A	144 *shi*; 1,440 *guan*	144 *shi*; 1,440 *guan*
4B	126 *shi*; 1,260 *guan*	126 *shi*; 1,260 *guan*
5A	115 *shi*; 770 *guan*	115 *shi*; 770 *guan*
5B	101 *shi*; 670 *guan*	101 *shi*; 670 *guan*
6A	72 *shi*; 480 *guan*	84 *shi*; 360 *guan*
6B	58 *shi*; 380 *guan*	67 *shi*; 290 *guan*
7A	72 *shi*; 180 *guan*	72 *shi*; 180 *guan*
7B	67 *shi*; 170 *guan*	67 *shi*; 170 *guan*
8A	62 *shi*; 160 *guan*	62 *shi*; 160 *guan*
8B	58 *shi*; 140 *guan*	58 *shi*; 140 *guan*
9A	66 *shi*; 0 *guan*	53 *shi*; 130 *guan*
9B	60 *shi*; 0 *guan*	48 *shi*; 120 *guan*

SOURCE: *DAMING HUIDIAN*, 789:681

Notes: In 1411 the Yongle emperor reduced the percentage of officials' salaries in paper currency as follows: 50 percent for officials with rank 1A to 4B; 40 percent for those with rank 5A to 5B; 30 percent for those with rank 6A to 6B; and 20 percent for those with rank 7A to 9B. As a result, officials those with rank 1A to 6B benefited from this new policy as they could obtain more rice and less depreciated paper money. The conversion rate remained 10 *guan* for 1 *shi.*

paper currency. The cost for avoiding particular punishments was 8,000 *guan* for beheading, 6,000 *guan* for strangling, 3,000 guan for banishment, 2,000 *guan* for penal servitude, 1,000 *guan* for heavy flogging, and 500 *guan* for light flogging.[94]

Through these two measures, the amount of paper money circulating in markets fell, and its value rose. It was a lengthy process; before the market price of the currency increased to a satisfactory level, the Ming capital had moved

94 *DaMing huidian*, 789:143.

to Beijing. As shown later, this created even more problems with paper money. But, by this time, the economic outlook had improved on another front. The resumption of the tribute missions and the foreign trade that accompanied them had stimulated a sluggish economy, as a result of Admiral Zheng He's voyages across the Indian Ocean.

5 Reopening China to Trade

5.1 *The Treasure Fleet*

In 1403, the first year of the Yongle reign, construction was initiated at the Longjiang shipyard just outside Nanjing.[95] Shipwrights, carpenters, caulkers, ironsmiths, and sailmakers began to build and repair warships, trading ships, and support vessels for the "foreign expeditionary armada" (*xiafan guanjun*), later known as the Treasure Fleet.[96] In July 1405, the fleet set sail on its first voyage, commanded by Admiral Zheng He. The other high-ranking officers in the fleet were also court eunuchs in the civil service. The admiral was accompanied by naval soldiers, most of whom were from Fujian Province on the coast, as well as linguists and translators, and gifts for foreign rulers. The admiral's mission was to invite other countries to send tributary missions again, to improve and add to existing maps, and to clear the seas of pirates and make the ocean safe for travel and trade.

On the fleet's return in 1407, Admiral Zheng He's navy fought the pirate Chen Zuyi and his fleet, who had taken Palembang in South Sumatra and controlled the Malaccan Strait. The Ming navy defeated the pirates with the help of Shi Jinqing, a local Muslim chieftain; Admiral Zheng made him the pacification superintendent of Palembang, assuring China of a port there. The treasure fleet brought back valuable gifts for the emperor as well as envoys from many countries in Southeast Asia who wanted to present their tribute in person (and engage in trade while in China). The emperor gave them gifts in return and invited them to send more missions to China.[97]

95 Longjiang was the largest shipbuilding center in the Ming dynasty. Regarding its operation, see Louise Levathes, *When China Ruled the Seas: The Treasure Fleet of the Dragon Throne 1405–1433* (New York: Simon & Schuster, 1994), 75–85.

96 Edward L. Dreyer, *Zheng He: China and the Oceans in the Early Ming Dynasty, 1405–1433* (New York: Pearson Education, 2007), 99.

97 Tansen Sen, "The Impact of Zheng He's Expeditions on Indian Ocean Interactions," *Bulletin of SOAS* 79, no. 3 (2016): 613.

The tribute missions gave merchants a chance to trade while incurring minimal transaction costs. China traded porcelain, tea, and silk for pepper, cloves, cinnamon, cotton goods, gold, silver, pearls, coral, amber, ivory, rhinoceros horns, camphor, frankincense, other kinds of incense, sappanwood (an herbal medicine), and other scented kinds of wood.[98] Sappanwood and pepper were especially popular, and Chinese merchants distributed them throughout China, stimulating interregional trade. By the time Beijing became the official imperial capital in 1421, Zheng He had made five voyages, reestablished old trade routes, and established China's naval dominance in Southeast Asia and the Indian Ocean.

5.2 *Building the New Capital in Beijing*

The Yongle emperor announced that, after nearly two decades of repair and construction, Beijing would become the imperial capital at the lunar new year in 1421.[99] At that time, Beijing was a triple-walled city, with one wall enclosing the innermost Palace City, a second wall around the Imperial City, and a third wall around the outer Capital City. In 1553, a fourth wall was built at the southern end of the outermost wall. (See Map 2)

The innermost wall was 7.9 meters high, built of brick, with a perimeter measuring 3.4 km.[100] The wall surrounding the Palace City (or Forbidden City) had four main gates, one in each of the cardinal directions. (See Map 3.) As Hok-lam Chan notes, the Palace City and the entire Capital City with all it enclosed were laid out according to the principles of geomancy (*fengshui*), ancient Chinese cosmology explaining the celestial-terrestrial correspondence. Because he was the Son of Heaven, the emperor's dwelling place was built to be a heaven on earth.

The interactions of yin and yang, opposite but complementary cosmic forces, were vividly reflected in the design and arrangement of these palaces and halls. Of the three Great Halls in the front, the Hall of Service to Heaven, which symbolized the "superior yang," was a magnificent imperial audience hall. Its central focal point was a throne decorated with a carved marble dragon, the symbol of imperial power and authority. The throne was placed atop a platform of nine steps that corresponded to the nine layers of Heaven. Among the three palaces in the rear, the Palace of Heavenly Purity and the

98 Dreyer, *Zheng He*, 37.

99 Chen Xuelin (Chan Hok-lam), *Liu Bowen yu Nazha cheng: Beijing jiancheng de chuanshuo* (Beijing: Shenghuo, dushu, xinzhi sanlian shudian, 2008), 34.

100 The Palace City wall enclosed an area of 0.72 sq. km.; its length was 960 meters from north to south and 760 meters from east to west.

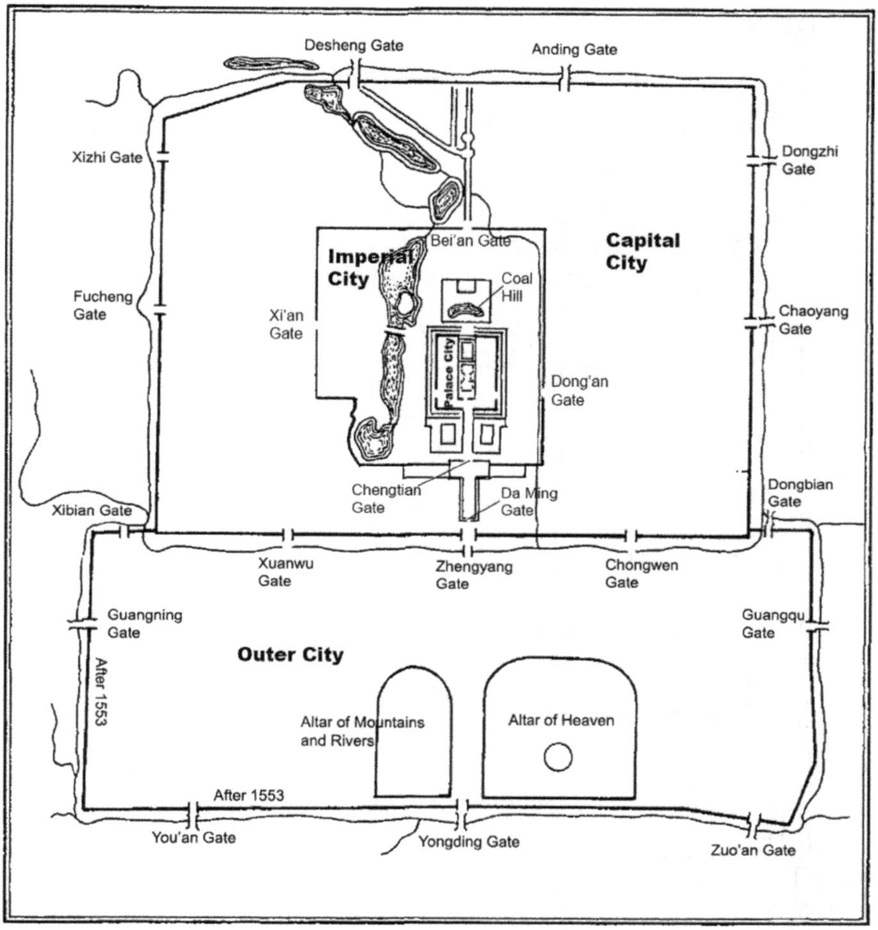

MAP 2 Beijing
SOURCE: ADAPTED FROM "MAP 12. CITY PLAN OF PEKING," IN *THE CAMBRIDGE HISTORY OF CHINA*, VOLUME 7: *THE MING DYNASTY, 1368–1644, PART 1*, EDITED BY FREDERICK W. MOTE AND DENIS TWITCHETT (NEW YORK: CAMBRIDGE UNIVERSITY PRESS, 1998), 240.

Palace of Earthly Tranquility were the bedchambers of the emperor and the empress, respectively. The middle palace, the Hall of Peaceful Unity, was the "dragon cave" where the yang and yin interacted and (hopefully) produced life and nourishment. The architectural arrangement and the dimensions of the palaces and halls in the Palace City replicated those in Nanjing, symbolizing continuity and legitimacy as well as geomancy.

The walled Imperial City surrounded and further protected the Palace City. The Imperial City wall had four gates, each one a bastion against attack. Inside

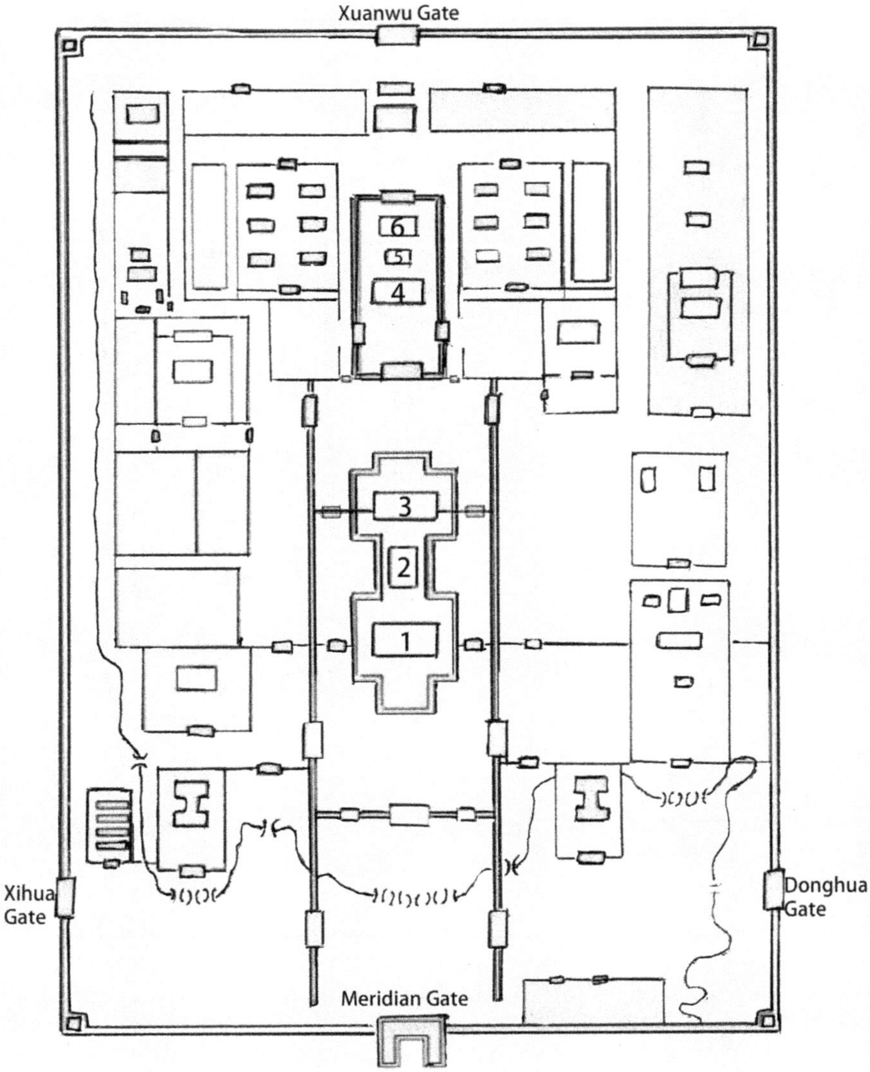

MAP 3 Plan of the palace city in Beijing. 1. *Fengtian dian* (Hall of Service to Heaven) 2. *Huagai dian* (Hall of Celestial Parasol) 3. *Jinshen dian* (Hall of Prudence) 4. *Qianqing gong* (Palace of Heavenly Purity) 5. *Jiaotai dian* (Hall of Peaceful Unity) 6. *Kunning gong* (Palace of Earthly Tranquillity)

the Imperial City gardens, parks, and more palaces lined the shores of man-made ponds and islands. Wansui Hill, popularly known as Coal Hill, had five peaks and commanded a panoramic view of the entire city. An elevation at its top was dubbed Zhenshan, meaning "mount for suppression," to symbolize the Ming victory over the previous regime.[101]

To make Beijing the all-powerful political center of the empire, the government had mobilized hundreds of thousands of workers for its construction projects. These workers included 27,000 artisan households in Nanjing that the emperor ordered to relocate permanently to Beijing, where eunuch agencies supervised their work. The need for workers was not limited to Beijing. To rebuild the Huitong Canal in Shandong, for instance, a total of 300,000 laborers were recruited from the prefectures of Xuzhou, Yingtian, and Zhenjiang in the Yangzi River valley.[102]

The mobilization of laborers did not end when the emperor's building projects were completed, as the new capital needed thousands of workers to maintain the palace and government institutions. To supply workers for the rest of the city, the Ministry of Works organized 180,000 of the 240,000 artisan households in the provinces to serve in the new capital. Many of these artisan households had formerly gone to Nanjing to perform their labor service; now, they had to travel to Beijing, instead.[103] They served in a seasonal or yearly rotation, as was the case in Nanjing.

To support two capitals, the state began to print more paper money to pay the additional officials. Although Beijing became the imperial capital, Nanjing maintained its original government and six ministries, hence, the empire had two courts. Beijing was the throne capital, and its status was supreme,[104] but the Ming government still had to pay two sets of court officials in rice as well as paper money.

But because the grain supply had run short, especially in Beijing, the emperor decided that, instead of increasing the total rice payment to cover both sets of officials, he would divide the original rice payment between them. For example: in 1411 an official in Nanjing with a rank of 1A was paid 522 *shi* of rice and 5,220 *guan* of paper money. Under the new policy, in 1421 he received only 209 *shi* of rice, and the remaining 313 *shi* went to an official of the same rank in Beijing. As shown in Table 4, to cover the shortage in their rice salaries, the emperor made up the difference in paper money at the rate of 10 *guan* of

101 Chan, *Legends of the Buildings of Old Peking*, 110.

102 *Mingshi*, 4204.

103 Xu Daling, "Mingdai Beijing de jingji shenghuo," *Beijing daxue xuebao* 4 (1959): 47.

104 The court at Nanjing, as Frederick Mote put it, had "very limited actual responsibility and with power over regional government only, except in fiscal administration and a few other areas" ("The Transformation of Nanking," 152).

TABLE 4 Annual salaries of officials in Nanjing and Beijing, 1411 and 1421 (in *shi* and *guan*)

Rank/Year	1411	1421 Nanjing	1421 Beijing
1A	522 *shi*; 5,220 *guan*	209 *shi*; 8,352 guan	313 *shi*; 7,308 *guan*
1B	444 *shi*; 4,440 *guan*	178 *shi*; 7,104 guan	266 *shi*; 6,216 *guan*
2A	366 *shi*; 3,660 *guan*	146 *shi*; 5,856 guan	220 *shi*; 5,124 *guan*
2B	288 *shi*; 2,880 *guan*	115 *shi*; 4,608 guan	173 *shi*; 4,032 *guan*
3A	210 *shi*; 2,100 *guan*	84 *shi*; 3,360 *guan*	126 *shi*; 2,940 *guan*
3B	156 *shi*; 1,560 *guan*	62 *shi*; 2,496 *guan*	94 *shi*; 2,184 *guan*
4A	144 *shi*; 1,440 *guan*	58 *shi*; 2,304 *guan*	86 *shi*; 2,016 *guan*
4B	126 *shi*; 1,260 *guan*	50 *shi*; 2,016 *guan*	76 *shi*; 1,764 *guan*
5A	115 *shi*; 770 *guan*	38 *shi*; 1,536 *guan*	58 *shi*; 1,344 *guan*
5B	101 *shi*; 670 *guan*	34 *shi*; 1,344 *guan*	50 *shi*; 1,176 *guan*
6A	84 *shi*; 360 *guan*	24 *shi*; 960 *guan*	48 *shi*; 720 *guan*
6B	67 *shi*; 290 *guan*	19 *shi*; 768 *guan*	38 *shi*; 576 *guan*
7A	72 *shi*; 180 *guan*	18 *shi*; 720 *guan*	36 *shi*; 540 *guan*
7B	67 *shi*; 170 *guan*	17 *shi*; 672 *guan*	34 *shi*; 504 *guan*
8A	62 *shi*; 160 *guan*	16 *shi*; 624 *guan*	31 *shi*; 486 *guan*
8B	58 *shi*; 140 *guan*	14 *shi*; 576 *guan*	29 *shi*; 432 *guan*
9A	53 *shi*; 130 *guan*	13 *shi*; 528 *guan*	26 *shi*; 396 *guan*
9B	48 *shi*; 120 *guan*	12 *shi*; 480 *guan*	24 *shi*; 360 *guan*

SOURCE: *MING SHILU*, TAIZU, 2778; *DAMING HUIDIAN*, 789:681

Notes: In 1421 the Yongle emperor adopted different salary scales for Nanjing officials and Beijing officials. In Nanjing, all officials were paid 20 percent of their salaries in rice and 80 percent in paper money. But in Beijing, the percentage of officials' salaries in paper currency was much higher: 70 percent for officials with rank 1A to 5B; 60 percent for those with rank 6A to 9B. The conversion rate remained 10 *guan* for 1 *shi*.

paper money per *shi* of rice. Thus, this Nanjing official would receive an additional 8,352 *guan* to make up the shortfall, whereas the Beijing official would receive an additional 7,308 *guan*. In this way, the total grain payment for two sets of officials remained the same, and the emperor's paper money payments tripled (in the case of the official ranked 1A, from 5,220 to 15,660 *guan*).

The markets, especially in Beijing and Nanjing, responded immediately to the flood of precious notes by devaluing it. In 1422 the emperor attributed the problem to a common market practice of refusing to accept worn-out notes. He became so angry that he decreed that anyone who refused to accept a worn-out note could be sentenced to death and his or her family sent into exile, after paying a fine in paper money.[105] Even such a severe punishment did not raise the value of precious notes in the market; and the emperor's strategy remained unsuccessful even by the time he died two years later.

In August 1424, on his return to Beijing after a military campaign in the Gobi Desert, the Yongle emperor died of a sudden illness. His legacies included a new capital in the north, a bloated bureaucracy, underpaid officials, and a depreciated state currency in the form of paper money—"precious notes" that were nearly worthless. At the same time, he had reopened China to foreign trade, strengthened its relationship with other countries, rid the seas of pirates, and stimulated the economy.

6 Retrieving Precious Notes: Commercial Fees and Charges

Zhu Gaochi, the Yongle emperor's eldest son, ascended the throne in September 1424, but died only ten months later. As the Hongxi emperor, he frequently expressed anxiety over the low circulation of precious notes.[106] He tried to raise officials' salaries by increasing the commutation rate of paper money for rice, from 10 *guan* for one *shi* of rice to 25.[107] But this raised salaries only in theory; as it dumped even more paper money into the market, the measure only exacerbated its devaluation.

In early 1525, the Hongxi emperor ordered Xia Yuanji, the minister of revenue, to meet with other officials to find a solution to this problem. Xia replied that the government had issued too much paper money and should retrieve more money from the market while reducing its issuance. He suggested increasing the operating fee or shop fee for commercial enterprises in the Capital City, called the *mentan*.[108]

The operating fee had originated in Nanjing. When the dynastic founder built civilian housing within his new capital, he neglected to set aside space for businesses. Years later, many of these civilian houses, especially those on the main streets, became shops as well. As the ground floors were long and rectangular, owners divided their houses into a shop front on the street, with private living quarters in back. The operating fee was similar to a licensing fee

105 *Ming shilu*, Taizong, 2350.

106 *Ming shilu*, Taizong, 2350; *Ming shilu*, Renzong, 39, 89, 138, 219.

107 *Mingshi*, 2003.

108 *Ming shilu*, Renzong, 219.

(but without an actual license) in that it permitted the owner to conduct business in his shop.

The Hongxi emperor endorsed Xia Yuanji's proposal and raised the price of the operating fee, which was paid in paper money. He also reinstated the ban on using gold or silver in exchanges. He insisted that the tax increase was only a temporary measure, which he would rescind after the market value of paper money returned to normal.[109] But he died a few months later, in late May of 1425.

The Hongxi emperor was succeeded by his son Zhu Zhanji, then twenty-six years old. Reigning as the Xuande emperor, Zhu Zhanji had to grapple with the low morale among officials due to their meager salaries. Despite his father's efforts, the market value of paper money had not risen to a level that provided a living wage. Only a few months after his ascension to the throne, he received a petition from a scholar named Yin Song in Huguang Province, requesting payment in rice for all local officials. Yin stated that the price of rice was so high that, depending on the district, it cost 40–70 *guan* per *shi*. If an official had a large family, his salary would not be sufficient for food. Yin postulated that, in such a case, the official would no longer consider his honor and would stoop to illegal activities in order to feed them. Yin suggested that, to guarantee that officials remained honest, the state disburse the entire official salary in rice.[110]

Instead of taking even more rice in taxes, and possibly bankrupting farmers to pay his officials, the Xuande emperor consolidated and expanded commercial charges and fees, hoping to increase the value of paper money. These commercial charges consisted of taxes on government land and on farms used for commercial purposes and charges for traveling merchants.

Landowners, merchants, artisans, officials, and anyone else who used government land in and around the cities for commercial purposes (e.g., shops and warehouses) paid the commercial tax offices and bureaus for the privilege. In 1429, the government issued a list of commercial properties and their monthly operating fees as follows: an inn cost 500 *guan*, a mill 500 *guan*, a lumberyard or a warehouse 400 *guan*, a shop that manufactured or sold tiles and bricks 400 *guan*, a shop that mounted calligraphy and paintings 30 *guan*, and a carriage house 20 *guan*. In rural areas, farms were taxed at 300 *guan* per

109 *Ming shilu*, Renzong, 219.
110 *Ming shilu*, Xuanzong, 175–76.

mu (0.14 acre)[111] of vegetable garden and 100 *guan* for every ten fruit trees in an orchard.[112]

The prefectural and county magistrates taxed traveling merchants by setting up tax offices and bureau branches at transshipment points and city gates, where the rate for carts carrying goods was 10 *guan* for a small cart, 50 *guan* for an oxcart, and 200 *guan* for a donkey cart.[113] The magistrates collected these charges in paper money; then, after spending it locally, for instance, to pay official salaries, they sent the remainder to the palaces of the two capitals, to be stored in the inner treasuries.[114]

The Ministries of Revenue in Beijing and Nanjing oversaw the inland customs toll for merchants sailing on the Grand Canal and divided the canal into five segments to charge a toll for each one.[115] The toll was assessed by a boat's loading capacity. Unless it was empty, a boat was charged 100 *guan* for every 100 *shi* of its loading capacity. This meant that a boat would pay 500 *guan* in tolls if it could carry 100 *shi* from Nanjing, through all five segments of the canal, to Tongzhou.[116] As it was difficult to measure a boat's loading capacity, it became common practice to obtain the figure by calculating the length of its cross beam.[117] The paper money collected through seven customhouses was transported directly to an inner treasury in Beijing and later used to pay officials' salaries.[118] For the locations of inland customhouses, see Map 4.

These measures were remarkably successful. Shortly after the reform, the value of paper money rose at markets. In 1431, the Xuande emperor stated that he was satisfied with this progress, and, to raise the farmers' income, he cut the farm tax from 300 *guan* per *mu* to 150.[119] One year later, he extended the benefit to merchants by reducing the rent of government warehouses in

111 See "Ming Weights and Measures."

112 See Sakuma Shigeo, "Mingdai no shôzei seido," *Shakai keizai shigakkai* 13, no. 3 (1943): 257–58.

113 *DaMing huidian*, 789: 553–54.

114 Sakuma Shigeo, "Mingdai no shôzei seido," 249–50.

115 The five segments of the Grand Canal were: Nanjing to Huai'an, Huai'an to Xuzhou, Xuzhou to Ji'ning, Ji'ning to Linqing, and Linqing to Tongzhou.

116 *DaMing huidian*, 789:554.

117 Li Longqian, *MingQing jingji tanhui chubian* (Taipei: Daoxiang chubanshe, 2002), 490–91; see also Li Xun, *Mingshi shihuozhi jiaozhu* (Beijing: Zhonghua shuju, 1982), 245.

118 These customhouses, called *chaoguan* (lit., paper-money customs) were, from south to north, at Upper Xin River (at the West gate of Nanjing), Yangzhou (Jiangsu Province), Huai'an (Jiangsu Province), Xuzhou (Jiangsu Province), Ji'ning (Shandong Province), Linqing (Shandong Province), and Kuo County (Tongzhou). *DaMing huidian*, 789:610. See also Sakuma Shigeo, "Mingdai no shôzei seido," 253.

119 *Ming shilu*, Xuanzong, 1783; *DaMing huidian*, 789:554.

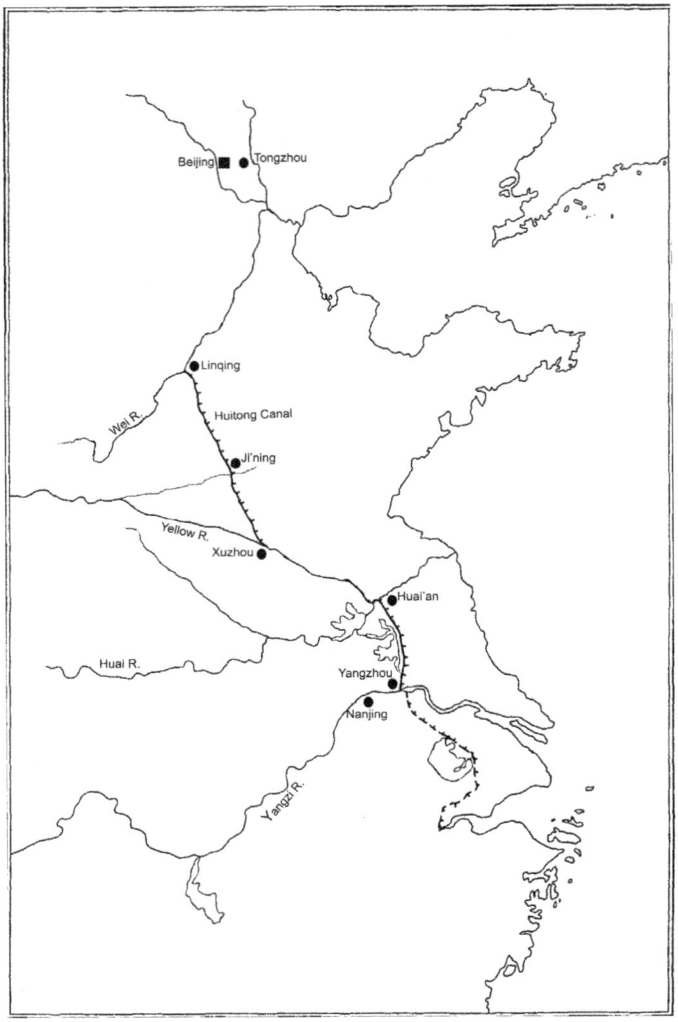

MAP 4
Inland customhouses in 1429

provinces by 50 percent as well.[120] In 1433, as the value of paper money had risen, the emperor accepted the suggestion of his new minister of revenue, Hu Ying, and lowered the commutation rate in the official salary from 25 *guan* to 15 per *shi* of rice.[121]

120 *Ming shilu*, Xuanzong, 2018.

121 *DaMing huidian*, 789:610. The new rate aroused criticisms and grievances among officials against Hu Ying. See *Mingshi*, 2003.

7 Conclusion

No matter what form it takes, money is a token, a kind of credit. Its value depends on its fiat value in the market—what the market will accept as fair payment, which most often is based on supply and demand. When the Hongwu emperor attempted to exert his political authority to maintain the fiat value of precious notes in the market, he failed. By the time of the Yongle reign, officials had realized that if the government wished to encourage the circulation of paper money in the market, it had to allow people to use the precious notes to pay taxes. The Yongle emperor began to levy a salt consumption tax and commercial fees in paper money in order to soak up the excess notes that had flooded the market when the emperor(s) paid officials in paper currency. Through these taxes, tolls, and fees, the notes returned to state coffers. These measures proved so successful in raising the value of paper money that two successive emperors, the Hongxi and Xuande emperors, continued and expanded them.

By the early fifteenth century, four major channels existed for paper money: the salt consumption tax; the crime restitution fees; the operating charges for businesses, farms, and merchant transit (e.g., at city gates); and the inland customs tolls on the Grand Canal. These measures stabilized the value of paper money in the 1430s.

As shown in Chapter 2, state currency was never the only currency of exchange in the market—it was not even the main one. Despite the imperial ban on using gold and silver in exchanges, market exchanges were dominated by silver bullion and copper coins, and their value remained stable—commodity prices in coins and silver were unaffected by the devaluation of the precious note. Paper money circulated in markets solely because it could be used to pay particular taxes, and the only reason that it needed to circulate was to be usable currency for official salaries.

CHAPTER 2

From Illegal to Official: Copper and Silver, 1400–1487

The Hongwu emperor had prohibited copper and silver as exchange currencies in the market, in a failed attempt to promote the use of precious notes, his state currency. Later emperors, searching for a more viable state currency, turned to copper and then silver. To understand what led to this change, we look first at the conditions at the beginning of the dynasty.

Throughout the reign of the Hongwu emperor, all of China, from North China to the southeast coast, underwent an economic recession. It was not until around 1400, after the death of the founder of the dynasty, that the economy recovered.[1] The historian William Atwell suggested that the recession was caused by dramatic changes in the climate. In the fourteenth century, China, like Europe, experienced prolonged economic hardship because of a lethal combination of global volcanic activity, other natural disasters, and climate change. By the beginning of the fifteenth century, with the return of a climate more favorable for agriculture, China's economy recovered. This recovery allowed the Yongle emperor (r. 1403–1424) to collect enough tax income in the form of tribute grain to launch grand state projects such as creating a new capital in Beijing, building the Grand Canal to carry the rice tribute northward, and dispatching armies to the northern frontiers to fight the nomadic Mongol tribes. Tribute grain had been received in such abundance that: "In addition to the several million *shi* of grain that were shipped to the capital every year, district and prefectural granaries were so full that grain spoiled and could not be eaten."[2] However, transporting the enormous amount of rice to Beijing, in order to pay the soldiers who protected the capital, would prove difficult.

Atwell noted that the agricultural and economic recovery enabled the Yongle emperor to issue more precious notes and copper coins and to open or reopen silver mines in China and in parts of Southeast Asia that China controlled.[3] In

1 See G. William Skinner, "Presidential Address: The Structure of Chinese History," *Journal of Asian Studies* 44, no. 2 (1985): 279.

2 From the *Mingshi*, the general history of the Ming compiled in the early Qing dynasty, quoted in William Atwell, "Time, Money, and the Weather: Ming China and the 'Great Depression' of the Mid-Fifteenth Century," *Journal of Asian Studies* 61, no. 1 (2002): 86.

3 Although the Yongle emperor took in 80,185 taels in his first year, and less than 30,000 taels was the most silver that had been taken previously, in 1390, the silver and copper mines in

 | DOI:10.1163/9789004687530_004

addition, the Yongle emperor had the money and resources to build the gigantic treasure fleet, commanded by the eunuch Admiral Zheng He, reestablishing trade and foreign relations from the coasts of the South China Sea to the Indian Ocean.

According to Atwell's logic, the Hongwu administrative model was simply a passive response to an economic downturn caused by natural disasters, as volcanic ash and poor weather affected agricultural and, then, market activities. Without sizable markets, the Hongwu emperor could not obtain the money he needed to administer the empire, so he made do with labor services and taxes in kind, instead. But, in fact, the Hongwu emperor was *actively* nationalistic and isolationist.

1 Recession, Piracy, and Foreign Trade

As the Hongwu emperor, Zhu was suspicious of foreigners, foreign trade, and the Chinese merchants who engaged in it. Travel on the Silk Road, the trade route that had connected Asia to Europe since the second century BCE, had been in decline since the twelfth century, when the imperial capitals moved from the west to the east, closer to the coastlines. At that time, maritime trade on the eastern coast experienced a corresponding rise, making it more important than the overland route, and more Southeast Asian countries became tributary states of China. Although at the end of the Yuan, private maritime trade was thriving, unobstructed by the state, the only reason that maritime trade existed at all during Hongwu's early reign was that it was part of the official tribute system, the basis of China's relationship with surrounding countries and the embodiment of the Chinese world order. As John King Fairbank explained, "The relations of the Chinese with surrounding areas, and with non-Chinese peoples generally, were colored by ... an assumption of Chinese superiority" and were "hierarchic and nonegalitarian, like Chinese society itself."[4]

Mark Mancall noted that, in the tribute relationship, the ruler of China was presented as the Son of Heaven and the man at the apex of civilization, whereas the other country sent tribute in return for Chinese recognition and

---

Ming China were small. William Atwell writes: "For a population that probably approached 90 million people in 1400, silver receipts even of 10,000 kilograms per year may not seem very significant either to government revenues or to the Ming economy as a whole," in "Time, Money, and the Weather," 86.

4 John K. Fairbank, "A Preliminary Framework," in *The Chinese World Order: Traditional China's Foreign Relations*, ed. John K. Fairbank (Cambridge: Harvard University Press, 1968), 2.

protection.[5] When the dynasty in China changed, the new dynastic founder informed surrounding countries that it was time to renew Sino-foreign relations. Thus, in 1367, a year before he ascended the throne and for the purpose of launching the tribute system, the Hongwu emperor set up an agency for managing it, the Office of Maritime Trade and Shipping (*Shibo si*), at Taicang, a port city near Nanjing. In 1368, as soon as he had formally ascended the throne, he sent envoys to Goryeo (the Korean Peninsula), Annam (northern Vietnam), Japan, Champa (central and southern Vietnam), Java, and other Southeast Asian countries, inviting their rulers to present tribute to China's new ruler.[6] Chinese emperors permitted the envoys from these countries to engage in some trade after offering tribute from their kings to the Son of Heaven. The formal explanation for this trade was that it was needed to cover the envoys' personal travel expenses. But why would these countries bother to make the journey to China, if it were simply to kowtow?

In practice, Southeast Asian rulers sold their envoy appointments to maritime merchants who wished to trade with China, and the Hongwu emperor was well aware of this. In the late Yuan dynasty, when Quanzhou became the busiest trading port in Fujian, a native of the area named Zhu Daoshan rose to prominence as a merchant leader. The Yuan emperor invited him to organize the "tribute" missions. In doing so, the emperor had to permit Chinese merchants to leave China and travel to other countries, which was why maritime trade was prosperous in the early years of the Ming.[7]

The Hongwu emperor, however, restricted visits from tributary states, basing their frequency on their intimacy with the Ming government.[8] Only three years after inviting countries to pay tribute, he believed that he had cemented his rule in Sino-foreign relationships and became progressively more intolerant of foreign merchants. In 1371, the emperor closed the Office of Maritime Trade and Shipping in Taicang and decreed that when a tributary mission arrived there, the local garrison soldiers would escort the envoys and their tribute directly to Nanjing.[9] In this way, the emperor intended to end the foreign

5 Mark Mancall, "The Ch'ing Tribute System: An Interpretive Essay," in Fairbank, *The Chinese World Order*, 63–66.

6 Danjô Hiroshi, "Min hatsu no kaikin to chôkô: Minchô sensei shihai no rikai ni yosete," in *Min shin jidaishi no kihon mondai*, ed. Mori Masao et al. (Tokyo: Kyûko shoin, 1997), 206.

7 Li Qingxin, *Mingdai haiwai maoyi zhidu* (Beijing: Shehui kexue wenxian chubanshe, 2007), 44–47.

8 For example, representatives from Liuqiu (now Okinawa) were allowed to visit China once every two years, while those from Siam (Thailand) and Champa were allowed once every three years. *DaMing huidian*, 74–76; see also Li Qingxin, *Mingdai haiwai maoyi zhidu*, 74–75.

9 *Ming shilu*, Taizu, 969.

trade aspect of tributary missions, turning the tribute mission into a political performance. Many years later, the Ming scholar Shen Defu commented on this policy change. He suggested that the emperor had been wary of the envoy-traders, those cunning "oceanic barbarians," who might take advantage of the proximity of Taicang to Nanjing to spy on the Ming court.[10] By placing the envoys under close surveillance, Zhu Yuanzhang wanted to be sure that they could do nothing but present tribute.

The Hongwu emperor did not reserve his distrust for foreign merchants; his suspicion of clandestine maritime activities led him to impose a travel ban on his own coastal populations.[11] The earliest record of such a ban noted that, in 1371, the emperor was "still" banning coastal inhabitants from overseas travel, which implied that the Hongwu emperor had never permitted private interactions between Chinese and foreigners. The emperor forbade his subjects not only to have any contact with foreigners but also to take ships to other countries without his permission. When the Office of Maritime Trade and Shipping opened at southern ports to oversee tributary missions, they were put under close military surveillance to prevent commoners from fraternizing with foreigners.

The emperor's misgivings extended to Chinese merchants in the Yangzi River valley and along the southern coasts who had become wealthy during the Yuan dynasty through private foreign trade, which had flourished until he took the throne in 1368. These Chinese merchants had trade connections across South and Southeast Asia, to the coast of East Africa and the Middle East. Their wide-ranging trade had created demand for foreign imports in China, and they became rich under the Yuan emperors, who lived in the north and did not interfere with their business. Some of these wealthy merchants had openly opposed Zhu in his war for the throne. But when the Hongwu emperor prohibited private foreign trade without supporting official foreign trade through the tributary missions, these merchants had no legal way to satisfy ongoing demand for foreign goods. To continue to trade, the merchants could become smugglers, work with pirates, or leave the country and settle elsewhere. At least some of them did: throughout the Hongwu reign, maritime trade continued, albeit illegally.[12]

In short, the Hongwu emperor's comprehensive ban on foreign trade, whether private or official (through the tributary missions), created an

10 Shen Defu, *Wanli yehuo bian* (1606, repr. Beijing: Zhonghua shuju, 1959), 317.

11 *Ming shilu*, Taizu, 1300.

12 For a general history of maritime trade in the early Ming, see Zhang Weihua, *Mingdai haiwai maoyi jianlun* (Shanghai: Xuexi shenghuo chubanshe, 1955), especially p. 17.

atmosphere of tension and mutual antipathy between the throne and maritime merchants and coastal populations. In the coastal provinces, even some government officials engaged in illegal foreign trade.[13]

In 1374, for an unknown reason, the Hongwu emperor reopened the Office of Maritime Trade and Shipping in three ports in southeastern coastal provinces, giving the impression that the tributary trade might be revived, but all three of them were closed again that same year.[14] He instructed the Ministry of Rites to send a message to various countries in Southeast Asia saying that they had fulfilled their tribute duty and that they did not need to continue to visit.[15] In 1381, to emphasize this point, he renewed the 1371 ban on sea travel to trade with foreign countries.[16] In the absence of official trade to control the seas, piracy and smuggling became rampant.

The Hongwu emperor did not oppose domestic trade as long as it was conducted among Chinese. (As mentioned in Chapter 1, in 1391 he built several government warehouses on the banks of the Qinhuai River outside Nanjing and rented them at low cost to traveling merchants who needed storage space.) He reserved his animosity for foreign trade or any hint of it. In 1394, he stated that many foreign barbarians were cunning, and that was why he had been so careful in selecting tributary states, taking years to do so, and finally permitting only three (Liuqiu [Okinawa)], Zhenla [Khmer kingdom], and Siam [Thailand]). But despite his efforts to limit foreign influence, many coastal inhabitants smuggled foreign products into China, especially incense. To put an end to the smuggling, he not only renewed the 1371 and 1381 bans on any and all association with foreign barbarians but also banned all foreign goods in China. People who owned foreign products had to destroy them within three months or risk severe punishment. The emperor suggested that the Chinese buy local incense for worship and then banned the sale of incense made in Guangdong and Guangxi to other provinces, because he suspected the "cunning merchants" from these provinces of selling foreign incense disguised as Chinese products.[17]

---

13 See Roderich Ptak, "China and Portugal at Sea: The Early Ming Trading System and the *Estado da India* Compared" (1991), repr. in *China and the Asian Seas: Trade, Travel, and Visions of the Other (1400–1700)*, ed. Roderich Ptak (Aldershot; Brookfield, Vt.: Ashgate, 1998), 23.

14 The ports where the Office of Maritime Trade and Shipping were reopened briefly were Mingzhou (now Ningbo) in Zhejiang Province, Quanzhou in Fujian Province, and Guangzhou in Guangdong Province. Shen Defu, *Wanli yehuo bian*, 317; *Mingshi*, 1848.

15 *Ming shilu*, Taizu, 1565.

16 *Ming shilu*, Taizu, 3640.

17 *Ming shilu*, Taizu, 3373–74.

In summary, Zhu Yuanzhang ruled China for thirty-one years, but, except for the first few years, he did his best to suppress maritime trade. He eliminated official foreign trade from the tribute system, banned all contact between Chinese and foreigners, and, in the case of incense, even disrupted trade between coastal and inland provinces.

Historians have suspected that his actions were in response to piracy, which was endemic in Chinese coastal waters in the late Yuan and the early Ming. Many pirates were coastal boat people, who made their living not just as fishermen but also as smugglers (or merchants; there was little distinction between the two). The boat people carried weapons to protect themselves from the navy, but they also attacked and looted coastal villages and other merchant junks. In the interest of state security, it made sense for the dynastic founder to reduce the commercial activities of coastal populations.[18] As a result, market activities in China were seriously curtailed, but this would not have swayed the dynastic founder because, as the Ming historian Wu Han commented, Zhu thought no good would come from maritime trade.[19] But, as a deterrent to piracy, Zhu's actions failed: when the government shut down the trading ports without corresponding measures to guard the coast and patrol the seas, piracy continued unabated.

2 Reopening China: Silver in the Market

The Ming government's attitude toward maritime trade took a sharp turn during the Yongle emperor's reign. As mentioned earlier, in the early fifteenth century, the Yongle emperor adopted a zealous diplomatic policy, reviving and expanding the tribute trade. Because he had taken the throne through warfare, he was eager to present himself to rulers of surrounding countries as the legitimate authority of China, and tribute missions were one way to do that. The treasure fleet was another.

In 1403, the first year of his reign, he had sea-going junks built and existing ships repaired at Nanjing, assembling a fleet of trading ships, warships, and support vessels that would once again open China to foreign trade. In the same year, he reopened the Office of Maritime Trade and Shipping at the three tribute ports in the southeast coastal cities of Mingzhou in Zhejiang Province,

18 Danjô Hiroshi, "Min hatsu no kaikin to chôkô," 208; Wu Han, "Shiliu shiji qian zhi Zhongguo yu Nanyang" (1936) in his *Wu Han shixue lunzhu xuanji*, 615; Li Qingxin, *Mingdai haiwai maoyi zhidu*, 47.

19 Wu Han, "Shiliu shiji qian zhi Zhongguo," 613.

Quanzhou in Fujian Province, and Guangzhou in Guangdong Province. At each office, he appointed a eunuch to supervise the tribute trade.[20] He made Zheng He, his childhood servant and trusted battlefield commander in the civil war, the head eunuch in the palace and supervisor of all its construction work. In 1404 the emperor made Zheng He the admiral of the treasure fleet and in 1405 dispatched him overseas, in order to encourage the rulers of surrounding countries to present tribute to (and to trade with) China again.[21] Zheng made seven spectacular maritime journeys around the South China Sea and the Indian Ocean, six of them during the Yongle reign.[22]

When the historian Li Qingxin compiled a table of tributary missions, he found that, during the thirty-one-year Hongwu reign, there were only 109 tributary missions from 15 countries, compared to 339 missions from 40 countries during the twenty-two-year Yongle reign.[23] The Yongle emperor did not relax the ban on *private* maritime trade, but official, government-controlled trade through the tribute missions flourished. Because Admiral Zheng He and other eunuchs bought foreign goods for the palace during their voyages, coastal civilians, soldiers, and even some officials traded overseas by claiming that the eunuchs had entrusted them to do so.[24] Now that a strong navy controlled the seas and the demand for foreign goods was met legally, piracy and smuggling were all but wiped out.

2.1 *Feeding the Capital: Tribute Rice and the Grand Canal*

Despite the economic recovery and the overabundance of rice, scholar-officials and soldiers in Beijing had trouble collecting their rice salaries. The poor navigability of the Grand Canal, particularly in the middle, where it became the dangerous Yellow River, made transporting the rice tribute from the Yangzi valley in the south to Beijing in the north an arduous process. The Huai and

20 *Mingshi*, 1848.

21 This was the first time that a eunuch had been appointed to such a powerful position. Zheng He was only 33 years old at the time but had already proven himself an able commander, military strategist, and diplomat. In 1404 the emperor had ordered him to build a navy to clear the coasts of Japanese pirates. According to several Chinese and Japanese documents, Zheng He traveled to Japan, where he successfully enlisted the aid of Ashikaga Shogun to deal with the raiders. See Tsai, *The Eunuchs in the Ming Dynasty*, 155–57.

22 The voyages during the Yongle reign were in 1405, 1407, 1409, 1413, 1417, and 1421. For a brief introduction to the maritime expeditions commanded by Zheng He, see Chan, "The Chien-wen, Yung-lo, Hung-shi, and Hsuan-te Reigns," 232–36.

23 Liuqiu (Okinawa), Siam (Thailand), and Champa maintained the closest tributary relationship with China, with 55 missions from Liuqiu, 18 from Siam, and 17 from Champa. Li Qingxin, *Mingdai haiwai maoyi zhidu*, 56–58.

24 *Ming shilu*, Xuanzong, 2308.

Yangzi Rivers that crossed the canal were prone to flooding, and the Yellow River, which connected the northern and southern sections of the canal deposited tons of silt annually, making the river too shallow for the large boats needed to carry the bulky rice tribute. Because of its load of silt, the Yellow River also tended to flood, jump its banks, and change course.[25] Although the Yongle emperor had new canals built in northern China and in the south, which greatly improved the inland waterway, the Yellow River was still used as the middle of the Grand Canal.[26] Additionally, the final 35 kilometers of the journey north, from Tongzhou to Beijing, were uphill and over land, which meant the rice was stored in granaries at Tongzhou or transshipped to carts in order to finish the journey to Beijing.[27]

But soldiers in the capital had to be fed. They were the main reason for the Grand Canal because the stability and protection of the northern capital, which was much closer to the Mongols at the northern border than Nanjing was, depended on them.[28] To protect the new capital, the Yongle emperor stationed more than seventy military units in Beijing and its environs, totaling about 250,000 soldiers,[29] over half of them relocated from Nanjing.[30] Every month, these soldiers each received a salary of 1 *shi* of rice, for an annual outlay of 3 million *shi* of rice.

The Yongle emperor paid his officials and his soldiers in rice coupons, to be redeemed from specific granaries. Any rice that they did not need for themselves could be traded or sold to buy other necessities—meat and vegetables, clothing for their families, fuel, and so on. When the amount of tribute rice that could be transported on the canal was insufficient, it was Beijing soldiers who suffered. The tribute rice stored in the Beijing or nearby Tongzhou granaries went to the common soldiers, whereas Beijing military and civil officials received their rice coupons for granaries in Nanjing, a thousand miles away.

25 In the Ming and Qing dynasties, the lower course of the Yellow River shifted to the south and merged with the Huai River, which was north of the Yangzi.

26 In later years, the Ming and then the Qing governments built canals independent of the Yellow River in the middle section of the Grand Canal. The project was not completed until the late seventeenth century, during the Qing dynasty.

27 Although a short canal had been built between Tongzhou and Beijing in the Yuan dynasty, it had fallen into disrepair. It was rebuilt in 1527 but, due to the uphill route, was too shallow for the large grain boats. Small boats called lighters were used to carry the rice on the last leg of its journey to Beijing.

28 As mentioned in the Introduction, the Yuan dynasty lost Beijing when the rice shipment for its soldiers went astray. Without their rice salaries, the Mongol soldiers simply deserted.

29 This figure is from 1435. See Yu Zhijia, "Mingdai liangjing jiandu," 155.

30 Yu Zhijia, "Mingdai liangjing jiandu," 140.

Although Beijing officials, regardless of rank, were allowed 0.5 *shi* of rice a year from the state granaries in Beijing or Tongzhou, the (much larger) remainder of their rice salary coupons were for granaries in Nanjing.[31]

The policy of paying Beijing salaries in Nanjing rice coupons was utterly impractical. Even if these civil and military officials had sent their servants to collect the Nanjing rice, the cost of the journey would have been prohibitive. In 1424 the Yongle emperor increased the annual amount of rice each Beijing official could take from local granaries, but only from 0.5 *shi* to 1 *shi*,[32] a negligible amount.

Instead of making the long-distance journey to Nanjing four times a year to collect their rice, many simply sold their coupons to local merchants. The merchants speculated with the rice coupons, buying them at low cost and holding on to them in the hope that their value would rise, causing rice to be stockpiled in the Nanjing state granaries. Probably because of the distance between Beijing and Nanjing, the state did not impose a strict cut-off date for the Beijing rice coupons. As a result, many merchants kept the coupons for years, waiting for the price of rice to rise; when it did, they went to the granaries and exchanged their coupons for rice. Therefore, rice coupons became a kind of security backed by the rice in state granaries. In years when the rice harvest was normal, and the merchants held on to their rice coupons, the state would have to build more storage space for the excess grain and store the rice for years. Then, when rice prices rose, and merchants traded in their coupons, the state suddenly found its granaries empty. In this way, merchants profited at the expense of the state, which had to pay to maintain the granaries.[33]

In 1436, when Zhu Qizhen became the Zhengtong emperor, many officials, including the minister of revenue, entreated him to solve this problem. The emperor agreed that the Ministry of Revenue should commute an annual total of 4 million *shi* of tribute rice from the lower Yangzi provinces into a monetary payment, transfer the money to Beijing, and use it to pay military officials there.[34] Because the reform only covered military officials, the civil officials in Beijing continued to sell their coupons to merchants,[35] but the new policy did alleviate some of the management problems at Nanjing granaries.[36] It also initiated a shift in taxation from grain to silver.

31 *DaMing huidian*, 789:681.

32 *DaMing huidian*, 789:681.

33 Liu Yichen, "Zhengtong yuannian (1436) zheyin ling chutai shimo zaitan," *Zhongguo shehui jingji shi yanjiu* 5 (2020).

34 Li Xun, *Mingshi shihuozhi jiaozhu*, 60, 136; *Ming shilu*, Wuzong, 299.

35 The common soldiers in Beijing received rice in kind.

36 As a consequence of the reform, the rice tribute to Beijing via the Grand Canal decreased by 4 million *shi* but did not stop.

2.2 *Commuting the Grain Tax: the Gold Floral Silver Reform*

In 1436, when stipends for Beijing military officers began to be paid in silver, instead of rice, the land taxes for the wealthiest Yangzi provinces, including South Zhili, Zhejiang, Jiangxi, and Huguang, were converted to silver, at the rate of 0.25 tael of silver per *shi* of rice. This reform was known as the Gold Floral Silver (*Jinhua yin*) reform, through which a total of 1 million taels of silver (for 4 million *shi*) was transferred to Beijing.[37] As far as we know, this was the first time that the Ming government converted the grain tax into a silver payment on such a large scale.[38]

In the fifteenth century, China was not short of silver. Throughout the Ming, emperors obtained about 200,000 taels of silver a year from mines in Yunnan, Zhejiang, and Fujian,[39] and over half of it was from Yunnan.[40] In the form of ingots, the silver went first to the imperial treasuries in the capital and then to the market as the emperor spent it. China's silk and porcelain exports brought in even more silver from neighboring countries, although the massive importation of silver from Nagasaki and Spanish Manila did not occur until the mid-sixteenth century.

In 1442 the Ministry of Revenue set up the Taicang Treasury to store silver in Beijing. (See Figure 3.) The treasury's main purpose was to buy supplies for frontier garrisons. In the first year, it only stored silver from changing the cost for feeding war horses from grass to silver. But in the following decades, as an increasing number of taxes in kind were converted into silver, the Taicang Treasury became the largest silver storehouse in the government. It was also the primary source of salaries for soldiers as well as other military expenses at the frontier (although soldiers in Beijing continued to be paid in rice coupons).[41]

The Gold Floral Silver reform was implemented in steps. First, landowner-farmers in the lower Yangzi provinces had to sell their tax tribute grain for

---

37 For the details of the history of the Gold Floral Silver reform, see Horii Kazuo, "Kinkagin no senkai," *Tōyō shi kenkyō* 5, no. 2 (1940); Hoshi Ayao, "Kinkajin kô," *Yamagata daigaku kiyô* (Jinbun kagaku) 9, no. 1 (1978); Kikuo Taniguchi, "Minmatsu no Kinkajin nitsuite," in *Chûgoku gendai no hô to shakai*, ed. Kaoru Umehara (Kyoto: Institute for Research in Humanities, Kyoto University, 1993).

38 Although Horii Kazuo noted that Zhou Chen had started the reform in the heavily taxed Jiangnan district in 1433, Horii Kazuo based his information on the *Xianhai xianzhi* [*Gazetteer of Shanghai County*], which was not published until nearly a hundred years later, in 1524. See Horii Kazuo, "Kinkagin no senkai," 42, 49n. Therefore its reliability may be in question.

39 Jiaozhi Province, which the Yongle emperor invaded in 1407, was also rich in silver mines, but Ming control over that territory (modern-day northern Vietnam) was short-lived. Local resistance against Ming rule was consistently fierce, and in 1427, following a local rebellion, the Ming government retreated from the district.

40 See Liang Fangzhong, "Yunnan Yinkuang zhi shi de kaocha" (1939), in his *Mingqing fushui* (Beijing: Zhonghua shuju, 2008), 463–71; idem, "Mingdai Yinkuang kao" (1939), in his *Mingqing fushui*, 472–514.

41 *DaMing huidian*, 789:548.

FIGURE 3 Silver ingots. In the Ming, local officials melted down the silver that they collected in taxes into large, standardized ingots, to make the silver easier to transport to the Taicang or other treasuries in the central government. Each ingot was supposed to weigh 50 taels and was inscribed with the name of its local government office in case it was underweight.
CREDIT: NATIONAL MUSEUM OF CHINA, BEIJING

silver in order to pay their tax in its new form. Then, the tax silver was sent to Beijing, probably via the Grand Canal, which would have been an ideal transport route because it was fast and safe, due to the troops stationed along its length. Unlike shipping rice, which was cheap and bulky, transporting enough silver from the south to pay military officials in Beijing required only a small boat. Finally, military officials were paid in silver and used the money to buy necessities in Beijing, where it entered the market.

2.3 *Silver and the Precious Note*

One might wonder why the government did not use paper money in the conversion considering that, as mentioned in Chapter 1, earlier strategies to retrieve the notes from the market had succeeded so well that, by this time, the market value of paper money was high.[42] The use of silver, instead of paper

42 The market value of paper money was still high during the Zhengtong reign (1436–1449). See Qiu Yongzhi, "Zhanzheng, shichang yu guojia: Zhengtong Jingtai zhi ji tonghuo liutong tizhi de bianqian," *Zhongguo jingjishi yanjiu* 6 (2017): 33–34.

money, in the reform showed the market preference for silver, which had been used as money in China for over a thousand years. The reform formally marked the end of the futile official ban on using silver in exchanges.

Whereas silver was widely used in market exchanges, paper money had mostly been used to pay the commercial taxes, charges, and fees that the Xuande emperor had levied to retrieve depreciated paper money from the market. Although he later reduced these fees, his measures had been so successful that paper money was in short supply in the market. In 1436, the year of the Gold Floral Silver reform, the Zhengtong emperor decided to reverse the flow of paper money after the eunuch who took charge of the Siyao Treasury (which stored paper money) in the palace reported that the Treasury was full. For years, the quantity of incoming precious notes had been so much greater than the outflow that there was no more room for them. To solve the storage problem, and in view of the high value of paper money in the market, the Zhengtong emperor continued what the Xuande emperor had begun: reducing the commercial charges due in precious notes in Beijing and Nanjing. In 1441 the charges on vegetable farms, orchards, and small carts entering the two capitals were exempted, and fees for warehouses and the larger carts pulled by oxen or donkeys were reduced.[43]

As already mentioned, the amount of paper money that officials received in their salaries fluctuated with the conversion rate between rice (as the original form of official salaries) and paper money. In 1433 the Xuande emperor, in another attempt to retrieve the by-then-devalued paper money from the market, had reduced the conversion rate from 25 *guan* to 15 *guan* per *shi* of rice. In 1441, when the Zhengtong emperor wanted to make space in the Siyao Treasury and return precious notes back to circulation, he reinstated the earlier rate of 25 *guan* in officials' salaries.[44]

Although these measures increased the quantity of precious notes in circulation, by 1446 the value of paper money had increased even more. According to a Ministry of Revenue report, one tael of silver had been worth 1,000 *guan* of paper money but had fallen to only 400–500 *guan*.[45] To reduce the monetary burden on merchants, the emperor offered further reductions: from 81 *guan* to 20 *guan* for the donkey-cart charge and from 20 *guan* to 8 *guan* for the oxcart charge. In 1447 the toll on the Grand Canal was also reduced from the 1429 price of 100 *guan* per boat to 20 *guan*.[46]

43 *DaMing huidian*, 789:555.
44 *DaMing huidian*, 789:685.
45 *Ming shilu*, Yingzong, 2723.
46 *Ming shilu*, Yingzong, 3072.

These measures reduced the inflow of precious notes and successfully depleted the Siyao Treasury, to the point that, in 1446, the Zhengtong emperor took the advice of Revenue Minister Wang Zuo and restored the earlier conversion rate of paper money to rice in the official salary, dropping it to 15 *guan*.[47] In order to supply the market with more of the high-value paper money, the Precious Notes Bureaus in Beijing and Nanjing operated their woodblock printing machines daily. In Beijing, the Precious Notes Bureau recruited 600 workers, divided into two shifts, to run the machines continuously and print 700,000 notes a year.[48] Even if each note printed was worth only 1 *guan*, the annual output would have totaled 700,000 *guan*.

Then, in 1448, the value of paper currency plummeted. In Beijing, the price fell so low that one *guan* was worth only 2 copper cash. The Zhengtong emperor accepted Censor Cai Yuji's proposal to save the precious note by immediately banning copper coins and punishing anyone who used them with a fine of ten times the value of the coins that they had spent.[49] But this punitive measure had no effect on the market valuation of paper money.

The Ming government seems to have had a rudimentary idea of how the worth of its currency was affected by that currency's supply (or oversupply). The emperor and his officials knew that if they wanted to raise its market price, they had to retrieve the excess paper money from the market. Although they understood basic economic concepts, they also seem to have relied on the awe and respect due to the Son of Heaven, making them overconfident that, if the emperor ordered it, his subjects would accept and abide by any of his policies, no matter how little economic sense it made to them.[50]

A year after the ban on copper coins, the Zhengtong emperor was captured by a Mongol group, the Oirats, at the Battle of Tumu. Zhu Qiyu, one of the emperor's younger brothers, was enthroned in his place, beginning the Jingtai reign in 1450.[51]

The Jingtai emperor took the throne in a time of crisis. The Oirats had begun a new wave of invasion, and their target was Beijing. The new emperor's first priority was defending the capital, and the second was boosting the morale of

---

47 *Ming shilu*, Yingzong, 2987.

48 *Ming shilu*, Yingzong, 3983.

49 *Ming shilu*, Yingzong, 3209.

50 Paintings of the emperors always portrayed them as larger than life, like the queen bee in a hive. The emperor and his officials may have expected his subjects to regard him in that light and simply acceded to his wishes.

51 For the details of this battle, see Twitchett and Grimm, "The Cheng-t'ung, Ching-t'ai, and T'ien-shun Reigns," 322–25.

the civil officials there. In the first year of his reign, he shut down the Precious Notes Bureaus, dismissed all its workers,[52] and began to pay the rice salaries of his civil officials in silver.[53] Beijing military officials had been paid in silver, instead of the inconvenient rice coupons, since the Gold Floral Silver reform in 1436. The Jingtai emperor extended this policy to civil officials. In 1452, he further raised the income of capital officials by converting all their paper money salaries into silver at a fixed rate of 1 tael per 500 *guan*.[54] These measures reduced the use of paper money but depleted the state's silver stocks. In 1456, therefore, the Jingtai emperor found it necessary to pay part of the official salaries in silk cloth from in-kind taxes and revised the conversion rate from 500 *guan* to 700 *guan* (making their salary in paper notes worth less in silver).[55]

The use of silver for official salaries ended a year later, when Zhu Qizhen, the former Zhengtong emperor, retook the throne. Zhu Qizhen had been released by the Oirats in 1450, seven years earlier, but put under house arrest by the Jingtai emperor, who feared a coup. Then, in the first lunar month of 1457, the Jingtai emperor fell critically ill. Zhu Qizhen, with the assistance of certain high officials and eunuchs, seized the throne. The Jingtai emperor was demoted to the status of prince and put under house arrest himself. He died a few days later, rumored to have been murdered. Zhu Qizhen became the emperor again, but with a new reign title: Tianshun (literally, "Following the Way of Heaven").[56] He immediately began to undo what the Jingtai emperor had put in place; as a result, civil and military officials once again received their salaries in paper money, and civil officials once again had to fetch their rice salaries from Nanjing.[57]

In short, during the first half of the fifteenth century, the government, especially the Ministry of Revenue, took advantage of market development to convert some taxes in kind into payments in silver. But silver did not replace paper money for tax payment; it was only used for taxes not paid in paper money. As shown in the next section, the currency that actually encroached on the function of paper money was copper cash.

52 *Ming shilu*, Yingzong, 3983.

53 *DaMing huidian*, 789:682.

54 *Ming shilu*, Yingzong, 4698.

55 *DaMing huidian*, 789:682.

56 For the details on this coup d'état, see Twitchett and Grimm, "The Cheng-t'ung, Ching-t'ai, and T'ien-shun Reigns," 338–39.

57 *DaMing huidian*, 789:682.

3 Copper Coins in a "Filthy" Reign

In 1465 the eldest son of the Tianshun emperor, Zhu Jianshen, ascended the throne and, at the age of eighteen, became the Chenghua emperor. Many scholar-officials at the time found the boy emperor unprepared for taking the throne. They were scandalized when he took Lady Wan, a middle-aged woman who had been in service to his grandmother, as his senior consort, and then allowed her, not the empress, to dominate the imperial harem.[58] Lady Wan gave birth to the emperor's son, but the infant prince died within a year. A few years later, Lady Bo, another of his wives, also gave birth to a son, and this child also died shortly after birth. It was rumored that Lady Wan had killed him. Afterward the Chenghua emperor seemed unable to have children who survived. Although some of his consorts became pregnant, they soon miscarried.[59] Lady Wan was rumored to have conspired with powerful eunuchs to induce the miscarriages. Five years later, in 1470, a palace woman named Ji bore a child, named Zhu Youtang, who was the emperor's first surviving son and later became the Hongzhi emperor.[60] According to contemporaneous rumors, Ji, with the help of eunuchs, had given birth and raised her child in secret until he was six years old. After a eunuch told the emperor that he had a living son, the emperor joyfully told the court that he was going to make the child the crown prince. An enraged Lady Wan secretly ordered Ji's death (Ji was forced to hang herself), and the eunuch who had helped Ji was so terrified that he poisoned himself. To protect the young prince after Ji's death, the empress dowager took him to live with her.[61] This story remains unproved, but demonstrates that the scholar-officials who noted and recorded all the rumors had a low opinion of the Chenghua emperor's ability to manage his personal life. In the eyes of the scholar-officials, even worse than the boy emperor's attachment to Lady Wan

58 Although his father had chosen Lady Wu as his empress, the Chenghua emperor cast her aside after he ascended the throne, making Lady Wang the empress. But he always preferred Lady Wan, who was of humble origin and could not be named the empress.

59 An emperor usually had more than ten wives, as well as royal concubines and the empress.

60 Ji was a palace woman who caught the emperor's eye when she was working in one of the palace treasuries. The emperor had a single sexual encounter with her and had forgotten her by the time that he learned she had borne him a son. Ji's background was mysterious and remained so, even to her son; her contemporaries believed that her father was the chieftain of a minority tribe in southern China. She died six months before her son, the future emperor, was named crown prince.

61 The Chenghua emperor would have another eleven sons, none of them by Empress Wang. Xu Wenji and Chen Shilong, *Zhengshuo Mingchao shiliu di* (Beijing: Zhonghua shuju, 2005), 133–39, 152.

was his continuation of his ancestors' predilection for appointing eunuchs to high positions in state administration.

Tensions between the scholar-officials and the emperor's eunuchs had been ongoing for decades. The historian Shih-shan Henry Tsai noted that the eunuchs were "a central, constituent element of the imperial government" and one "through which emperors could, and did, exercise their power in all areas of government."[62] As an administrative hierarchy, the eunuchs were in step with the emperor but sometimes ran counter to the scholar-officials. That a senior eunuch at the palace was always appointed to supervise the emperor's secret police, the Eastern Depot, did nothing to repair the rift between the two groups.

When the Yongle emperor established the Eastern Depot in 1420 to gather intelligence and reveal treason, he staffed the depot with his own bodyguards, the guards dressed in embroidered uniforms, as investigators. But he later made a high-ranking eunuch the director of these secret police. Over time, the Eastern Depot became notorious for spying on the population, accusing honest officials of corruption, and taking them to the Eastern Depot within the palace to be tortured into confessions (or killed if they persisted in declaring their innocence) unless they could afford to pay a hefty bribe. The officers of these guards did most of the "investigation," becoming "the most feared secret police in Ming China as they tortured, maimed, and murdered countless innocent people," while "about 100 agents … were routinely sent out to obtain information and seek out conspirators." Their eunuch supervisor, who reported directly (and immediately) to the emperor, may have been, initially at least, a passive observer of the guards' excesses. Under the direction of a humane and honest eunuch, such as Chen Zhun (during the reign of Chenghua), who told his agents "to stop engaging in frivolous, hearsay investigation and harassment," the eunuch director was even able to rein them in.[63] But the fact that a high-ranking eunuch directed the Eastern Depot was bound to rankle, especially when so many scholar-officials had been unjustly accused by it. And later eunuch directors were at least as bloodthirsty and power hungry as these guards.

Then, Chenghua expanded his secret police, adding a Western Depot and appointed the infamous eunuch Wang Zhi to take charge of it. Its goal of finding "witches or weird people capable of spreading malicious rumors" enabled its agents to allege misconduct on the slightest pretext. Wang Zhi and his subordinate eunuchs did apprehend a witch and broke up a salt-smuggling ring,

62 See Tsai, *The Eunuchs in the Ming Dynasty*, 9.

63 Tsai, *The Eunuchs in the Ming Dynasty*, 98–102.

but they also seized high positions in the bureaucracy by accepting bribes and torturing innocent officials who were not their allies. They inspired such terror "that everyone hid as soon as they heard the depot agents coming to their vicinity." The Grand Secretary and noted scholar Shang Lu sent a memorial to the emperor, saying that no one, from scholar-officials to merchants to common people, felt safe since Wang Zhi had taken charge of the Western Depot.[64]

Far from considering their behavior a problem, the emperor chose these same eunuchs to supervise his military campaigns against the border tribes. He made Wang Zhi the army-inspecting censor, a crucial military position "to accompany an army on campaign, monitor its activities, and independently report to the throne."

Accepting all the stories and rumors as fact, many political historians have considered the reign of Chenghua a period of unbridled corruption. For example, the historian Meng Sen described the political environment at this time as "filthy and muddy."[65] In this "filthy and muddy" political environment, a monetary reform occurred that shifted some of the traditional functions of paper money to copper coins and even devalued the precious note to reflect its market value more closely.

3.1 *Government Taxes and Fees in Copper Cash*

In 1465, when the Chenghua emperor took the throne, Ma Ang, the minister of revenue, noted that paper notes had failed to circulate and recommended the payment of certain taxes in copper cash, instead. As shown in Chapter 1, the state had set up four major channels for retrieving paper money: the salt consumption tax, the shop and transit fees, the inland customs tolls, and the crime restitution fee. Ma Ang suggested that the state accept payment of half the paper money charges in copper cash, excepting only the crime restitution fees, which would still be paid in paper money. The Chenghua emperor endorsed the proposal and ordered that each *guan* of paper money equal only 4 copper cash, not the official rate of 1,000.[66] This was the first time that a Ming emperor had reduced the value of paper money, and he did so to reflect its market price. Although the conversion rate was not the precise market price—paper money had been devalued to 2 copper cash per *guan* in 1448—it was close.[67]

64 Tsai, *The Eunuchs in the Ming Dynasty*, 115–16.

65 Meng Sen, *Mingshi jianyi* (Shanghai: Shanghai guji chubanshe, 2002), 176. For an introduction to the political environment during the reign of Chenghua, see Mote, "The Ch'eng-hua and Hung-chih Reigns," 343–402.

66 *Ming shilu*, Xianzong, 385; *Wanli kuaiji lu* (1581), in *Xuxiu kiku quanshu*, 832: 137–38.

67 *Ming shilu*, Yingzong, 3209.

This monetary reform also increased the emperor's income. Assuming that the market value of a *guan* was still 2 copper cash in 1465, a government institution with an annual tax income of 1,000 *guan* had 2,000 copper coins in purchasing power. After the reform, half the tax, or 500 *guan*, was collected at the rate of 4 copper coins per *guan*. Thus the institution would collect 2,000 copper coins and 500 *guan* in paper money. At the market rate of 2 copper cash per *guan*, this 500 *guan* was equivalent to 1,000 copper coins. As a result, the total income of that institution became 3,000 copper cash. By applying the new policy, the institution could increase its income by 50 percent, from 2,000 copper coins to 3,000. Though the market price of a *guan* fell below 2 copper cash, the actual gap was even larger.

The sudden tax increase dealt a harsh blow to traveling merchants who had been paying their inland customs charges in paper money. The customhouses were located mostly on the Yangzi River and the Grand Canal.[68] Beginning in 1465, when the customhouses could demand half their payment in copper cash, many merchants refrained from doing business along these routes. Immediately after the new taxation measure went into effect, customs officials in charge of Jiujiang and Jinshazhou, on the middle Yangzi River, asked the imperial court for a temporary tax exemption. They stated that the districts where these two customhouses were located had suffered poor harvests, and a tax exemption could encourage the importation of more food. The court granted their request, but only for two months.[69]

After the Chenghua emperor agreed that a portion of tax be paid in copper cash, Ming officials asked for the same rule to apply to their salaries. In 1466 an official from the Ministry of Revenue submitted such a petition, but the emperor refused to endorse it. He noted that, as the new taxation policy had just begun to be implemented, it was too soon to make the change in official salaries.[70] Officials in that ministry made a similar request the following year, but received no reply.[71] The following year, the emperor finally agreed to convert 70 percent of the official salaries that had been paid in precious notes into copper cash, at the rate of 3 per *guan*.[72] Although the conversion rate was one

68 In 1465, the first year of the Chenghua reign, there were customhouses on the Yangzi River at Hangzhou, Suzhou, Jiujiang, and Jinshazhou, and on the Grand Canal at Upper Xin River at Nanjing in the south and Hexiwu at Tianjin in the north. *DaMing huidian*, 789:610.

69 *Ming shilu*, Xianzong, 689–90.

70 *Ming shilu*, Xianzong, 648, 651.

71 *Ming shilu*, Xianzong, 845.

72 *DaMing huidian*, 789:683.

cash less than the tax collection rate, officials still benefited from being paid in copper coins, instead of the devalued paper money.

In short, the Chenghua emperor did not abolish precious notes, but by accepting copper coins for tax payments and substantially devaluing paper money, he greatly diminished their role in state administration. After 1465, the Ming government had to consider whether copper coins were a stable currency.

4 Counterfeit Coins and Gresham's Law

In fifteenth-century China, the only rich copper mines were in Yunnan, a province in the Ming empire since 1381. Because transportation between Yunnan and the imperial mint in Beijing was mostly over land, it was too difficult and costly for the government to undertake. As a result, merchants bought and sold copper, and the government bought from them.

Despite a shortage of mines, copper coins circulated widely in markets. Some of the coins had been cast in previous dynasties, but many of them must have been made by commoners. Copper coins, which were actually bronze, were easy enough to make by heating copper and tin, mixing the liquid metals together, and pouring them into a mold. Official coins were made with molds, so the easiest, least costly way to make a counterfeit was to cast a mold of an authentic coin and pour the liquid metals into that mold. After the liquid cooled, the fake coin looked authentic enough, although to the discerning eye the characters and figure on the coin were less clear and sharp than those on an authentic coin. The counterfeits all bore the reign titles of the early Ming or of previous dynasties such as the Tang and Song. As long as the counterfeiter maintained the original ratio of copper and tin in the mixture, it was difficult to tell the difference. Lightweight coins were easier to spot.

When money was only used in market exchanges, Gresham's law that "bad money drives out good money" did not apply. Despite the many different kinds of copper cash and the inevitable variations in their amount of copper and their weight, merchants were mostly able to recognize inferior coins. This left little room for passing off privately made, low-quality coins. For example, if a local market accepted coins made in the Tang era, and a shopper went to a rice shop with counterfeit coins that looked like Tang coins but weighed only half as much, a sharp-eyed shopkeeper would either refuse the coins or double the price for purchasing the rice. This is not to say that inferior coins did not circulate in markets. From time to time, swindlers mixed the genuine with the false coins to put the counterfeit into circulation. But cheating a shopkeeper was not easy, and even if one of them carelessly accepted inferior coins from a customer, in a small community that customer was fairly easy to track down.

In the market, no one cared who had made a coin, only whether the coin's weight, condition, and copper content were adequate. Merchants generally divided the bronze coins into two categories: "big things" were high-quality coins, and "small things" were low-quality coins. A "big thing" was worth one cash in the market, and a "small thing" was worth only half a cash.[73]

In 1465 when the Ming government accepted tax payments in bronze coins, it took any coins cast by previous legitimate dynasties and rulers in the Ming, so long as they were not broken or clipped,[74] and assigned every coin the same value. Because both "big things" and "small things" circulating in the market bore the reign titles of previous dynasties, they had the same value in tax payments, even though their price varied in markets. In accordance with Gresham's law, taxpayers kept the "big things" in their pockets and used the "small things" to pay their taxes.

Unlike merchants, officials followed government guidelines for collecting tax money. They had no need to assess the value of any coin they accepted, as long as it was legal money—that is, as long as it *looked* as if it had been made by a government, past or present. But because coins were cast from molds of other coins, they all looked government made. This is why the theory that bad money drives out good money applied only when inferior coins were used to pay taxes. As a major destination for the copper coin tax, Beijing was flooded with inferior coins.

The influx of inferior coins became a problem in 1470, when grain prices in Beijing spiked as a result of poor harvests of millet and wheat in northern China. To keep commodity prices low in Beijing, the Chenghua emperor withdrew half a million *shi* of rice and millet from Beijing and Tongzhou granaries for a reduced-price sale in the metropolitan areas. Each *shi* of rice was sold for 0.6 tael of silver and millet at 0.5 tael. People who did not have silver were allowed to pay in copper cash.[75]

The famine exacerbated market discrimination against inferior coins. In 1472 a court official laid the blame for rising prices in Beijing on choosy shop merchants. He argued that merchants should not charge more when customers

73 Dai Jin, ed., *Huangming tiaofa shili leizuan*, in *Zhongguo zhenxi falu dianji jicheng* (Beijing: Kexue chubanshe, 1994), 2nd series, 4: 585–87.

74 Counterfeiters sometimes shaved or clipped the edges of a coin, using the clippings to cast new coins.

75 *Ming shilu*, Xiaozong, 1621–24. The order did not give the conversion rate between silver and copper cash. It may have allowed the officials who took charge of the reduced-price grain sales to collect cash based on the market price between the two monies.

paid in inferior coins. His petition received support from the Ministry of Revenue as well as the emperor, and an imperial order prohibited merchants from accepting only good coins.[76] But, once again, an imperial order did nothing to solve the problem.

Soon afterward, court officials blamed the problem on counterfeiters. In 1476 Wang Fu, the minister of works, warned the imperial court:

> In recent years, as the government notes do not circulate effectively, copper coins prevail. [But] is it good for people? Stubborn people are ignorant, and cases of counterfeiting are increasing. Your humble servant thinks that [because] counterfeiters lack fear even in the imperial capital, won't the counterfeiting be more rampant elsewhere in the empire?[77]

Wang Fu also noted the profitability of counterfeiting:

> Every catty of copper is sold at only 0.05–0.06 tael of silver, but [with it the counterfeiter] may strike 150–160 cash. [Then,] for [only] a day, [he] can make a profit from 100 to 200 percent. This is why counterfeiting is so widespread.[78]

The minister suggested that the state take the Ming law against counterfeiting seriously and enforce it.[79]

According to the Great Ming Code, the penalty for counterfeiting bronze coins was death by strangulation.[80] But, early on, the Ming government had adopted a more lenient approach. For example, in 1370, instead of putting five counterfeiters to death, the Hongwu emperor noted that they were poor people, punished them with flogging, and sent them to work in the Baoyuan Mint in Nanjing.[81] But in 1476, when Nanjing officials reported cases of counterfeiting and requested lighter penalties, the Chenghua emperor decreed that the crime was too serious to reduce the punishment.[82]

Despite being punishable by death, counterfeiting was widespread. Along with many cities along the Grand Canal, Beijing became a principal market for counterfeit coins. In 1477 the Chenghua emperor received a report from the Ministry of Punishment in Nanjing about a retired military official at the

76 *Ming shilu*, Xianzong, 2131.
77 Dai Jin, *Huangming tiaofa shili leizuan*, 5:700.
78 Dai Jin, *Huangming tiaofa shili leizuan*, 5:701.
79 Dai Jin, *Huangming tiaofa shili leizuan*, 5:701.
80 *DaMing lu*, in *Zhongguo zhenxi falu dianji jicheng*, 2nd series, 1:375.
81 See *Ming shilu*, Taizu, 1151.
82 *Ming shilu*, Xianzong, 2741.

Suzhou garrison who had been using his home to trade raw copper and manufacture illegal coins. The report also stated that many bronze coins recently circulating in Beijing had been manufactured by outlaws in the canal cities, including Suzhou, Songjiang, Changzhou, Zhenjiang, Hangzhou, and Linqing. Traveling merchants bought the counterfeit coins for half a cash each and took them to Beijing to pay their taxes at a rate of one cash. To stem the tide of inferior coins, the emperor ordered provincial governors to reinstate the ban on counterfeiting and extend the punishment for counterfeiting to commoners who helped to circulate illegal coins. Under the new law, if someone found out about counterfeiting but failed to report it or circulated counterfeit coins, he was punished by having to wear a cangue weighing 100 catties (about 132 lbs.) for a month, [83] and then he and his entire family were sent to serve in a nearby garrison. If the lawbreaker already lived in a garrison, he and his family were sent to a frontier garrison.[84]

A 1478 report described the case of a smuggler and money changer named Wang Yuan, who had been registered in a military household and on the reserve list as an honor guard at the palace. But he left this household and returned to his home province, Henan, where he built a business trading scrap copper and counterfeit coins. In the second lunar month of 1478, Wang went to Xuzhou (in Henan) with scrap copper and exchanged it for coins made by the counterfeiters there. Wang took the coins to Beijing, hid them in his uncle's house, and from there distributed them to local shopkeepers. In the seventh month, with two partners (a soldier and a civilian), Wang made another business trip, first, to purchase scrap copper in Shandong and Henan. When the three partners returned to Xuzhou, they exchanged the scrap for 10,000 counterfeit coins. The coins were so heavy that they needed donkeys to carry them back to Beijing. Wang again used his uncle's house as a warehouse. The men set a retail price of a tael of silver in exchange for 1,550 cash. At least three local shopkeepers went to the house to buy fake coins.[85]

In 1480, a Beijing civilian named He Tong wrote to the emperor about how difficult life had become since the devaluation of copper coins:

> In former times, a tael of silver was sold at 800 copper cash. The [price of] cash was high [in terms of rice or silver], and grain was cheap, therefore,

83 Essentially a portable pillory, a cangue was a flat square or rectangle of wood that fit around a person's head and shoulders so that he could not lie down or feed himself. A cangue imposed slow torture; the longer it was worn on a person's neck and shoulders, the more painful it became, and there was no way to relieve this pain or shift the weight.

84 Dai Jin, *Huangming tiaofa shili leizuan*, 5:701–2.

85 Dai Jin, *Huangming tiaofa shili leizuan,* 702–4.

> both soldiers and civilians lived in peace and enjoyed their work. In recent years, however, counterfeit coins are made in the provinces, transported to Beijing, and spent in markets. A *qian* [0.1 tael] of silver is sold at 130 cash now. If a family has five to seven members, and they all earn their living by selling vegetables or carrying loads for others, for the entire day's work they can earn no more than 20 to 30 cash. [In the old days] the money was just about enough for the family to buy firewood and grain, and, therefore, they could survive. Now, they are hungry and cold, and this is the reason that cases of burglary and robbery are increasing. During the past twelve months, [merchants in] the markets were too choosy [to accept counterfeit coins]. As a result, the circulation of copper coins is blocked, and the price of grain has increased.[86]

He Tong's petition painted a picture of devaluation of copper cash, whose value changed from 800 to 1,300 per tael of silver. The prices of all goods, not only grain, nearly doubled when they were cited in terms of copper cash.

Once again, devaluation was blamed on merchants and their habit of accepting only good coins. He Tong advised the government to reinstate the ban and force merchants to accept inferior coins at their face value. The Ministry of Revenue supported this proposal to the emperor, arguing that money should circulate freely, and, therefore, no one should reject coins unless they were obviously counterfeits (thin or poorly made) or clipped. The emperor endorsed the proposal.[87] Laws and penalties failed to curb counterfeiting or prevent shopkeepers from choosing good coins over inferior ones, and currency speculation was particularly active in Beijing thanks to the tax guidelines.

In addition to the 1477 and 1478 reports on smuggling counterfeit coins to Beijing, an official memorial in 1480 stated that merchants bought large amounts of paper money in the Jiangnan region for the low price of 1 tael of silver per 1,000 *guan*, then transported the currency to Beijing for sale to taxpayers there.[88] At this point, all the tax money, except silver, had lost value.

5 Conclusion

In the early fifteenth century, market activities in China revived, and the Ming government stabilized the market price of paper money. But the use of this

86 Dai Jin, *Huangming tiaofa shili leizuan*, 704–5.

87 Dai Jin, *Huangming tiaofa shili leizuan*, 705–6, 708.

88 Dai Jin, *Huangming tiaofa shili leizuan*, 582.

state currency was confined mostly to paying commercial taxes and official salaries. Silver bullion and copper coins were the currencies of exchange in markets, even though they were repeatedly banned from circulation.

In midcentury, probably because of overproduction, the price of paper money plummeted. In the 1460s, the state began to accept copper coins as well as paper money for taxes, tolls, and other charges. The government had not yet cast its own copper coins but accepted all coins issued by previous dynasties to pay for half the state taxes and fees that had previously been settled entirely in paper money. This was the first step toward restoring copper coins as a state currency in the Ming.

Unlike the precious note, which was a unique product of the Ming government, the copper coins in the market varied in size and copper content and thus in value. After low-quality coins were allowed for tax payments, Gresham's law of bad money driving out good took over, leading to a precipitous drop in the purchasing power of copper coins. The new policy also encouraged counterfeiting, and Beijing, as a tax destination, was inundated with fake coins. Whereas the devaluation of paper money had affected mainly official salaries, the depreciation of copper cash affected all those who used coins for small exchanges—that is, everyone.

For most people, silver ingots were less convenient than copper coins, because they were worth more and could not be used for small purchases, and because their value was discernable only by the silver's fineness and weight. But these qualities were advantages for the state: silver's high purchasing power made it easy to transport and store, and because it was no longer used for coins and had no face value, it could not be counterfeited. Its worth was based on its weight, which simplified tax collection. As the Ministry of Revenue was making silver the basis of financial restructuring, the Chenghua emperor collected 1 million taels of silver annually to pay the salaries of military officials in Beijing, through the 1436 Gold Floral Silver tax reform.

But the household registration system was breaking down, and with it the emperor's means of running the palace, as the state's currency of copper coins continued to decline in value. In Chapter 3, we see that, by 1487, when the Hongzhi emperor took the throne, he lacked a sound currency, one that his eunuchs could use to buy his daily necessities, especially meat, at local Beijing markets. The Son of Heaven no longer had the means to feed his imperial household.

CHAPTER 3

Household Registration, Foreign Trade, and the Emperor's Table, 1444–1566

As shown in Chapter 2, market activities recovered after foreign trade resumed via the tribute missions; the resulting economic upturn allowed the government to convert some of its in-kind taxes and labor services into silver taels and copper coins. But as the market grew and flourished, the household registration system fell apart, although its collapse was not entirely due to market development. People had been avoiding household registration from its inception to escape their labor service or taxes in kind or simply because they wanted to work at a different occupation from their forebears or live somewhere other than their home village. Because Ming subjects were registered only by name and place, they could evade taxation by leaving their birthplace and changing their name. Market growth speeded up the breakdown of the household registration system because people could leave their home village more easily when they could find work in market cities. As we discuss in this chapter, the growing market even provided new kinds of work.

As more people avoided registration, the loss of resources from taxation affected not only government finances in the provinces but palace finances in Beijing. Successive emperors found it increasingly difficult to collect in-kind taxes and labor services as local people disappeared. Before examining the significance of this loss of labor services and in-kind taxes for palace finance, we take a closer look at the foreign trade that indirectly precipitated this loss.

1 Maritime Merchants and Household Registration

The Ming government had banned private maritime trade from its inception, but China's southeastern coastal population had a long tradition of private trading in Southeast Asia. When the Ming government made private foreign trade illegal, this maritime trade continued secretly—an early example of evading household registration. Then, in 1444, the Chaozhou prefect in Guangdong Province reported that fifty-five local people had left Chaozhou by sea to engage in commerce in Java. Twenty-two of them remained in Java; the other thirty-three returned to Chaozhou but planned to travel to Java again. Later that year, as they were about to set sail, the prefect apprehended four of

 | DOI:10.1163/9789004687530_005

them. The Zhengtong emperor ordered provincial officials to hunt down the rest of them.[1] That report did not explain why those thirty-three people, who had already settled in Java, returned to China at all. They may have had their own, different reasons, or they may have been maritime merchants.

After private foreign trading became illegal, many maritime merchants became smugglers or found ways to work within the system, albeit from outside China. A good example of the latter is the story of Du Wenbin. A salt smuggler from Dingzhou in Fujian, Du Wenbin had escaped his household registration in 1448 by moving to Siam (Thailand),[2] where he began a new life as Naiying-bimeiya, in time becoming one of the vice-envoys to the Ming court. In 1476 he organized a tribute mission from Siam to China, sailing with another vice envoy, named Kunluqunxieti, an ethnic Siamese who was his trade partner.[3] This kind of partnership was ideal for the tribute trade; Du Wenbin knew the China market, and Kunluqunxieti could handle the formal relationship with Ming officials and meet the emperor.

In the fourth lunar month of 1476, the ship that carried Du Wenbin and Kunluqunxieti left Siam with about 200 other passengers who were trading in China under the guise and protection of a tribute mission.[4] On its way to the Office of Maritime Trade and Shipping at Guangzhou,[5] a storm disabled the ship, which drifted to the Leizhou Peninsula in southern Guangdong in the eighth lunar month. With the help of local officials, the traders on board stored their tribute and private goods (mostly ivory and sappanwood) in a government warehouse there and awaited the arrival of Maritime Trade and Shipping officials. Four months later, accompanied by these officials, a eunuch finally arrived in Leizhou to meet with the tribute mission. Because the tribute had been delayed so long, the eunuch simply selected some ivory and sappanwood for the throne and then ordered the envoys to depart on their return journey, because by then their ship had been repaired. Along with the 200 passengers,

1 *Ming shilu*, Yingzong, 2278.

2 The official report did not state Du Wenbin's category of household registration but mentioned that his nephew, Du Lin, was a reservist at a garrison in Dingzhou Prefecture, Fujian. Because they were in the same family, Du Wenbin may also have belonged to a military household before he escaped to Siam. (See this report in Wang Shu, *Wangduanyi zouyi*, in *Qinding siku quanshu* [1787, repr. Taipei: Taiwan shangwu yinshuguan, 1986], 427:525.)

3 This case was reported to the imperial court by a high official in Nanjing named Wang Shu (1416–1508); see Wang Shu, *Wangduanyi zouyi*, 427: 529–30. For a good summary of the case, see Chen Xuelin (Chan Hok-lam), "Xianluo gongshi 'Xie Wenbin' shijian pouxi."

4 Wang Shu, *Wangduanyi zouyi*, 525: 529–30.

5 Foreign merchants had to sign in at one of the three ports (at Mingzhou, Quanzhou, or Guangzhou), so that officials could verify their status as tributary emissaries and clear them for travel to Beijing via the inland waterways.

the two vice-envoys knelt before and begged the eunuch and officials to allow them to continue their journey so that they could pay their respects to the Ming emperor in person, on behalf of the Siamese ruler. This request was difficult for Ming authorities to refuse, and that was the point; the eunuch and officials allowed the tribute mission to continue.[6]

With official permission, the two vice-envoys set off, ostensibly to pay tribute in Beijing, but actually to trade. Using his network, Du Wenbin, and probably Kunluqunxieti, rented a boat to travel from Leizhou to Guangzhou. At Guangzhou, Du sold 355 *dan* of sappanwood and 20.1 *dan* of ivory for 3.5 taels and 6 taels per *dan,* respectively, or a total of 1,363.1 taels, to two contractors whom he knew.[7] The contractors bought the goods on credit, promising to pay him when they met up again in Nanjing. The contractors transshipped the products to their own boats and went to find brokers with connections to local retail shops.[8] As this arrangement shows, the China market was well equipped to handle the foreign import trade. Before imported goods became available to ordinary customers, they had changed hands three times, from seller to contractor, contractor to broker, and broker to retailer.

Accompanied by Chinese officials and soldiers, the tribute trade was safe. It was also lucrative because the merchants' only competitors were envoys from other tributary states. Considering that private maritime trade was prohibited, merchants acting as tributary envoys basically monopolized the China market. Additionally, as envoys, they were honorable guests of the emperor, with the attendant privileges of free transportation, meals, and accommodation, tax exemption when passing through customs, and gifts (usually silk and money) from the Ming emperors.

From Guangzhou, a tribute mission ship took Du Wenbin and his partner to Nanjing, a city famous for its silk weavers. Nanjing was where the dragon robes and other garments for the emperor and his imperial household were made. As the city boasted the best silk weavers in the empire and was located midway between all three cities that hosted Offices of Maritime Trade and Shipping, where tribute missions landed, and Beijing, which was their official destination, Nanjing had become a thriving commercial center in the prosperous tribute trade. In the early Ming, its weavers probably worked only for the palace, but when the market expanded, many Nanjing weavers found ways to sell their wares to foreigners and obtained high-grade raw silk locally and in the neighboring Lake Tai districts.

---

6 Wang Shu, *Wangduanyi zouyi*, 30.

7 *Dan* was a measure of weight equal to *shi* in volume and 130 lbs. See "Ming Weights and Measures."

8 Wang Shu, *Wangduanyi zouyi*, 525:530.

On the third day of the eighth lunar month in 1477, Du's mission ship berthed at the Shangxin River outside the western city gate, at the busiest commercial district in Nanjing. Although this location was propitious, it was not easy to conduct business. The mission's official objective was to visit Beijing to see the emperor, and Ming regulations still forbade fraternizing between Chinese and foreigners. The two envoys were supposed to remain on their junk and not disembark to wander in the streets of Nanjing. They needed brokers who did not mind breaking the law to act as middlemen between them and the silk weavers. Luckily for the envoys, as a result of all the foreign trade, many brokers were in Nanjing. Whenever the brokers saw a tribute ship arrive, they looked for ways to work for the merchants. Some of them even boarded the ship to introduce themselves if they had no one to refer them.

Du Wenbin stayed in Nanjing for sixteen days. First, he collected payment from the two contractors who had bought his ivory and sappanwood on credit in Guangzhou. Then, he hired brokers to order satin that would be taken back to Siam. On the twentieth day of the eighth month, for instance, a female broker named Zhou Zhen, who belonged to a local military household, visited Du on board ship. Du agreed to pay her 328 taels of silver for satin cloth, satin handkerchiefs, and satin betelnut bags. He gave Zhou 287.5 taels as a down payment, with the remainder plus her brokerage fee to be paid when he collected the goods on his way back from Beijing. Thereupon, Du's ship headed for Beijing.[9] In Beijing, the envoys met the Chenghua emperor, offered tribute, and received gifts. Then, Kunluqunxieti asked for a new ship so that they could sail back to Siam, and the emperor granted his request.[10]

The story of Du Wenbin paints a vivid picture of how market activities supported "free workers"—people who worked outside the household registration system—in fifteenth-century Nanjing. Many local people who were skilled in sericulture (silkworm farming) or weaving and registered in artisan households also worked as "free" artisans outside the system, to make money via the flourishing external trade. Anyone who acted as a broker or retailer also worked outside the household system, which had no category for them. Their work was a function and a result of the market economy.

Nanjing was not the only city that benefited from foreign trade. In 1488, when the Hongzhi emperor ascended the throne, a Korean official named

9 Wang Shu, *Wangduanyi zouyi*, 526.

10 The emperor ordered the Guangdong government to build the ship, but a high official in Guangdong tried to make a deal with Kunluqunxieti, offering the mission 200 taels of silver, instead. Kunluquxieti preferred to have a new ship; he even informed the imperial court, and the official was impeached. Chen Xuelin, "Xianluo gongshi 'Xie Wenbin' shijian pouxi," in his *Mingdai renwu yu chuanshuo* (Hong Kong: Chinese University Press, 1997), 297.

Choe Bu traveled via the Grand Canal to northern China and left an account of his journey.[11] Choe admired the prosperity of Hangzhou and wrote that a local official had told him: "In our country, private maritime junks set sail from Suzhou, Hangzhou, Fujian, and Guangdong to Champa and to Huihui [Huihui refers to Muslim countries on the Indian Ocean] to purchase annatto, pepper, and foreign incense. These junks [travel] endlessly."[12]

On the canal near the north gate of the city, Choe saw that, in addition to numerous colorfully painted pleasure boats, merchant boats gathered from southern prefectures such as Wenzhou, Chuzhou, Taizhou, Yanzhou, Shaoxing, and Ningbo.[13] When he reached Suzhou, he found a city even more prosperous than Hangzhou. At the northwestern gate of the city, the Changmen Gate, merchant boats gathered "like clouds in the sky," and shops lined both sides of the canal.[14] He was dazzled by the prosperity of canal cities on the other side of the Yangzi River, in central and northern China, including Huai'an, Xuzhou, Ji'ning, and, most of all, Linqing.[15]

In short, by the fifteenth century, Ming society was already dominated by a healthy market economy as a result of the tribute missions. As in the case of the Nanjing silk market, trade from the tribute missions was reshaping society, providing opportunities for free workers, and hastening the deterioration in the household registration system. In the midst of this flourishing market, emperors struggled to meet palace expenses using an outdated household registration system that operated without money so that the emperor would not have to depend on the market.

To add to the expense, the earliest Ming emperors considered the capital, not just the palace, as their domain. Therefore, an emperor took responsibility for everyone who depended on him, worked for him, or visited him there. This included the imperial family and household (eunuchs and palace women) as well as nobles, officials, soldiers, Buddhist monks and Daoist priests, guests (from tributary missions or others)—in short, everyone except the commoners in the capital. The emperor relied on the twenty-four eunuch institutions

11 Choe Bu was a Korean official. In 1488, he and 42 other Koreans took a ship from Jieju Island to mainland Korea but encountered a storm and drifted to the Zhejiang coast in Taizhou Prefecture. Choe left an account of about five months of his experiences in China. See Ge Zhenjia, *Cuipu "Piaohai lu" pingzhu* (Beijing: Xianzhuang shuju, 2002). Timothy Brook has a good analysis of Choe's travel record in his *The Confusions of Pleasure: Commerce and Culture in Ming China* (Taipei: SMC, 1998), 39–51.

12 Ge Zhenjia, *Cuipu "Piaohai lu" pingzhu*, 95.

13 Ge Zhenjia, *Cuipu "Piaohai lu" pingzhu*, 101.

14 Ge Zhenjia, *Cuipu "Piaohai lu" pingzhu*, 105, 107.

15 Ge Zhenjia, *Cuipu "Piaohai lu" pingzhu*, 193.

(see details below) and the six government ministries to maintain the granaries and storehouse treasuries providing the food and other supplies (from in-kind taxes) that he needed to fulfill these obligations.

Under the Hongwu emperor, labor services and in-kind taxes had worked well enough to keep the emperor's storehouse treasuries and granaries well stocked. But by the Yongle era, the emperor had to pay his officials in currency, instead of rice, and as the market improved and household registration broke down, the Son of Heaven sometimes lacked the wherewithal to pay for imperial meals. To make matters worse, the emperor had a position to uphold, hosting state banquets, tributary missions, and festivals with the splendor befitting his rank and making offerings to the gods and his ancestors with the magnificence befitting theirs.

2 The Emperor's Table

The sacrifice at the Temple of Grand Offerings, conducted in the first lunar month, was the most important state observance in the early Ming.[16] It marked the emperor as the Son of Heaven and signified his right to rule.

The emperor made the sacrificial offering, which was usually a calf, to the god of Heaven at the temple. Before the Jiajing emperor separated the worship of the god of Heaven and the god of the Earth, Ming emperors made their offerings to the various other gods in the temple at the same time. The sacrificial animals included, but were not limited to, calves, goats, pigs, and deer. On the day of the ceremony, the emperor, guided by officials from the Department of Imperial Offerings and attended by all high civil and military officials in the capital, presented the sacrificed animals, wine, and fruit to the gods, to the accompaniment of sacred music. With this ritual, the emperor maintained his status as the Son of Heaven and the legitimate ruler of China.[17]

---

16 The Temple of Grand Offerings built by the Yongle emperor in 1420 was modeled after the same temple in Nanjing. It housed the wooden tablets of the god of Earth and the god of Heaven until 1530, when the Jiajing emperor separated the worship of the two gods and built them their own altars and temples. See Li Yuanlong, *Tiantan* (Beijing: Chaohua chubanshe, 1998), 2.

17 Li Yuanlong, *Tiantan*, 10–12, 127–28, 131, 135. See also *DaMing huidian*, 790:437. The current Altar of Heaven in Beijing was rebuilt by the Qianlong emperor in 1754, when he ordered the Ministry of Rites to have it repaired without delay, as it was falling to pieces. See L.C. Arlington and William Lewisohn, *In Search of Old Peking* (Hong Kong: Oxford University Press, 1991), 105.

The emperor also offered seasonal sacrifices to the wooden spirit tablets of previous Ming emperors in the Imperial Ancestral Temple just outside the palace,[18] and daily offerings to his personal ancestors in the Hall for Honoring the Forebears within the palace.[19] The offerings to an emperor's personal ancestors were varied and abundant to show the emperor's filial piety. The full list of actual food outlay gives an idea of what this meant: in the first lunar month, fragrant leeks, fresh greens, shepherd's purse, clams, perch, and chicken and duck eggs; in the second lunar month, new tea, rapeseed greens, celery, southernwood leaves, and goslings; in the third lunar month, new bamboo shoots, amaranth greens, cabbage, carp, and chicken and duck eggs; in the fourth lunar month, turnips, cherries, loquats, plums, apricots, cucumbers, piglets, and pheasants; in the fifth lunar month, pumpkins, gourds, wild lettuce, eggplant, haw apples, peaches, plums, pullets, wheat grain, barley grain, wheat noodles, and shad; in the sixth lunar month, fresh lotus seedpods, watermelons, muskmelons, winter melons, dried shad, shredded shad cured with red wine dregs, and herring; in the seventh lunar month, pears, fresh horned nuts (water caltrop nuts, shaped like a bull's head with horns), waterlily seeds, fresh jujubes (red dates), and grapes; in the eighth lunar month, small-panicle millet, large-panicle millet, rice, lotus root, taro, water reeds, new ginger shoots, mandarin perch, and crab; in the ninth lunar month, chestnuts, oranges, bream, and small red beans; in the tenth lunar month, yams, chrysanthemums, tangerines, and hares; in the eleventh lunar month, buckwheat noodles, sugarcane, venison, roebuck venison, wild geese, swans, cormorants, storks, quails, partridge, and sunfish; in the twelfth lunar month, spinach, mustard greens, silver pomfret, and bream.[20]

Additionally, the emperor made daily offerings to his forebears of bread, cakes, and other treats. To provide plenty of variety for the ancestors, the offerings changed every day of the lunar month as follows: on the first day, rolled fried cakes; on the second day, finely granulated sugar; on the third day, tea from Ba County (in eastern Sichuan Province); on the fourth day, sugared butter cookies; on the fifth day, twice-cooked fish; on the sixth day, steamed rolls with steamed mutton; on the seventh day, clover honey biscuits; on the eighth

18 The current Ming emperor performed seasonal rites to previous Ming emperors at the Qingming festival for the spring season, the Duanwu festival for the summer season, the Zhongyuan festival for the autumn season, and the winter solstice for the winter season. *DaMing huidian*, 790:523.

19 Aurelia Campbell, *What the Emperor Built: Architecture and Empire in the Early Ming* (Seattle: University of Washington Press, 2020), 28.

20 Mote, "Yuan and Ming," 217–18. It was a translation by Mote of a record provided by the late Ming scholar Yao Shilin (1559–1644). See Yao Shilin, *Jianzhi bian*, n.d., in *Congshu jicheng chubian*, ed. Wang Yunwu (repr. Shanghai: Shangwu yinshuguan, 1936), 167–68.

day, sugared steamed biscuits; on the ninth day, pork shortbreads; on the tenth day, sugared jujube cakes; on the eleventh day, open-oven baked breads; on the twelfth day, sugar-filled steamed breads; on the thirteenth day, mutton-filled steamed breads; on the fourteenth day, rice-flour cakes; on the fifteenth day, fat-filled pastries; on the sixteenth day, honey cakes; on the seventeenth day, puff-paste baked breads; on the eighteenth day, "elephant eye" (rhomboid shaped) cakes; on the nineteenth day, flaky filled pastries; on the twentieth day, marrow cakes; on the twenty-first day, rolled cookies; on the twenty-second day, crisp honey biscuits; on the twenty-third day, scalded-dough baked breads; on the twenty-fourth day, sesame-oil noodles; on the twenty-fifth day, Chinese salt-and-pepper breads; on the twenty-sixth day, water-reed shoots; on the twenty-seventh day, sesame-sugar-filled baked breads; on the twenty-eighth day, smartweed flowers; on the twenty-ninth day, sour cream; and, on the thirtieth day, thousand-layer baked breads. If the month had twenty-nine days, the offering for the thirtieth was offered on the first day of the next month, along with the offering for that day.[21]

Food for the living, including the emperor and his vast household, would have been even more elaborate. The emperor ate three meals a day, in addition to the tea and dim sum that palace women served him before breakfast, after they had helped him dress. Meals for the Son of Heaven had to be plentiful, far exceeding what an ordinary person could finish at a single sitting. The Ming government record left us with the menus of breakfast and lunch for the dynastic founder in 1384. They show twelve dishes of food for his breakfast and twenty for his lunch. In addition to rice, soup, and tea, every meal included a variety of meats and vegetables. The record does not give the details about his dinner, but it must have been more bountiful than lunch. As well, Ming emperors usually did not drink wine at breakfast and lunch, but wine had to be served with dinner. The emperor normally ate his meal alone, unless he invited a guest or a concubine to join him. The emperor usually invited whichever concubine with whom he had decided to spend the night to dine with him.[22]

After 1420, during the Yongle reign, twenty-four eunuch agencies managed the emperor's household in Beijing. They had been established gradually, taking over most of the duties performed by palace women in the early Ming. The agencies comprised twelve directorates, four offices, and eight services. (See Table 5 for details.) The agency known as the Directorate of Palace Foods prepared the emperor's daily meals in a gigantic kitchen, with nearly 200

21 See Mote, "Yuan and Ming," 216–17; see also Yao Shilin, *Jianzhi bian*, 166–67.

22 See Qiu Zhonglin, "Huangdi de canzhuo: Mingdai de gongshan zhidu ji qi xiangguan wenti," *Taida lishixi xuebao* 34 (December 2004): 5–7.

eunuch kitchen servants and a eunuch director.[23] In addition to cooking for the emperor, they prepared the food offerings for the spirit tablets in the Hall for Honoring the Forebears. The Directorate of Palace Foods used firewood from the Office of Firewood and obtained its supply of food from two bureaucratic departments outside the palace: the Ministry of Rites in the Department of Imperial Offerings and the Department of Imperial Banquets. In general, the Department of Imperial Offerings provided the food for the dead, and the Department of Imperial Banquets provided the food for the living, especially the emperor and his dependents.

The Department of Imperial Banquets also provided the food and cooking for the state banquets that followed the many festivals and ceremonies that took place every year. Other than the grand sacrifices to the god of Heaven and the Earth god were ceremonies for minor gods such as those for mountains and rivers, sun and moon, rain, and heavenly soldiers. The altars for these gods were usually located in the suburbs of Beijing. The Department of State Sacrifices provided the offerings, and the Department of Imperial Banquets meals for all the participants, such as princes, high ministers, and other guests, in the celebratory banquets that followed. The feasts at these banquets included many dishes of meat, vegetables, and sweets, but unfortunately the Ming literature did not record in detail the dishes actually served.

In addition to supplying the food for imperial meals through the Directorate of Palace Foods, the Department of Imperial Banquets prepared the state banquets for metropolitan officials at traditional celebrations, such as the multitude of seasonal festivals.[24] Moreover, important birthdays—including those of the emperor, the empress, the empress dowager, and the crown prince—were celebrated with a state banquet held outside the Meridian Gate (the front

---

23 See Liu Ruoyu, *Zhuozhong zhi*, in *Siku jinhuishu congkan, shibu* (Beijing: Beijing chubanshe, 2000), 71:152.

24 These included Chinese New Year (the first day of the lunar new year); the spring equinox (first of the 24 solar terms that divide the year into 24 equal parts); the Qingming festival (or Tomb-Sweeping festival, for cleaning and visiting the graves of ancestors, the fifth of the 24 solar terms); Buddha's Birthday (the eighth day of the fourth lunar month); the Duanwu festival (now known as the Dragon Boat festival, to commemorate the drowned poet Qu Yuan with dragon boat races, the fifth day of the fifth lunar month); the Double Seven festival (now known as Chinese Valentine's Day, for the reunion of the legendary lovers, the Cowherd and the Weaving Maid, the seventh day of the seventh lunar month); the Zhongyuan (Hungry Ghost) festival (for making offerings to wandering spirits, the fifteenth day of the seventh lunar month); the Laba (Rice Porridge) festival (the beginning of the new year celebrations and the day of Buddha's enlightenment, the eighth day of the twelfth lunar month); and the winter solstice (the twenty-second of the 24 solar terms).

TABLE 5 Twenty-four eunuch agencies

Directorates

	Directorate	Duties
1	Ceremonial	In charge of palace entertainment, ceremonies, and punishment; supervised special royal missions and eunuch personnel; directed all eunuch services, transmitted and gave advice on petitions, recorded imperial documents, and kept the palace books.
2	Palace Servants	Responsible for all palace construction and civil engineering; procured fireworks, copper, tin, wood, and iron utensils; repaired royal mansions and mausoleums.
3	Palace Carpentry	Made screens and all the wooden furniture; games and toys; and decorative objects from sandalwood, lacquerware, ivory, and pearl.
4	Outfits	Made draperies, cushions, rattan blinds, and raincoats and umbrellas for outfitting the emperor.
5	Imperial Stables	Took care of horses, exotic animals, and firearms and supervised the Imperial Guards.
6	Imperial Temples	Cleaned the temples and mausoleums and lit incense and altar candles.
7	Palace Foods	Prepared court meals and banquets, as well as the offerings to the emperor's ancestors three times a day.
8	Palace Seals	Stored sacred seals, imperial decrees, proclamations, and seals for grand commanders.
9	Documents	Stored peerage appointments and other official documents.
10	Palace Custodians	Cleaned palaces and other imperial structures.
11	Royal Clothing	Made ceremonial robes, everyday apparel, headgear, and footwear.
12	Entourage Guards	Acted as front guards and swept roads during every imperial visit to the Outer Court.

TABLE 5 Twenty-four eunuch agencies (*cont.*)

Offices

	Office	Duties
13	Firewood	Handled firewood and charcoal and kept the tanks full of water for firefighting.
14	Bells and Drums	Played bells and drums and performed theatricals and shadow-picture plays.
15	Paper	Made toilet paper and other paperware.
16	Bathing	In charge of bathhouses and bathing equipment.

Services

	Service	Duties
17	Palace Armament	Produced and cared for various weapons and armor.
18	Silverware	Made gold and silver pieces for imperial use and gifts.
19	Nursing Home	Took care of retirees and court ladies expelled from the palace so that court secrets would not be revealed. (The only eunuch office located outside the Imperial Palace.)
20	Headgear	Made headgear, footwear, and banners for princes and princesses.
21	Garments	Made summer, winter, and special clothing for palace personnel.
22	Weaving and Dyeing	Made indigo and dyed linen, silk fabric, and other kinds of cloth.
23	Wine, Vinegar, and Noodles	Supplied wine, vinegar, sugar, soy sauce, noodles, etc.
24	Vegetables	Supplied vegetables, fruit, nuts, and seasonal delicacies.

SOURCE: SHIH-SHAN HENRY TSAI, *THE EUNUCHS IN THE MING DYNASTY* (ALBANY: STATE UNIVERSITY OF NEW YORK, 1996), 231–32 (APPENDIX 1).

gate of the Palace City), and hundreds of officials would attend.[25] On occasions when the emperor hosted the banquet,[26] the imperial women—the empress, empress dowager, imperial consorts, wives of imperial sons, and imperial daughters—held a feast for the wives of chief ministers and high officials in the Palace of Earthly Tranquility in the Inner Quarters of the palace.[27]

The tributary missions were another expense for the Department of Imperial Banquets. When emissaries from tributary states went to Beijing, this department provided their daily meals.[28] The expenditure was enormous and unpredictable (depending on the number of envoys that year) but necessary, as it concerned the emperor's "face." Whereas in the palace about two hundred eunuchs worked in the Directorate of Palace Foods to cook for the emperor, for state banquets the Department of Imperial Banquets needed thousands of servants in its kitchens. Its quota was 9,462 kitchen servants. These kitchen servants were performing their obligatory labor service.[29]

The food for all these banquets came from nearby state-owned farms and taxes in kind from various provinces.[30] The Department of Imperial Banquets managed four farms in the suburbs south of Beijing: for pigs, cows, and goats; for chickens, ducks, and geese; for fruit trees; and for vegetable gardens.[31] Every farm had annual quotas for deliveries to the Department of Imperial Banquets: 800 live cows, 1,000 live pigs, 1,000 salted pigs, 20 lambs, plus 120,000 chicken eggs, 18,000 live geese, in addition to many ducks and chickens.[32] Although produce from these local farms was fresh, it had too little variety and insufficient quantity to supply the throne, so the Department of Imperial Banquets

25 *DaMing huidian*, 792:575.

26 Ming records did not specify which banquets the emperor hosted, but these records and other documents make it likely that, at a minimum, he presided over the banquets for the major traditional festivals such as Chinese New Year and the Duanwu Festival; the birthdays of important people; the completion of building projects such as palace halls and tombs of former emperors; offerings that he made to major gods, such as the god of Heaven; and the ritual for agriculture in which he performed a farming task and the empress engaged in sericulture (cultivating silkworms and extracting silk from them). The emperor probably did not preside over offerings to minor gods and their subsequent banquets, whose altars were in the Beijing suburbs but sent officials to do so on his behalf.

27 Mote, "Yuan and Ming," 230.

28 *DaMing huidian*, 792:576.

29 *DaMing huidian*, 579.

30 These farms were located south of the street called Dongjiang mixiang, renamed Dongjiao minxiang in the Qing dynasty. See Xu Daling, "Mingdai Beijing de jingji shenghuo," 48.

31 Hucker, *A Dictionary of Official Titles*, 409.

32 *DaMing huidian*, 792: 578–81.

relied heavily on in-kind taxes from the provinces. Every year, it collected 32,050 live geese and 18,900 live pigs from Zhejiang Province alone.[33]

In short, in the late fifteenth century, although the market was thriving, the emperor's table—which included imperial daily meals and ancestral offerings, as well the many ceremonies and banquets that he hosted throughout the year—was supplied outside the market, through the household registration system. By 1488, when the Hongzhi emperor ascended the throne, the system was breaking down. The emperor needed money to buy food to make up the shortfall, and he did not have it.

3 The Emperor's Coffers

The Palace Treasury comprised all the storehouse treasuries in the palace, including, but not limited to, the Jiazi Treasury for cotton cloth and dyes, the Yizi Treasury for clothing and quilts, the Bingzi Treasury for raw silk and raw cotton, the Dingzi Treasury for copper, iron, tin, incense, tea, and wax, and the Wuzi Treasury for timber and pepper. These treasuries were the emperor's personal storehouses, and palace eunuchs managed them for him.[34]

The emperor kept his money in the Siyao Treasury and the Inner Chengyun Treasury. The Siyao Treasury had been set up in the early Ming to hold all the keys to palace entrances, but soon it also became storage for the precious notes that the Hongwu emperor gave as gifts.[35] Along with keys and precious notes, the Siyao Treasury stored copper coins, from both earlier dynasties and Ming castings.[36] When the Yongle emperor moved his main capital north to Beijing, both capitals had Siyao Treasuries. Palace eunuchs could withdraw copper cash from these treasuries to buy what the emperor needed in local markets.

Beginning in 1465, the Siyao Treasury also took in coins from the taxes and other charges—the salt consumption tax, the shop and transit fees, and the inland customs tolls—that originally had been payable only in precious notes.[37] Because half these charges were now payable in copper coins,

33 *DaMing huidian*.

34 Su Xinhong, "Mingdai Neiku de huangshi caizheng zhuangshuhua yanbian," *Mingdai yanjiu* 24 (June 2015): 37.

35 *Ming shilu*, Taizu, 2503; Li Xun, *Mingshi shihuozhi jiaozhu*, 210.

36 The dynastic founder issued copper coins between 1368 and 1375 and then again in 1377, 1387, and 1389, although precious notes were the state currency. The Yongle and Xuande emperors reopened the imperial mints in 1408 and 1433, respectively, to cast coins. Peng Xinwei, *Zhongguo huobi shi*, 435–36.

37 As shown in Chapter 2, these charges—the salt consumption tax, the shop and transit fees, and the inland customs tolls—were first levied solely in paper money, to take excess

the Siyao Treasury in Beijing received them continuously as income, copper coins, used for paying civil officials there. In 1474 its coin income fell when the government cut the conversion rate of these charges and fees in half, from 4 copper cash per *guan* of precious notes to 2, and a year later applied the new rate to officials' salaries, reducing the outlay of coins as well.[38]

According to a 1480 report, the Siyao Treasury, through Beijing's Ministry of Revenue, took in 24 million *guan* in paper money from the inland customs toll every year. Because the other half of the customs toll was paid in copper coins at the rate of 2 per *guan*, the 48 million cash went to the Beijing Siyao Treasury annually, from this fee alone,[39] without even counting the salt consumption tax or the shop and transit fees.

The emperor also stored money in the Inner Chengyun Treasury. This was one of his several personal treasuries, for precious materials such as gold, silver, and satin. When the market value of the paper money in the Siyao Treasury fell, the emperor withdrew more of these precious materials from the Inner Chengyun Treasury to give guests as gifts. The Inner Chengyun Treasury became more important in 1436, when the Zhengtong emperor implemented the Gold Floral Silver reform, converting the grain tax into a silver tax to pay Beijing military officials. As shown in Chapter 2, the resulting 1 million taels of silver went directly to the Inner Chengyun Treasury in the palace. But the annual salaries of his military officials totaled less than 200,000 taels, hence, the emperor kept over 800,000 taels a year for his own personal use.[40]

Although no precise record survives on of how emperors spent their money, we know that they gave silver as gifts to nobles, high officials, and tributary mission representatives. They also bought paintings, antiques, precious stones, and exotic pets from the markets in Beijing. Although emperors found these luxury items enticing, and may have seen them as their due as Sons of Heaven, the tax system did not cover them; emperors had to find other ways to obtain them.

The emperors had access to the Siyao Treasury for paper money and copper coins and the Inner Chengyun Treasury for silver. Each currency was used for different expenses, depending on tradition and need. In the early Ming, the emperor covered all expenses in the capital with resources from his storehouses, paying officials with rice from his granaries there. In the Yongle emperor's time, it became traditional for the emperor to pay Beijing officials with

---

precious notes out of circulation. Then the value of precious notes rose, and in 1465 half the amount of these charges became due in copper coins and half in precious notes.

38 *DaMing huidian*, 789: 683, 724; Dai Jin, *Huangming tiaofa shili leizuan*, series 2, 4:580.

39 Dai Jin, *Huangming tiaofa shili leizuan*, 4:582.

40 Li Xun, *Mingshi shihuozhi jiaozhu*, 60, 136; *Ming shilu*, Wuzong, 299.

precious notes from his Siyao Treasury. When the value of precious notes declined, officials were paid in copper coins and, later, in silver. Beginning in 1436, silver from the Gold Floral Silver reform in the Inner Chengyuan Treasury was earmarked for military officials.

By the fifteenth century, when paper money had only nominal value in markets, the emperor had to maintain a stock of copper coins and silver, which was more welcome in the market, to fund his needs. In 1488, the first year of the Hongzhi reign, as a temporary solution, the emperor converted the salt consumption tax and all commercial charges into silver, which he stored in his Inner Chengyun Treasury.[41]

The 1488 measure revealed the Hongzhi emperor's desperate need for silver. He had to pay incidental expenses for his father's funeral and his own succession ceremony. Bureaucratic departments paid the bulk of these costs—the Ministry of Works built a new mausoleum, and the Ministry of Rites managed all the ceremonies. But the new emperor still had to buy gifts for his new empress and concubines; and he had to hire Buddhist monks or Daoist priests for his father's funeral.

Theoretically, the emperor's finances were separate from state finances. But if the emperor found himself short of money and was unable to raise it, as the Hongzhi emperor had done with the 1488 measure, he probably asked the government ministries to "lend" some of their silver to the Inner Chengyun Treasury. The ministers were certainly not happy to see their funds disappear in this way, but they could not let the Son of Heaven live a miserable, hand-to-mouth existence. As their only recourse, they tried to curb what they saw as imperial profligacy. The result was ongoing conflict between ministers and their emperor.

4 An End to Extravagance?

Whenever a new emperor took the throne, high ministers filed petitions to "review" (and abolish) unpopular state policies. The new emperor, to show that he was determined to promote good government, usually went along with them. When Zhu Youtang became the Hongzhi emperor, Zhou Hongmo, the minister of rites, used his petition to "eradicate heresy." The "heresy" to which he was referring was Buddhism, an "imported" religion.

41 The conversion rates for these government charges were 0.3 tael for 1,000 *guan* in paper money and 1 tael for 700 copper cash. Dai Jin, *Huangming tiaofa shili leizuan*, 4:588. The conversion ceased when the financial strain eased in 1489, but resumed and became a long-term rule for the inland customs tolls in 1493. See *DaMing huidian*, 789:612.

The Chenghua emperor had been a devotee of Buddhism. During his twenty-three-year reign (1465–1487), he had invited many reputable monks from different provinces and even foreign countries to visit him, conferred upon them honorable titles such as Zen master (*chanshi*) and *lama*, and built imposing monasteries for them in the capital. The Ministry of Works paid for the construction, but through the Department of Imperial Banquets, the Ministry of Rites paid for the monks' daily food. The emperor's expenditure on Buddhism had been enormous. After the death of the Chenghua emperor, the minister of rites hoped to reduce the number of Buddhist monks in Beijing. The Hongzhi emperor approved his request and ordered the repatriation of over 1,000 monks.[42]

In the fifth lunar month of 1488, the Ministry of Rites pushed for a more radical step to trim expenses on state banquets. An official in the ministry named Zhang Xiang criticized the imperial banquet for the Duanwu (Dragon Boat) Festival, which had just passed. As noted earlier, at the conclusion of a festival, the emperor invited hundreds of metropolitan officials and foreign envoys to a state banquet. Zhang Xiang objected to holding a banquet so soon after the death of the Chenghua emperor, when officials should have been in mourning. Instead of being subdued and abstinent, these officials, most of whom had served in the Chenghua court, had dressed in their finest clothes to drink wine, eat meat, and converse in loud voices, shamelessly. To encourage integrity among officials, Zhang asked the emperor to ban state banquets for traditional festivals for three years. Further, to eliminate the "heresy" of Buddhism, he wanted to cancel the state celebration of Buddha's birthday permanently.

The Hongzhi emperor believed that Zhang's criticisms and punishments were unfair. He questioned Zhang's superior, Rites Minister Zhou Hongmo, as follows: If the ministry considered the banquet inappropriate, why had it not called for canceling the banquet beforehand, instead of condemning the celebration after organizing the event? Zhou replied that it was because his subordinate office, the Department of Imperial Banquets, had not consulted him in advance. Zhou's answer only irritated the emperor further. He ordered that all festivals, and the state banquets that accompanied them, proceed according to tradition.[43]

The Ministry of Rites also kept an eye on court activities to prevent food costs from escalating. The Hongzhi emperor was not obsessed with Buddhism, but he was a devout Daoist. In the sixth lunar month of 1489, an earthquake

42 *Mingshi*, 7885.

43 *Ming shilu*, Xiaozong, 335–38. Five months later, in the tenth lunar month, Zhou Hongmo stepped down as the minister of rites, though for another reason. See *Mingshi*, 3433.

erupted in Shaanxi Province.[44] One month later, an official from the Ministry of Rites wrote to the emperor that the earthquake was a warning from Heaven and that the court should halt all unnecessary Daoist ceremonies and rituals.[45] The Ministry of Rites achieved a great triumph in 1490, when it received imperial approval for a new policy, one that set a limit on food expenses, setting the cap on the cost for food at the level in 1488. All expenses that exceeded that amount were to be cut.[46]

The Ministry of Rites had good reason for fiscal anxiety. The household registration system was coming apart, as people moved around the empire more often; by the late fifteenth century, the Department of Imperial Banquets was having trouble collecting enough in-kind taxes (food) and labor services to support the throne. All it could do was avoid any new expenses that would deplete its remaining resources. Unlike a modern state, the empire had no single financial institution to cover the department's deficits. Instead, it had six ministries with separate duties and income sources, and the ministries were not responsible for helping one another.

The Department of Imperial Banquets in the Ministry of Rites was on the verge of bankruptcy. Many of its suppliers had escaped the household registration system, for example, the dairy farmers in Sanhe and Huai'rou Counties near Beijing. When Beijing became the imperial capital in 1421, the state had given 250 cows to families in these counties. Under household registration, these families had to raise the cows and give the Department of Imperial Banquets fresh milk for making cakes.[47] But decades later, all the dairy households and their cows had disappeared, leaving the department without milk.[48] To buy milk in local markets, the court needed money, and milk was not the only food in short supply. In order to continue to operate, the Department of Imperial Banquets asked the Ministry of Rites for help, even though the ministry did not have spare resources either.

Through the Ministry of Rites, the Department of Imperial Banquets tried to borrow money from the Ministry of Revenue. The Ministry of Revenue was the best-financed ministry, as it was in charge of the land tax. After the household system broke down, the Ministry of Revenue simply collected the land tax directly from those who held it, regardless of whether they were the registered

44 *Ming shilu, Xiaozong*, 597.

45 *Ming shilu, Xiaozong*, 614.

46 *Ming shilu, Xiaozong*, 825–26, 881–82.

47 See Qiu Zhonglin, "Huangdi de canzhuo," 19. Milk was used in baking; there is no evidence that it was consumed as a beverage.

48 *Ming shilu*, Xiaozong, 2299. Those households may have died out, but it was more likely that they had left the area to evade taxes.

household. Owners could move, but the land could not, so the Ministry of Revenue was able to continue collecting the tax. Since the mid-fifteenth century, the Ministry of Revenue had gradually converted its land taxes into silver, which it stored in its Taicang Treasury, established in Beijing in 1442.

In 1492, Ye Qi, the minister of revenue, further increased silver income through a reform in the salt administration. Ye Qi changed the regulation such that salt traders no longer had to transport grain to frontier garrisons in order to obtain salt certificates to take to the salt fields, but could buy salt certificates—with silver—directly from officials in the salt fields. The new measure saved salt traders substantial time and money, and the Ministry of Revenue gained a corresponding increase in silver. After the reform, the silver income in the Taicang Treasury rose to more than 1 million taels a year.[49]

In short, the Ministry of Revenue became the institution to which the Department of Imperial Banquets could turn for money. By 1497 its debt to the Ministry of Revenue was 30,700 taels of silver.[50]

But the transfer of silver from the Taicang Treasury to the Department of Imperial Banquets posed a risk to frontier security. The original purpose of the Taicang Treasury had been to pay soldiers and buy supplies for frontier garrisons, so the drain on its silver made many court officials uneasy. In 1497, Duke Zhang Mao, who was famous for his admonitions to the throne, suggested that the Department of Imperial Banquets lower its costs: first, by cutting back on its annual quota of farm animals (100,000 a year) by 10–20 percent; and, second, by buying more chickens, ducks, and geese, instead of the more expensive cows, pigs, and goats. The Hongzhi emperor agreed to the proposal initially but later rejected it when Lin Feng, the head of the Department of Imperial Banquets, convinced the emperor that the real problem was that the department had been unable to collect its full quota of food as in-kind taxes and that this was why it had had to borrow money from the Ministry of Revenue in order to purchase the rest of the food they needed. In this light, what the Duke had suggested would only have diminished the already-reduced food supply for the department.[51]

As a result of this argument, the department continued to borrow silver. By 1500 it had a debt of about 100,000 taels. That year, several officials from various ministries submitted a joint memorial to the emperor to halt this extravagance. They pointed out that China was experiencing a comet and

49 Li Xun, *Mingshi shiluozhi jiaozhu*, 166.

50 *Ming shilu*, Xiaozong, 2283.

51 *Ming shilu*, Xiaozong, 2282–83.

earthquakes—warnings from Heaven of state mismanagement.[52] But the real drain on the Taicang Treasury was not from the Department of Imperial Banquets but, rather, from the Inner Chengyun Treasury, the emperor's own treasury. By 1500, the Inner Chengyun Treasury had "borrowed" 1.3 million taels from the Taicang Treasury for palace expenses.[53]

Palace expenses comprised more than the emperor's personal spending. Beginning in 1497, the Hongzhi emperor had agreed to convert rice salaries into silver for all the officials in both capitals.[54] This was an especially considerate policy for civil officials in Beijing; it meant that they no longer had to travel to Nanjing for their rice salaries or sell their rice coupons. But the policy increased the drain on the Inner Chengyun Treasury. In 1501, the emperor demanded yet another transfer of silver, this time 450,000 taels, from the Taicang.[55]

Officials in the Ministry of Revenue could not disobey an imperial order, but they repeatedly asked the emperor to control spending on his "hobby," by which they meant Daoism.[56] Daoism had prevailed in the inner court since the time of the Yongle emperor. According to a legend that likely originated at that court, in 1399 the Yongle emperor, who was then the Prince of Yan, consulted his primary spiritual adviser, the Buddhist monk Daoyan, regarding the proper time to initiate a rebellion against his nephew. Daoyan told the prince that he had to wait until his "master" had arrived to assist him. During a military ceremony held on the day that Daoyan had chosen to begin the attack, an apparition of a man with long untied hair and a sword appeared in the sky before the prince. When the prince asked Daoyan to identify the mysterious figure, Daoyuan replied that it was his master, the deity Zhenwu.[57]

Zhenwu, or Xuanwu, literally means the Perfect General or Dark General. In Daoism he is the God of the North and the God of War.[58] The Yongle emperor believed that Zhenwu had helped him triumph and was the protector of his reign. He constructed dozens of temples in Beijing dedicated to Zhenwu, including the *Qin'an dian*, the last building before the North Gate of the

52 *Ming shilu*, Xiaozong, 2917–19.

53 The emperor's treasury borrowed 300,000 taels in 1495, 500,000 taels in 1496, and 500,000 taels in 1500. *Ming shilu*, Xiaozong, 2919.

54 The conversion rate was 0.7 tael per 1 *shi* of rice. *DaMing huidian*, 789:683.

55 *Ming shilu*, Xiaozong, 1809–10, 2186, 2919, 3120.

56 For a brief introduction to the Daoist faith of the Hongzhi emperor, see Yang Qiqiao, *MingQing huangshi yu fangshu* (Shanghai: Shanghai shudian chubanshe, 2004), 62–67.

57 Campbell, *What the Emperor Built*, 89–90.

58 Wang Yi'e, *Daoism in China*, trans. Zeng Chuanhui (Beijing: Wuzhou chuanbo chubanshe, 2004), 79.

palace, where he conducted his own personal worship of Zhenwu.[59] The Yongle emperor also launched the large-scale construction or repair of temples on Mount Wudang, one of the sacred mountains of Daoism, and of the roads and paths leading to and up the mountain, and then renamed Mount Wudang the Great Mountain of Supreme Harmony (Dayue Taihe shan).[60]

In 1501, the Hongzhi emperor, another Daoist devotee, borrowed 450,000 taels from the Taicang Treasury, which he bestowed on the Daoist priests of the Xianling palace (Palace of Divine Manifestation), a large Daoist temple in Beijing that the Yongle emperor had dedicated to the deity Divine General Wang.[61] Moreover, the Hongzhi emperor sent a pilgrimage mission of over eighty eunuchs and artisans with a new statute of Zhenwu, gifts, and money to the Mount Wudang temples. Officials suggested canceling the pilgrimage to avoid the extra expense. The emperor replied that he respected their suggestion, but the pilgrimage had already left.[62]

At the same time, the Hongzhi emperor was faced with an immediate financial crisis, one that affected the daily palace meals as well as state banquets. In the fourth month of 1501, the Department of Imperial Banquets requested another loan, this one for 30,000 taels to settle a debt for livestock. Due to opposition by the Ministry of Revenue, the emperor did not grant the loan initially; but after he realized that he no longer had food for his daily meals and state banquets, he changed his mind. The Ministry of Revenue grumbled about increasing food expenses, and the emperor again instructed the Department of Imperial Banquets to follow his previous order, the one that had been ignored, and spend no money for food beyond the quota set in 1488.[63]

The Hongzhi emperor did attempt to be more frugal. He had never spent much on his own meals. Presumably for religious reasons, he already ate

---

59 Vincent Goossaert, *The Taoist of Peking, 1800–1949: A Social History of Urban Clerics* (Cambridge: Harvard University Asia Center, 2007), 193.

60 For details of the Yongle emperor's Mount Wudang construction project, see Campbell, *What the Emperor Built*, 92–99.

61 Divine General Wang was a fearsome celestial general and thunder divinity, and the protector of all Daoist monasteries. (See Goossaert, *The Taoist of Peking*, 341–42). He was portrayed with a red face, a long beard, and three eyes. He wore a red robe with gold armor and stood on a wheel of wind and fire, with finger charms in his left hand and a metal whip in his right. During the Yongle era, a Daoist named Zhou Side from Hangzhou, who claimed to possess Wang's mystic techniques of divination through thunder magic, was so well known that everyone in Beijing had heard of him, and the Yongle emperor often summoned him for consultation. To accommodate Zhou in the capital, the emperor had a temple built for Divine General Wang in the western suburbs of Beijing. See Wang, *Daoism in China*, 91.

62 *Ming shilu*, Xiaozong, 2924, 3255–56.

63 *Ming shilu*, Xiaozong, 3151, 3278, 3282.

vegetarian meals 111 days of the year. A lot of the palace's food expenses were for other imperial household members, such as the empress dowager, the emperor's wives and children, and the tribute mission envoys staying in Beijing, who would not be impressed by vegetarian meals. But to rescue the Department of Imperial Banquets, in 1501, immediately after instructing the Ministry of Revenue to grant the loan, the emperor agreed with the Department of Imperial Banquets that the state would offer no banquet during the three-day ceremonies of the Chongyang (or Double-Nine) festival on the ninth day of the ninth lunar month.[64] The emperor even ordered a "ban on slaughter" in 1502, in which everyone would follow the emperor's practice of eating vegetarian meals 111 days a year.[65]

This last order proved too radical for court officials. In response, the rites minister wrote that he appreciated the good intentions shown by the emperor's love for the welfare of living creatures, even though there might be some other reason for his order that was too embarrassing to articulate. Then he wondered whether it would be a good idea for the empress dowager and the tributary emissaries to eat meatless meals for such an extended period. The emperor did not respond directly to this. He only reminded the Department of Imperial Banquets to hold on to the money it had borrowed, for use in the future.[66]

In 1503, a year later, the Hongzhi emperor supported a plan to manufacture copper coins. If the ban on slaughtering animals for food was aimed at reducing expenses, then casting coins could be a way to augment his income.

5 Copper Coins as Income

In early 1503, after the Baoyuan Mint had been closed for seventy years, the Hongzhi emperor consulted the Ministry of Revenue about a proposal for casting coins.[67] The proposal had been made by a junior court official in Nanjing. The ministry argued against reopening the mint and suggested that the government first spend all the old coins left by early Ming emperors and collected in

64 *Ming shilu*, Xiaozong, 3295.

65 *Ming shilu*, Xiaozong, 3417.

66 *Ming shilu*, Xiaozong, 3417–18.

67 The dynastic founder had issued copper coins in the early Ming, but in 1375 he shut down the imperial mint and began to print paper money as his state currency. In later years, while continuing to issue paper money, the Yongle and Xuande emperors had both cast coins a few times but only in small amounts. See Peng Xinwei, *Zhongguo huobi shi*, 435–36.

taxes over decades. The emperor argued that casting coins had been successful before, and the need to "enrich the state and benefit the people" was urgent.[68]

The ministry acceded, submitting an initial plan for coin manufacture with three main points. First, even after the new coins had been cast, people should be able to use the old coins from previous dynasties and rulers to pay their taxes and other charges (e.g., customs tolls or crime restitution fees), though their coins would only be worth half their face value for these payments. Second, in order to address the emperor's financial crisis, the new coins had to be used to pay official salaries and to buy food by the Department of Imperial Banquets and the Department of Imperial Offerings. Third, they suggested that, in addition to the imperial mints in the capitals, each province set up its own mint for casting coins.[69]

The Ministry of Works, which had continually opposed the idea of casting coins, was precisely the institution responsible for doing so. In the third month of 1503, Zhang Wen, a Ministry of Works official, presented a long resentful memorial to the emperor. He stated:

> The cost for manufacturing 10,000 coins is 10 taels of silver. Now if the whole empire casts coins, how many thousand taels have to be spent? We should consider this question in the first place, but the Ministry of Revenue never mentions a word about this! ... it is not true that court officials do not know [that coin casting is] impractical, but none of them tells the truth. They all say that His Majesty is determined to implement it and therefore dare not speak to oppose him.[70]

Zhang concluded that if the emperor really wanted to be frugal, he would live within his means and then there would be no need to cast new coins; otherwise, no matter how many coins they cast, they would never be able to cover the emperor's expenditures.[71]

Although court officials voiced their disapproval implicitly or explicitly, the Hongzhi emperor was determined to cast more coins. In the third month of 1503, he stated that because the proposal of casting coins had been so widely discussed, it would be worthwhile to carry it out. But he cut back on his original

68 *Ming shilu*, Xiaozong, 3622.

69 *Ming shilu*, Xiaozong, 3622–23.

70 *Ming shilu*, Xiaozong, 3644–45.

71 *Ming shilu*, Xiaozong, 3647.

plan such that, instead of having the entire empire cast coins, only the two capitals did so.[72]

The cost of coin manufacture was for labor and copper. Theoretically, as artisan households, mint workers were supposed to work for free as their labor service. In practice, by this time, everyone who could evade their labor service did so. To retain their mint laborers, the ministries had started to pay them in copper coins as a meal allowance. Because the coins paid to the laborers were part of those produced, labor costs were not an expense before the casting began. The heavier burden for the Ministry of Works, which operated the Baoyuan Mint, was the raw material. Southeastern provinces such as Yunnan and Guizhou had rich copper mines, but because the Ming government had never built a direct transportation line to move the metal from the mines to the capital, it had to buy on the market, instead.

The Ministry of Works in Beijing and Nanjing could have bought raw copper from Jingzhou in the mid-Yangzi River valley, the biggest market for copper from Yunnan and Guizhou, but they did not have the silver to pay for it. If the manufacturing estimate from Beijing's Ministry of Works was accurate—that it cost 10 taels of silver to make 10,000 coins—then the mints in Nanjing and Beijing, respectively, needed an additional 25,660 taels and 20,990 taels annually to begin the emperor's project. Although the market prospered, both ministries were on the verge of bankruptcy. Nevertheless, in 1503, even without a way to pay for the copper, the emperor ordered the imperial mints to reopen. (See coin-making process in Figure 4 and copper coins in the Ming dynasty in Figure 5.)

Without funds, the Ministry of Works could not meet its quota for Hongzhi coins. In 1504 the Nanjing mint used the excuse of "a poor harvest"[73] to cut production by one third, and the emperor approved it.[74] The situation at the Beijing mint was even worse. The Hongzhi emperor never received a progress report, and, in the fifth month of 1505, he discovered that the Department

72 The annual quota of the Nanjing mint was 25.66 million coins. We lack data for the Beijing mint, but if we apply the ratio of 5.5:4.5 from the Jiajing dynasty, then the Beijing mint had to produce 20.99 million coins every year. In 1527, the Jiajing emperor ordered the mints to cast 41,491,200 in copper cash, with the Nanjing mint casting 22,660,800 (54.6%) and the Beijing mint 18,830,400 (45.4%). See *Wanli kuaiji lu*, 833:140.

73 The 1504 report simply noted a poor harvest caused by natural disasters. What may have had a bearing on the 1504 harvest was severe flooding of the Yangzi, affecting riverside cities, including Nanjing, in the eighth lunar month of 1502. This could have reduced harvests for a few years afterward. See *Mingshi*, 194.

74 *Ming shilu*, Xiaozong, 4005.

of Imperial Offerings was still withdrawing early Ming coins from the Siyao Treasury to buy food. His suspicions aroused, the emperor asked the Ministry of Revenue to check the stock of Hongzhi coins in the Siyao Treasury. The ministry replied that less than 20 percent of the new copper coins had been made

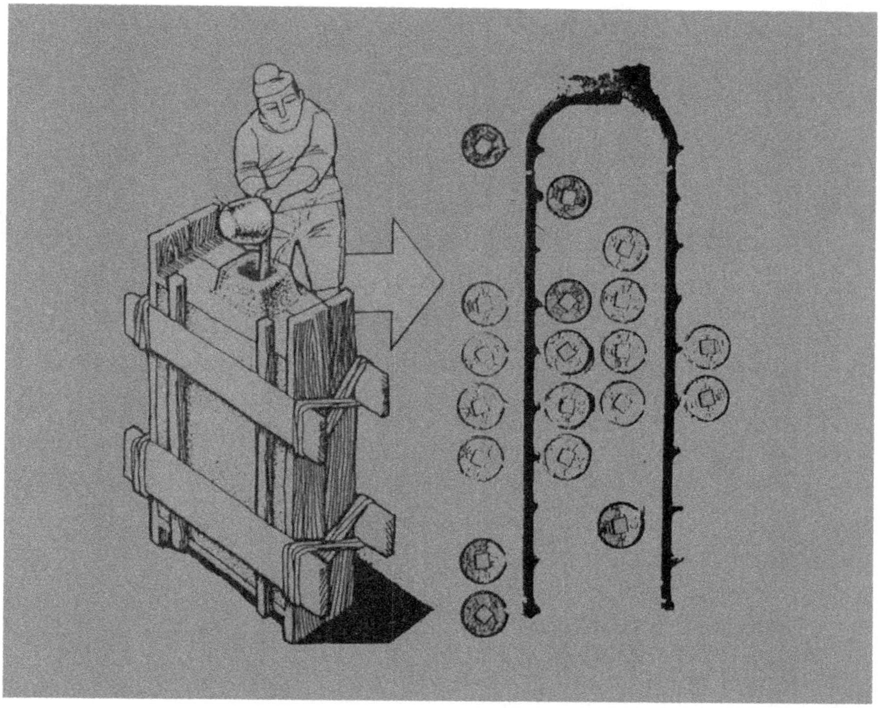

FIGURE 4 Casting coins. This is an image that shows the coin-making process used in both premodern Japan and China: Mint workers used finely powdered clay mixed with charcoal dust and water to create the clay for their coin molds. The clay was set into rectangular wooden trays and then impressed with metal coin patterns to form the molds. These metal patterns were joined together by little hollow tunnels to carry the liquid metal to all the molds. One tray and set of molds were imprinted with the face of the coin, one with the back of the coin. The two trays with their coin molds (faces and backs) were tied together, making a wooden container with a hole at the top. Liquid copper mixed with zinc or tin was poured into the hole and ran down into the clay tunnels, spreading out like the roots of a tree to fill all the molds. After the liquid metal had cooled and solidified, the two sides of the wooden container were opened to reveal hundreds of coins, joined by slender tunnels like flowers on a stem. The coins were broken off from these stems, and then, in most cases, their edges were sanded smooth (for exceptions, see long-stick coins, Figure 6).

CREDIT: EDO-TOKYO MUSEUM, TOKYO

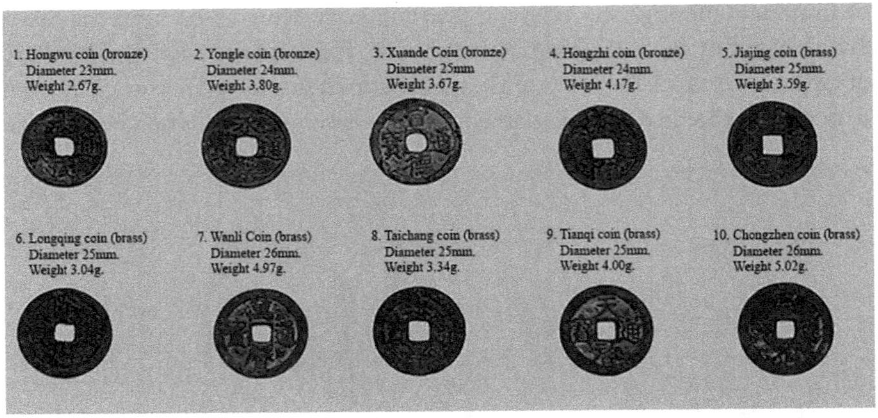

FIGURE 5 Copper coins in the Ming Dynasty. These Ming coins were collected by the author with the help of a coin collector. They had been used at marketplaces in Ming China. The coin collector reported that they were of such good quality that they must be genuine—but good-quality coins could also be made by counterfeiters.

so far. The emperor was furious and demanded a detailed report from the Ministry of Works.[75] But he died from a misdiagnosed illness a few days later, at age thirty-six, before the ministry could deliver its report.[76]

6 Prodigal Emperors

6.1 *The Zhengde Emperor (1505–1521): Extortion and Government Charges*

In the fifth month of 1505, the Hongzhi emperor's thirteen-year-old son Zhu Houzhao became the Zhengde emperor, inheriting the throne and all that went with it—including a lack of funds for maintaining the palace. Every year, the emperor took in about 1 million taels from the Gold Floral Silver reform, paid out about 200,000 taels to Beijing military officials, and kept a net income of 800,000 taels. But palace expenses were high, especially in the first year of

75 *Ming shilu*, Xiaozong, 4240–41.

76 The Hongzhi emperor became ill in the fourth lunar month. The imperial physicians treated him for a cold, but his condition worsened, and he died early in the fifth lunar month. His physicians were arrested and severely punished. See *Mingshi*, 196; Bu Shichang, *HuangMing tongji shuyi* (1605, repr. Taipei: Guangwen shuju, 1972), vol. 3, *juan* 8, 48a–49a.

the Zhengde emperor's reign, when he had to pay for his father's funeral, his own accession ceremony, and his wedding, because his father had wanted him to marry.

Long Shou, a eunuch who had taken charge of the Inner Chengyun Treasury, estimated that the cost of these three ceremonies would total 5,000 taels of gold and 1.8 million taels of silver. The Inner Chengyun Treasury did not store much gold, and although it could use silver to buy gold from the mines in Sichuan Province, the silver reserve in the treasury was far from sufficient to pay these amounts.[77] Han Wen, the minister of revenue, suggested that the new emperor pay military officials in copper coins, instead of silver, at a fixed rate of 700 cash per tael, for the three autumn months, thus saving 103,000 taels of silver to help cover urgent expenses. Military officials opposed the proposal, pointing out that the conversion rate reduced their actual incomes, and that, even though they did not mind the reduction, the proposal was unworkable because the Siyao Treasury in Beijing had only 25 million in copper cash on hand, which would cover only about 30 percent of their salaries for those months.[78]

The Zhengde emperor did as his father had done, and, in the eighth lunar month of 1506, he ordered a transfer of 400,000 taels of silver from the Ministry of Revenue's Taicang Treasury to his Inner Chengyun Treasury. Han Wen requested that he take only half this amount, as this initial order would empty the silver reserve in the treasury. The emperor changed his order to 300,000 taels to be transferred immediately, with the remaining 100,000 taels to be made up later.[79]

Despite the dearth of silver in the treasuries, the young emperor indulged in expensive hobbies, including music, dancing, wrestling matches, and collecting a menagerie of exotic animals. Meanwhile, the two imperial mints were still struggling to fulfill their quotas from 1504 and 1505. In 1507 Nanjing's minister of revenue reported to the throne that the Nanjing mint was still doing its best to make up the arrears in the manufacturing quota; even worse, the Hongzhi coins were not circulating well in the market there.[80] The Zhengde emperor did not shut down the mints, which continued to make coins bearing the Hongzhi reign title, but neither did he have his own coins made.

---

77 *Ming shilu*, Wuzong, 58–60.

78 *Ming shilu*, Wuzong, 299.

79 *Ming shilu*, Wuzong, 482–84.

80 *Ming shilu*, Wuzong, 735.

Instead, to raise money for his projects, the young emperor gave the eunuch Liu Jin free rein to raise revenue. Liu usually managed this task by threatening officials with charges of corruption or mismanagement and then taking bribes to withdraw the allegations. What may be evidence of the eunuch's success was that in 1507, Liu withdrew the immense sum of 350,000 taels from the Taicang Treasury to buy lanterns for the lantern festival that marked the middle of the first lunar month. Other funds were used to restore buildings in the imperial park south of Beijing. The emperor even began to build a new palace, known as the Leopard Quarter. Construction on this and other nearby residences and temples continued for years. All of it had to be paid for, and Liu Jiu was to raise the money by whatever means necessary. In addition to withdrawing silver from the Taicang, Liu Jin made money by selling salt certificates (for salt from state-owned fields), probably for less than the salt merchant buyers would have paid by going through official channels. Liu also imposed surtaxes in the provinces. In 1508, for example, a surtax of 20,000 taels of silver per year was assessed on the silver mines in Fujian and Sichuan Provinces, even though local officials had reported that the lodes were exhausted.[81]

The Zhengde emperor died in the third lunar month of 1521. Five months earlier, he had been fishing alone in a small boat on the Grand Canal when his boat overturned. He nearly drowned before his eunuchs were able to drag him from the water. As he was already in poor health from chronic drinking, he became seriously ill and remained so throughout the spring of 1521. In the third lunar month, he died in his Leopard Quarter at the age of twenty-nine.[82] The Zhengde emperor had no living sons and no brother; his fourteen-year-old cousin Zhu Houcong inherited the throne, becoming the Jiajing emperor.

6.2 *The Jiajing Emperor (1521–1566): Brass Coins*

In 1527, when the Jiajing emperor had been on the throne for six years, Zou Wensheng, the minister of revenue, advised the emperor to use the ideas of a former (Ming) minister of rites named Qiu Jun[83] to revive coin manufacture.[84] Qiu Jun had written that the state should make good-quality coins and rid the

81 James Geiss, "The Cheng-te reign, 1506–1521," in Mote and Twitchett, *Cambridge History of China*, 407.

82 Geiss, "The Cheng-te reign," 435–36.

83 Qiu Jun, who died in 1495, was one of the most prolific writers in Ming times. He left a monumental work, *Daxue yanyi bu* [*Supplement to the Extended Meaning of the Great Learning*], on a variety of subjects, especially government institutions. Chapters 26 and 27 discuss casting bronze coins. Qiu Jun, *Daxue yanyi bu*, 1506, Institute of Oriental Culture, University of Tokyo. For a biography of Qiu Jun, see Goodrich and Fang, ed., *Dictionary of Ming Biography*, 249–50.

84 *Ming shilu*, Shizong, 1851–55.

markets of inferior coins by replacing them with new, high-quality coins. His strategy for new coins was: "Don't scrimp on copper; don't save on labor."[85] He credited Kong Yi, an official during the Southern Qi dynasty (479–502), with this piece of wisdom. Kong had explained that, although heavy coins were cumbersome, light coins, which could be made at low cost, encouraged counterfeiting. Severe penalties did not deter counterfeiters when the state mints skimped on copper and skilled labor, making the counterfeiter's job both easier and more lucrative.[86]

Qiu Jun suggested that manufacturing costs could be covered without extra expense by taking the following steps. First, the state should set up mints in places that were flooded with inferior coins and dispatch officials to capture counterfeiters to work there as free laborers. Next, the government should select good-quality coins (Qiu considered coins from the Tang and Song dynasties the best) from the state treasuries to display in marketplaces, to familiarize the public with high-quality coins and make them wary of inferior ones. After they knew what to look for, people were encouraged to exchange their low-quality coins at a discounted rate for good-quality coins at local government offices. After collecting all these low-quality coins, local governments would have enough copper to operate their local mints. Qiu Jun assumed that it would take about ten years to replace all the low-quality coins with good-quality coins in this way.[87]

The Jiajing emperor began to cast coins in the last lunar month of 1527, ostensibly following Qiu's advice to make good-quality coins, but then rejected this method. To ensure high quality, the emperor ordered that each Jiajing coin weigh 1.3 *qian*, or 0.1 *qian* more than the Hongzhi coin. But he did not like the idea of setting up government mints in marketplaces throughout the empire to buy inferior coins, which he thought would only encourage counterfeiters to produce even more inferior coins. Instead, he continued to assign manufacturing quotas: the Nanjing mint was to cast 22.66 million cash and the Beijing mint 18.83 million cash per year. Therefore, the production totaled about 41 million cash, only 5 million less than the quota for Hongzhi coins. To pay for manufacturing, the emperor ordered the two Ministries of Revenue, the richest institutions in the government, to provide the imperial mints with the metal to make the coins.[88]

The emperor reactivated the Baoyuan Mints in Beijing and Nanjing (which had been open but inactive). He continued to allow bronze coins from previous

85 Qiu Jun, *Daxue yanyi bu*, chap. 26, 9a.

86 Qiu Jun, *Daxue yanyi bu*, 10a.

87 Qiu Jun, *Daxue yanyi bu*, 10a–11b.

88 *Wanli kuaiji lu*, 833:140.

dynasties to circulate, but he made his own reign's coins from brass—the first time that the Chinese state had done so. Brass, like bronze, is an alloy, made of copper and zinc, rather than copper and tin. The intrinsic value of a brass coin depended on its copper content—usually only 60 to 80 percent. Bronze coins generally had a copper content of 80 to 90 percent. More important, copper was more expensive than zinc. Therefore, unless the Ming government cast its brass coins with a high percentage of copper, even though the Jiajing coins weighed the stipulated 0.1 *qian* more than Hongzhi and other Ming coins, they contained less copper and were cheaper to make.[89] According to the record left by the Ministry of Revenue in Beijing, to fill the emperor's order (using Taicang Treasury silver to buy metal for coins), officials simply bought less costly, lower-grade brass on the market and then handed it over to the Ministry of Works to make the coins.[90]

Whereas the Beijing mint cast only inexpensive brass coins, the emperor had coins made from higher- and lower-grade brass at the Nanjing mint. The tail sides of the higher-grade coins were marked with golden paint, but the lower-grade coins were burned in order to scorch them; these new brass coins were called "golden back" and "fire paint," respectively.[91] Although it may have appeared that the Jiajing emperor was trying to revive the use of copper coins in state finances, he was more interested in using the copper cash to help pay for daily palace expenses and accumulating silver in the Inner Chengyun Treasury.

Early in the Jiajing reign, taxes collected in copper coins and paper money were converted to silver. In 1527, probably in return for supplying his mints with metal, the emperor permitted the Ministries of Revenue in Beijing and Nanjing to increase their stock of silver by converting the salt consumption tax from paper money and copper coins into silver at the rate of 1 tael of silver for every 250 *guan* or every 500 copper cash.[92] In 1528 the emperor extended the policy to the inland customs tolls, and through the Ministry of Revenue he diverted the silver to his own treasury, the Inner Chengyun Treasury. The conversion rates this time were 1 tael for 333 *guan* or 700 copper cash, with the

89 Although by state decree, the Jiajing coin should have been heavier than the Hongzhi coin, in my own collection the Jiajing coin, although larger, is slightly lighter than the Hongzhi coin. (See Figure 5). This discrepancy might reflect the difficulty of controlling the weight of a coin during casting.

90 *Wanli kuaiji lu*, 833:140.

91 Tan Qian, *Zaolin zazu* (1636, repr. Beijing: Zhonghua shuju, 2006), 9.

92 *DaMing huidian*, 789:725.

silver delivered four times a year to the Inner Chengyun Treasury.[93] That same year, the use of paper money for crime restitution fees was converted to silver at a rate of 1 tael for 80 *guan*.[94]

Converting government charges into silver dealt a heavy blow to people who had saved their copper coins for this purpose. For many decades, they had used copper coins to pay the salt consumption tax, the inland customs tolls, and the shop and transit fees, but now they could only use them for shop and transit fees in prefectural cities. Speculators transported their coins, especially the inferior ones, to commercial cities to pay these government charges as soon as possible. Beijing was also flooded with inferior coins. In 1528, Beijing officials were alerted to this development and demanded that tax collectors accept only good-quality coins. But when shopkeepers responded by striking, which led to a sudden shortage of goods in Beijing, the government backed off;[95] and inferior coins continued to pour into Beijing.

7 Closing the Baoyuan Mint

The Jiajing emperor had a poor relationship with his court officials. In the first decade of his reign, they argued fiercely over the titles of his parents. As the former emperor's cousin, Zhu Houcong shared a grandfather with the Zhengde emperor. His father, Zhu Youyuan, the Prince of Xing, had died at his fief in Huguang Province before his son ascended the throne, but his mother, Lady Jiang, was still alive. The boy emperor was so filial that he had invited his mother to live with him in Beijing. The problem was her title. Court officials considered the succession of Zhu Houcong a simple case of adoption and urged the young Jiajing emperor to treat his uncle (the deceased Hongzhi emperor) as his father and his aunt, Lady Zhang, Emperor Zhengde's mother, who was still alive, as his own mother. In that way, Lady Zhang could continue to be the empress dowager, and the reigning emperor's biological mother, despite living in the palace, would keep her title as the wife of a feudal lord. The new emperor wanted to give his deceased father the title of emperor so that he could give his mother the status of empress dowager.

In the seventh lunar month of 1524, in response to increasing pressure from the throne over his parents' titles, over two hundred court officials refused to

93 Liang Cai, "Yikan Guanglusi qianliang shu," ca. 1539, in *Ming jingshi wenbian*, ed. Chen Zilong (repr. Beijing: Zhonghua shuju, 1962), 913.

94 *Ming shilu*, Shizong, 2240–41. It is unclear where the silver was stored.

95 *Ming shilu*, Shizong, 4030.

disperse after their morning audience with the emperor and remained prostrate before him in the audience hall to protest his order. At about noon the emperor demanded a list of the protesters and had the leaders of the protest thrown in prison. At this point, another group of officials began to shout and beat on the doors of the audience hall. The emperor responded by throwing all the low-ranking officials in prison and told the rest to await sentencing. Five days later, over 180 officials were beaten at court. Seventeen died of their injuries, and the rest were banished. The next day, the emperor set up his father's spirit tablet and conferred an imperial title on him, thereby making his mother the empress dowager. Although in this way the emperor ended all discussion about his parents' titles in 1524, arguments about rituals for them continued. Having thus elevated his father to the status of emperor, the Jiajing emperor wanted his spirit tablet to be placed with those of other Ming emperors in the Imperial Ancestral Temple. This request was opposed by the Ministry of Rites, which insisted that the temple show only the *actual* line of succession. Therefore, despite his new title, his father was not qualified to be on it. When the emperor pressed the issue in 1525, the Ministry of Rites suggested as a compromise that a separate temple be built for his father, adjacent to the Imperial Ancestral Temple. The emperor accepted the proposal, though he demanded that offerings at his father's temple be conducted on the same day as those at the Imperial Ancestral Temple.[96]

During this controversy over imperial rites, the Jiajing emperor became an expert on rituals. Like the Hongzhi emperor, he was a devotee of Daoism. In the aftermath of the grand debate over his parents' titles, he studied Confucian classics to learn more about rituals. The imperial temples and altars (and their rituals) had been designed by the dynastic founder in the late fourteenth century, but beginning in 1530, the Jiajing emperor rebuilt them to make them more consistent with the Confucian classics. He criticized the practice of a singular offering to both heaven and earth in the Temple of Grand Offerings. In the fifth month of 1530, he ordered the Ministry of Works to build four separate altars, to worship the Heaven, Earth, Sun, and Moon.[97] In 1535 he rebuilt the Imperial Ancestral Temple and, a few years later, moved his father's spirit tablet into it.[98] In addition, the emperor had his own prince's residence in Huguang rebuilt.

The emperor's interest in ritual became yet another drain on the Ministry of Works. In 1540, Wen Renhe, the minister of works, made the following resentful comment to the throne:

---

96 James Geiss, "The Chia-ching Reign, 1522–1566," in Mote and Twitchett, *Cambridge History of China*, 448–49, 457–58.

97 Li Yuanlong, *Tiantan*, 11–12, 50–51.

98 Geiss, "The Chia-ching Reign," 459.

> In the last two to three years, such large constructions like palaces, halls, houses, altars, kitchen's storerooms, mausoleums, and stone tablets have cost a total of 6.347 million [taels of silver], and [the construction in] Your Majesty's former residence in Huguang additionally cost 1.7 million [taels]. [The Ministry is] still working on over 30 construction projects, and its [silver] reserve has already been exhausted.[99]

Without money, the Ministry of Works had no way to operate the Baoyuan Mint in Beijing, even though it now needed only to pay for laborers and fuel. The mint was supposed to produce 18.83 million cash each year, but production chronically fell short.

The lack of copper coins caused problems for the Department of Imperial Banquets. In order to prepare meals for the imperial household and foreign guests visiting Beijing, the department had to buy food from shops in Wanping and Daxing Counties in Shuntian Prefecture, because it could no longer rely on in-kind taxes from household registration. These shops offered price lists in silver, but those selling fruits and vegetables, because of their smaller scale of business, also accepted paper money and copper cash at market conversion rates. They sold fruits and vegetables to the Department of Imperial Banquets daily, but only collected on the debts seasonally. In the 1530s, to settle its produce debt for each season, the department needed to withdraw at least 4.5 million copper cash and 1 million *guan* in paper money from the Siyao Treasury.[100]

But after the salt consumption tax and the inland customs toll had been converted to silver, the Siyao Treasury had relied mostly on the Baoyuan Mint for copper coins. Since the autumn of 1536, the Siyao Treasury had lacked the copper coins and paper money to give to the Department of Imperial Banquets. The department continued to purchase fruits and vegetables from shops, adding to its debt in both copper coins and paper money. In the spring of 1540, after fifteen seasons of nonpayment, having accumulated debt of 15 million *guan* and 67.5 million copper cash, the emperor ordered the debt to be paid in silver from the Taicang Treasury. To cover the cost, the Ministry of Revenue took silver from the inland customs tolls, which had formerly gone to the Inner Chengyun Treasury, to replenish the silver in their Taicang Treasury.[101]

This arrangement changed the way in which the Department of Imperial Banquets bought food. Initially, Liang Cai, the revenue minister, had used silver to buy 4.5 million copper cash and 1 million *guan* on the market and then given the copper and paper currencies to the department to cover food

---

99 Cha Jizuo, *Zuiwei lu* (1672, repr. Hangzhou: Zhejiang guji chubanshe, 1986), 242.

100 Liang Cai, "Yikan Guanglusi qianliang shu," 909, 912.

101 Liang Cai, "Yikan Guanglusi qianliang shu."

expenses. But he soon realized that the government would lose money through the double currency conversion.[102] He began to pay the Department of Imperial Banquets directly in silver, instead, at a rate of 1 tael for 1,000 copper cash or 500 *guan*, totaling to a seasonal transfer of 6,500 taels directly to the Department of Imperial Banquets, which then settled its debt in silver.[103] As a result, the department no longer used either copper coins or paper money.

The Jiajing emperor had no feasible way to rescue the Baoyuan Mint; his 1540 order to the Nanjing mint, to make up part of the quota owed by the Beijing mint,[104] was tracked unrealistic. In 1541, Gan Weilin, Beijing's minister of works, pointed out that his mint could not even fulfill the annual quota. He told the emperor that, in coin manufacture, "the gains do not make up for the losses."[105]

To pay for the food expenses for the Department of Imperial Banquets, the emperor allowed the Treasury to share its income from the inland customs toll with the Ministry of Revenue. Beginning in 1548, the inland customs toll would be collected in paper money and copper cash for the Siyao Treasury one year and in silver for the Ministry of Revenue the next. The first year would be paper money and copper cash,[106] and it would go to the Siyao Treasury; the second year, instead of going to the Inner Chengyun Treasury, it would go to the Ministry of Revenue, probably to be stored in the ministry's Taicang Treasury.

As may be obvious, the Baoyuan Mint in Beijing was poorly managed. In 1553 the Jiajing emperor suddenly proposed an aggressive plan to increase its output. On top of the existing annual quota of 41.49 million copper cash (for both imperial mints), he ordered a one-time casting of 95 billion more.[107] The Beijing and Nanjing mints were to share manufacturing at a ratio of 6:4.[108] These new coins were to be used mainly by the Ministry of Works to pay laborers to rebuild Beijing. To defend the capital against Mongol invasion that same year, the emperor ordered the third, outer wall to be built.

The historian Peng Xinwei thought that it would have been impossible for the Ministry of Works to implement the order. The two ministries were

---

102 This report seems to suggest that the Ministry of Revenue, which had manufactured paper money for the emperor, had begun to buy old notes on the market, instead of printing new notes itself.

103 Liang Cai, "Yikan Guanglusi qianliang shu," 909–14.

104 *Ming shilu*, Shizong, 4865. In order to support the Nanjing mint, in 1541 the Ministry of Works in Nanjing was allotted 12,000 taels of silver from the tax revenue from the inland customs of Yangzhou, Huai'an, and Hangzhou. See *DaMing huidian*, 789:612.

105 *Ming shilu*, Shizong, 5004.

106 *DaMing huidian*, 789:612.

107 Of this amount, 50 billion coins were to carry the Jiajing reign title, while 5 billion would bear the reign title of each of the nine Ming emperors before him.

108 *Gujin tushu jicheng* (1726, repr. Shanghai: Zhonghua shuju, 1934), 704:13b.

already stretched to meet their annual quota; how could they possibly cast an *additional* 95 billion cash? He suspected that this was only an unsuccessful proposal, and the additional casting quota was recorded wrongly—a clerical error.[109]

However, the work was paid for, and Beijing was rebuilt. New gates were added to the southern wall, giving Beijing nine inner-wall gates and seven outer-wall gates.[110] But the original plan to extend a new outer wall completely around the city could not be realized; the lack of funds meant that only the southern section was built, enclosing both the Altar of Heaven and the Altars of the Mountains and Rivers.[111] (See Map 2.)

Inferior coins continued to flow into Beijing, making shop and transit fees more difficult to collect. If city officials followed the rules and refused to accept inferior coins, the shopkeepers went on strike, and commodity prices skyrocketed. In the eleventh month of 1564, another shopkeepers' strike in Beijing prompted Grand Secretariat Xu Jie to submit a proposal to end the chaos of the coinage system. In his proposal, Xu Jie stated that many inferior coins were actually produced by the Baoyuan Mint itself.

At least four categories of copper coins circulated in Beijing, and they were all legitimate for paying taxes. The top-quality coins were the brass "golden backs" from the Nanjing mint, but their output was very small. Second in quality were the coins known as "smoothed edges" because their edges had been sanded down, including bronze coins from the pre-Jiajing period and bronze coins from the Yunnan mint.[112] (Yunnan Province had established its own mint in 1555 with an annual budget of 20,000 taels from the Ministry of Revenue, to pay military expenses in the frontier. Some of these coins changed hands from soldiers to civilians, who took them to the markets in Beijing.)[113] The third-rate coins were the brass "fire paint" from the Nanjing mint. The lowest-quality coins were brass "fire paint," with bumpy edges made by the Beijing mint. Xu Jie noted that for two years, to save time and expense, the Beijing mint had replaced the sanders—the tools that smoothed the edges of each coin. Instead, a worker would thread several coins through their central holes onto a long stick and run a rasp over the edges of all the coins on the stick. The Jiajing coins

---

109 Peng Xinwei, *Zhongguo huobi shi*, 438.

110 The total area of the original walled city and the nearby walled southern extension was about 62 sq. km., making Beijing the world's largest capital city. Chan, *Legends of the Building of Old Peking*, 111–13.

111 This new city wall, which included 6.7 km of the southern edge of the old city's outer wall, was 16 km in perimeter.

112 Although "golden back" and "fire paint" coins from Nanjing had smoothed edges as well, they were not called "smoothed edges."

113 See *Ming shilu*, Shizong, 7297–99; *Wanli kuanji lu*, 833:141.

that were "sanded" in this way were called "long stick." Xu Jie noted that these "fire paint" long-stick coins not only had coarse and bumpy edges but were also adulterated with lead, making them difficult to distinguish from counterfeits. People refused to accept these low-quality coins, even though they were made at the Baoyuan Mint.[114] (See Figure 6)

Xu Jie argued that the emperor did not actually need a mint to finance the palace. He estimated that the Siyao Treasury required around 10 million cash a year, which could easily be supplied by a combination of "golden back" coins and Yunnan bronze coins from the shop and transit taxes. He thought the Baoyuan Mint in Beijing should shut down and that all lower-grade brass coins (the long-stick "fire paint") no longer be accepted.[115] The emperor endorsed his proposal. In 1564, after operating ineffectually for fifty-one years, the Baoyuan Mint in Beijing closed. At the same time, three mint officials and eighteen laborers were arrested on corruption charges. They were accused of having stolen 3,600 taels worth of copper and tin over several years, as well as exaggerating the number of laborers hired to receive extra money for their food allowances, totaling to another 3,300 taels.[116]

Shutting down the Baoyuan Mint immediately saved the Ministry of Revenue the 15,000 taels of silver a year that had been used to buy raw copper on the metal markets linked to the Yunnan mines the previous year.[117] The Ministry of Works also benefited because it had been paying about 13,000 taels a year for the mint's fuel and labor costs.[118] The Jiajing emperor also received a share of the silver a year later. In 1565 he ordered the Yunnan mint to shut down as well and had Nanjing's Ministry of Revenue, which had been paying that mint 20,000 taels a year, transfer that silver back to the ministry.[119]

The use of copper coins to settle government debts was limited considerably in the final years of the Jiajing reign. In 1565 the emperor decreed that a portion of the shop and transit fees, formerly due in copper cash, be paid in silver at a fixed rate of 1 tael for 700 cash.[120] The policy not only increased the

---

114 Xu Jie, "Qing tingzhi Baoyuanju zhuqian," 1564, in Xu Jie, *Shijing tangji*, in *Siku quanshu cunmu congshu, jibu* (repr. Ji'nan: Qilu shushe, 1997), 79:402.

115 Xu Jie, "Qing tingzhi Baoyuanju zhuqian," 79:402.

116 *Ming shilu*, Shizong, 8740–41.

117 As noted previously, the Ministry of Revenue had to buy raw copper on the market to operate the Baoyuan Mint. But a year before the shutdown, it had started to pay silver directly to the Ministry of Works for this purpose. See *Wanli kuaiji lu*, 833:141.

118 Xu Jie noted in his memorial that the two ministries paid a total of 28,000 taels a year to support the Baoyuan Mint. (See Xu Jie, "Qing tingzhi Baoyuanju zhuqian," 79:402.) Because the Ministry of Revenue paid 15,000 taels, the Ministry of Works paid 13,000 taels a year.

119 *Ming shilu*, Shizong, 8819–20.

120 *Wanli kuaiji lu*, 833:141.

FIGURE 6 Long stick. In the Jiajing period, to save time and expense, the Beijing mint replaced the sanding tools that had smoothed the edges of each coin. Instead, a worker threaded several coins through their central holes onto a long stick and ran a rasp over the edges of all the coins on the stick. The Jiajing coins that were "sanded" in this way were called "long stick."

SOURCE: A 1637 PAINTING IN SONG YINGXING'S *TIANGONG KAIWU* [*EXPLOITATION OF THE WORK OF NATURE*]. SEE LI CHIAO-PING, *TIEN-KUNG-KAI-WU: EXPLOITATION OF THE WORK OF NATURE: CHINESE AGRICULTURE AND TECHNOLOGY IN THE XVII CENTURY* (TAIPEI: CHINA ACADEMY, 1980), 244.

emperor's silver income but put an end to the arguments over high-quality coins versus low-quality coins when collecting taxes and other state charges. That same year, the emperor replaced copper with silver, at the same conversion rate, in officials' salaries. From then on, Ming officials were paid in paper notes and silver, instead of copper coins.[121]

8 Conclusion

From the mid-fifteenth to the mid-sixteenth century, as the household registration system broke down, Ming emperors needed a viable currency to make up for their loss of resources in labor services and in-kind taxes. Beginning in 1436, the emperors appropriated the lion's share of the silver from the Gold Floral Silver reform (collected by the Ministry of Revenue to pay military officials) to buy food for the emperor's table. In the second half of the fifteenth century, even the frugal Hongzhi emperor found the extra silver inadequate for meeting expenses. He demanded silver transfers from the Ministry of Revenue, but that sparked criticism by court officials. In 1503, he attempted to use copper coinage as his new source of income. The re-emergence of the coinage system in the sixteenth century was the Hongzhi emperor's last-ditch attempt to find the money to operate the Department of Imperial Banquets.

The two imperial mints reopened in 1503 without having solved the problem of how to pay for the copper. As a result, neither mint was ever able to make their manufacturing quota. When the mints failed to generate the needed income, the Zhengde emperor ordered silver transfers from the Ministry of Revenue to maintain his prodigious lifestyle. He also dispatched his eunuchs to levy surtaxes in the provinces, which caused widespread discontent in the government. After the Jiajing emperor ascended the throne, he reactivated the Baoyuan Mint to make brass, instead of bronze coins, but ordered the two Ministries of Revenue to step in and pay for the brass; the Beijing Ministry of Works had exhausted its stock of silver on construction projects and could not afford fuel and labor costs for the mint.

The story of the coinage system in the Ming should have ended in 1564 when the Jiajing emperor gave up his hopes for the Beijing mint and took the advice of Grand Secretariat Xu Jie to close the mint and use more silver in palace finances. But as shown in Chapter 4, in the late sixteenth century, Ming officials, under the leadership of Grand Secretariat Zhang Juzheng, still dreamed of wealth from coinage, an ever-flowing fountain.

121 *Ming shilu*, Shizong, 8820.

CHAPTER 4

Coins for the Government, 1567–1644

Previous chapters traced the rise and fall of copper coinage as subsidiary income to support the emperor's palace expenses for food—for daily meals, temple and ancestral offerings, festival banquets, tributary missions, and so on—after the loss of in-kind taxes to supply that food. To help pay for food, in the early sixteenth century, the throne obtained newly minted coins from the Baoyuan Mint and older copper coins from taxes, but there were problems with both the new and the old coins.

The problem with making new coins was that the Ministry of Works simply did not have the silver to buy the raw copper, bronze, or brass to make new coins.[1] The problem with the old coins from taxes was that the Siyao Treasury was full of inferior coins that had been accepted at face value for taxes but were of less value in the market. The merchants who provisioned the palace were reluctant to accept these inferior coins; they wanted to be paid in silver.

During the first half of the sixteenth century, Ming emperors made fewer and fewer payments in copper cash. Finally, in the mid-sixteenth century, the Jiajing emperor realized that the coinage system, like household registration for in-kind taxes, could not sufficiently provide for the throne. He began to pay palace expenses with silver, instead. In 1564, two years before his death, he shut down the Baoyuan Mint in Beijing.

As this chapter shows, despite the coinage system's failure to provision the emperor's table, government officials still believed that coin manufacture could provide unlimited wealth if only it were managed better, and they intended to share in the profit. Shortly after the death of the Jiajing emperor in 1566 the government resumed casting copper coins, and from 1567 to 1644, during the reign of the last four Ming emperors, bureaucratic institutions tried to generate revenue from their own mints.

1 Coins for the Country and the People

As shown in the Introduction, ever since debate among senior officials recorded in 81 BCE in the *Discourses on Salt and Iron*, coinage profits were intended for

1 Most of the new coins that the Ministry of Works made went to the Siyao Treasury in the palace to help pay for daily food and offerings to the ancestors.

 | DOI:10.1163/9789004687530_006

the emperor. Making copper cash was seen as a source of wealth that belonged to the throne, out of the belief that the throne would be threatened by allowing it to fall into the hands of common people, merchants, and gentry. During the Ming, the idea of issuing copper cash to enrich the throne still prevailed, but, as discussed earlier, by the final years of the Jiajing emperor, the imperial mint was actually a losing proposition. The emperor preferred to use silver bullion for palace finance as well as for state charges and fees.

In 1567 the incoming Longqing emperor took pity on Beijing merchants who had to scrape together enough silver to pay their shop and transit fees. He allowed these charges to be paid in copper coins at the exchange rate of 800 per tael, with each coin, regardless of weight and quality, of equal value.[2] In the same year, in a joint reply to the new emperor about the possibility of reopening the Baoyuan Mint, the Ministries of Revenue and Works, which shared the cost of coin production, firmly opposed the idea as a losing investment. For 1 tael of silver, the state could only cast 450 copper coins.[3]

The (limited) support for reopening the mint came mostly from provincial officials. In 1569, Jin Xueyan, the governor of Shanxi Province, criticized the Ming court for preferring silver to copper coins, which had enabled local ruffians to take over the casting of copper coins and seize the profit. He suggested that the state continue to manufacture coins and obtain the money to make them from new sources, such as crime restitution fees.[4]

A more influential memorial came from Tan Lun, the governor-general of Jiliao (Jizhou and Liaodong). Writing in his *Lun licai shu* [*Discourse on Managing Wealth*] in 1569, he placed the good of the country at the heart of his argument for casting coins. Tan Lun suggested that statesmen engage in a practice called *jianyin*. *Jianyin* did *not* mean reducing the value of silver, as has been suggested.[5] When he wrote that true statecraft would place "less importance" (*jian*) on silver (*yin*), Tan Lun was concerned not with the market price of silver but, rather, with its relative importance:

2 Ge Shouli, the minister of revenue, added that this imperial favor applied only when the shop tax was less than 1 tael or the transit tax less than 3 taels of silver. *Wanli kuaiji lu*, 833:142; see also *DaMing huidian*, 789:558.

3 *Wanli kuaiji lu*, 833:142.

4 *Qinding xu wenxian tongkao*, in *Qinding siku quanshu*, 626:252.

5 Richard von Glahn stated: "Tan lobbied in favor of increasing the output of coin, which he believed would relieve pressure on the money supply and thus cause silver to depreciate in value," in his *Fountain of Fortune Money and Monetary Policy in China, 1000–1700* (Berkeley: University of California Press, 1996), 143.

> If one wishes to succor the country, he should first enrich the people. If one wishes to enrich the people, he should first place more importance on cloth and vegetables than silver. If one wishes to place less importance on silver, he should carry out the coinage system. [He should] increase the production [of coins] so as to make up for the shortage of silver.[6]

Tan Lun was not the only official to support the return and expansion of the coinage system, but his argument was revolutionary. In contrast to the *Discourses on Salt and Iron,* which emphasized the authority of the throne, Tan focused on the good of the people and the country. He proposed using the coinage system to make the country strong. In other words, the beneficiary of the coinage system should be the government (the country), which served the people, not the throne.

By making the benefit of the country central to the coinage system, these local officials were angling for a share of the revenue from casting coins, which, for the prior century, had gone to the throne through the imperial mints in Beijing and Nanjing. If the throne allowed copper minting in the provinces, local governments would gain a new source of income. Although the manufacture of copper coins had failed in Beijing, provincial governments hoped to balance their costs and benefits. Unlike the Baoyuan Mint, which had to hand over its coins to the throne's Siyao Treasury, a provincial governor could use all the coins produced by his mint. In light of this, Tan Lun went on to propose that every province have its own mint and use the copper coins to pay their local officials and soldiers. He even proposed that the imperial court pay provincial mints the cost of making the coins, which he estimated at a total of about 1.2 million taels.[7]

Although the imperial court in Beijing, headed by Grand Secretariat Gao Gong, would have preferred to ignore these provincial proposals, it became increasingly difficult to remain silent. The proposals caused violent fluctuations in the coin market, which was sensitive to changing state policies. Common people and merchants wondered whether the new emperor would issue new coins and whether that would reduce the value of old coins in state charges and fees. Tan Lun's suggestion fed their fears. In the same memorial, Tan Lun had suggested that the state replace all existing coins with the "Great Ming coins." This new design was aimed at allaying market fears that coins would be devalued after an emperor died, but the proposal itself caused even

6 Tan Lun, "Lun licai shu," 1569, in *Ming jingshi wenbian,* ed. Chen Zilong (Beijing: Zhonghua shuju, 1962), 13:3438.

7 Tan Lun, "Lun licai shu," 3438.

more anxiety.[8] People worried that all the coins issued before the Ming would become worthless overnight. Tan submitted his memorial in the seventh month of 1569. The court ignored it, but after Yang Jiaxiang, another provincial official, sent a similar proposal eight months later, the imperial court moved quickly to calm the market.

In the fourth month of 1570, Grand Secretariat Gao Gong announced that no official should discuss the subject of coin manufacture, and a year and a half later, to prove that the state had no intention of halting the circulation of *any* copper coins, he instructed the Ministry of Revenue to make 2 million (new) Longqing coins for the Siyao Treasury.[9] Two million was not a large amount; it was simply Gao Gong's way of showing that the imperial court would continue to make coins. Additionally, all the coins cast by previous dynasties would be allowed to circulate and be used to pay government taxes and fees.[10]

Gao Gong did not agree with the proposal by Tan Lun and other provincial officials but revised monetary policies to ease public anxiety over copper coins. In 1571 the imperial court announced that Beijing would increase the amount of copper cash that could be used to pay transit taxes. First, when the tax was below 2 taels, merchants could pay their tax entirely in copper coins. When the tax reached 2 taels, merchants could pay half in silver and half in copper coins. Second, in the same year, in all state purchases, merchants who previously had been paid in silver received 20 percent of their payments in copper cash.[11] Third, in 1572 civil officials in Beijing received 10 percent of their salaries in copper cash. Of that amount, 60 percent was "golden back," 20 percent "fire paint" (probably Nanjing), and 20 percent "smoothed edges."[12] Their official conversion rates for 1 tael of silver were 800 cash for the "golden back" and 1,000 cashfor the "fire paint" and "smoothed edges."[13] Although "golden

8 Tan Lun, "Lun licai shu," 3438.

9 The Ministry of Revenue transferred 2 million Longqing coins to the court in the eleventh month of 1571. See *Ming shilu,* Muzong, 1519. The source did not record where these coins were made. As the Beijing mint had been closed, I assume the coins were made by the Nanjing mint.

10 *Qinding xu wenxian tongkao*, 626:252.

11 *DaMing huidian*, 789:558.

12 As noted in Chapter 3, "golden back" and (Nanjing) "fire paint" were both brass coins (with smoothed edges), whereas the coins called "smoothed edges" were bronze coins from Yunnan or previous dynasties.

13 See *DaMing huidian*, 789:684. This policy was followed by the Wanli emperor. See the 1578 memorial presented by Zhang Xueyan, the minister of revenue, in *Qinding xu wenxian tongkao*, 626:255.

back" coins were brass and "smoothed edges" were bronze (a more expensive alloy), "golden backs" had a higher value because they cost more to make.[14]

1.1 *Coins for the Ministries*

In the fifth month of 1572, the Longqing emperor died after a stroke, at the age of thirty-five. His ten-year-old son, Zhu Yijun, succeeded him, adopting Wanli as his reign title. Zhang Juzheng, who had been the boy emperor's tutor, became the new grand secretariat and the most powerful person in the imperial court. Tan Lun, who had been Zhang's protégé, was promoted to the position of minister of war in Beijing.

Zhang Juzheng based his new monetary policy on Tan Lun's earlier proposal.[15] On Zhang's advice, in 1576 the Wanli emperor ordered coins issued with his reign title at an annual quota of 100 million cash (compared with 2 million for the Longqing emperor). Of this amount, 70 million were to be "golden back" and 30 million "fire paint" coins. Both grades were to weigh 1.115 *qian*, to reassure the public of their worth. The Beijing and Nanjing mints would split the manufacturing quota at a ratio of 6:4. As usual, their respective Ministries of Revenue would provide the silver to buy brass to make the coins. Beijing's Ministry of Works replied that, for every 10,000 coins cast, it needed 14.89 taels of silver to buy brass. The emperor, probably after consulting the Ministry of Revenue, considered this price too high. The Ministry of Works accepted a 10 percent cut, but the project still cost 134,000 taels of silver a year.

With the issuance of the Wanli coins, Zhang Juzheng set a new precedent in the monetary system, in that only 10 percent of the 100 million cash was slated for the Siyao Treasury; the remaining 90 million went to the two Ministries of Revenue according to their respective manufacturing ratios.[16] This arrangement benefited the government (the ministries) rather than the throne. In 1579, when the emperor asked for an increase in his share, Zhang refused and restated that the coinage system was meant for the people, not the throne, and

---

14 "Golden back" coins were made with a method known as cementation, in which a mint worker added zinc ore to copper in a closed vessel. At around 1,000° C, the ore releases gaseous zinc, which is absorbed by copper to form brass. Because zinc evaporates (by about 25%) in burning, a mint worker had to continually add zinc to make the "golden back" coins. This increased the need for zinc, fuel, and labor, so the "golden back" coins became a valued commodity, even though zinc was of low value.

15 Hamaguchi Fukuju stated that the monetary policy adopted by Zhang Juzheng was basically modeled after what Tan Lun proposed. See his "Ryûkei-Banreki no sempô no shin tenkai," *Tôyôshi kenkyû* 31, no. 3 (1972).

16 *Qinding xu wenxian tongkao*, 626:253.

that his 10 percent quota was given to him only as samples, so that he could see for himself what kind of coins the mints were casting.[17] Zhang refused to increase the number of coins manufactured, probably because he knew that he would be unable to curb the emperor's spending. Zhang was not concerned about the overall economy, only with who would profit from the new coins. By giving them to the Ministry of Revenue, they could be used to pay for national defense in the frontiers.

1.2 *Provincial Mints*

To "benefit the people," Zhang Juzheng also allowed provinces to build their own mints as Tan Lun had proposed. The first one was built in response to a memorial from Guo Tingwu, the regional inspector of Yunnan, in the third month of 1576. (The Yunnan mint established in 1555 to pay soldiers had shut down in 1565.)[18] Guo stated that, although this southern frontier province was rich in copper mines, its people were still using cowries from foreign countries as money,[19] which meant that foreign governments made a profit from their use as currency in Yunnan.[20] Although Yunnan became part of the Ming empire in 1384, its location in the northern part of Southeast Asia meant that the province was still more Southeast Asian than Chinese.[21]

To make (and profit from) its own revenue, Guo suggested that Yunnan Province set up its own mint again. Beijing endorsed the proposal and a Ministry of Revenue official suggested that the Yunnan government save on labor costs by recruiting local troops to leave their garrisons and work at the provincial mint.[22] In the same month, an official named Zhou Liangyin proposed extending the

17 *Ming shilu*, Shenzong, 1802–3.

18 In 1558 the Yunnan governor petitioned the Jiajing emperor for permission to close the Yunnan mint. Even though raw copper was inexpensive and accessible, it was dangerous to transport the charcoal that the mint needed from Yunnan's central plateau, which was inhabited by hostile tribes. The emperor initially rejected the request but finally approved it in 1565. See *Wanli kuaiji lu*, 833:141; *Ming shilu*, Shizong, 8819.

19 Cowrie shells came from Maldives, an archipelago in the Indian Ocean. Cowries went to China by way of tribute ships from the Liuqiu kingdom (Okinawa) and other Southeast Asian countries and then with Chinese merchants to Yunnan, where they were exchanged for horses, gold, and other Yunnan products. Yang, *Cowrie Shells and Cowrie Money*, 94, 102, 105–7, 112.

20 *Ming shilu*, Shenzong, 1094.

21 Several Ming sources mentioned the use of cowrie money in Yunnan. For example, in 1532 a court official named Yang Shen was exiled to Yunnan, where he used 200 strings of cowries to buy a rare book printed in the Song dynasty. Yang, *Cowrie Shells and Cowrie Money*, 112.

22 *Ming shilu*, Shenzong, 1094; *Wanli kuaiji lu*, 143.

new policy to the other twelve provinces, as follows. First, the Provincial Commissioner in each province would take charge of each mint. Second, each provincial mint would produce the bronze coins known as "smoothed edges" (which had less value in the market than the brass "golden back" coins but were valued more highly than the brass "fire paint" coins, despite the official rate giving them equal value).[23] Third, provincial commissioners could use the newly minted coins to pay their officials.

The court then allowed provincial mints to produce coins unlike those made in imperial mints. In his endorsement of Zhou Liangyin's proposal, the Wanli emperor ordered all provinces to cast bronze coins at a unified standard weight of 1.3 *qian*.[24] This meant that, during the Wanli reign, there were three standards of state coins. The Beijing and Nanjing mints now both made "golden back" and "fire paint" brass coins, each weighing 1.115 *qian*, whereas the provincial mints made bronze coins that each weighed 1.3 *qian*. As noted, "smoothed edges" were worth less than "golden back," because they were easier to make. By increasing the weight of provincial coins, the imperial court hoped to increase their market value.

The new provincial mints were extremely successful in the following years. In the second month of 1577, Pan Jixun, the governor of Jiangxi Province, requested permission to transform his provincial arsenal into a copper mint. He estimated that, for only 1 tael of silver, a mint could produce 1,100 copper cash. In other words, for every 1,000 cash he spent at the official rate of 1,000 cash to 1 tael, he could make a profit of 100 cash (or 0.1 tael). He planned to have his subordinate prefects supply the bronze. The Ministry of Revenue supported the proposal, while reminding Pan Jixun to continue to accept the old coins as payment of taxes.[25]

In 1577 Pang Shangpeng, the governor of Fujian, also wished to turn a military barracks into a mint and put off-duty soldiers to work there. Pang estimated that he needed only 0.98 tael of silver to produce 1,000 cash, which meant that the mint would make a profit of 0.02 tael. Like Pan Jixun, he planned to make his subordinate prefects supply the bronze. Moreover, Pang Shangpeng had a plan to maintain the coins' credibility. He proposed the sale of the new coins for silver to retail shops in Fujian and allowing shop owners to exchange the

23 Zhou Liangyin did not specify why he proposed that provinces make bronze, rather than brass coins, but it may have been to avoid competition for raw materials between the imperial mint, which made the brass "golden back" and "fire paint" coins, and provincial mints.

24 *Qinding* xu *wenxian tongkao*, 626:254.

25 *Ming shilu*, Shenzong, 1357–58.

coins for silver at the same official rate from time to time, to reassure them that their new coins would not decline in value. The Ministry of Revenue also endorsed this proposal.[26]

By opening local mints, Zhang Juzheng and provincial governors both aimed to improve provincial finances. In a letter to support Pang Shangpeng's copper mint in Fujian, Zhang stated that if they were able to "transform raw copper to fortune, then people could have more money for their expenditures, and they could also find it easier to pay taxes. This is the reason why when the people are enriched, the state can be enriched as well."[27]

To increase their profit, some provincial governors made plans to build more mints. In the eleventh month of 1577, for example, Gao Wenjian, the governor of Shanxi, who had set up a provincial mint in Taiyuan Prefecture, wanted to build branch mints in Pingyang and Lu'an Prefectures. He estimated that the mint could show a 10 percent profit and that the more coins he made, the more profit there would be. The imperial court endorsed his proposal.[28]

Chen Rui, the governor of Huguang, had established a provincial mint in Wuchang Prefecture, and in the seventh month of 1578, he applied to build branch mints in Jingzhou and Hengzhou Prefectures. He planned to divide Hunan Province into copper-coin zones based on these three mints. Though headed by the governor, each mint would be supported financially by the prefectural government in its zone, with its coins disbursed within the same zone. For quality control, Chen Rui would dispatch twenty skilled laborers from the Wuchang mint to each branch. The imperial court also endorsed this proposal.[29]

It was not until the last month of 1578 that Zhang Xueyan, the minister of revenue, realized that the provincial mints were making their profit at the expense of the Siyao Treasury in the palace. Although the Baoyuan Mint in Beijing produced the "golden back" and "fire paint" coins, which had different conversion rates to silver when paid as officials' salaries, these rates did not apply to the shop and transit taxes, which retained their former rate of 1:800, from the Longqing period, regardless of which coins were used. Early in the Wanli reign, people kept the "golden back" coins in their pockets and paid their taxes in "fire paint" coins. While provincial coins circulated at a fixed official rate of 1:1,000 in the provinces, people brought these coins to Beijing, saving

26 *Ming shilu*, Shenzong, 1446–47.

27 Zhang Juzheng, "Da Minfu Pang Xing'an," in *Zhang Juzheng ji*, ed. Zhang Shunhui (Wuhan: Hubei renmin chubanshe, 1997), 2:701.

28 *Qinding xu wenxian tongkao*, 626:255.

29 *Ming shilu*, Shenzong, 1649–50.

20 percent on their tax payments. As a result, the Siyao Treasury was flooded with provincial coins.

To close this loophole, Zhang Xueyan changed the conversion rate for provincial coins in the shop and transit charges in Beijing, making one tael of silver in the shop and transit charges worth 800 cash in "golden back" coins, 1,000 cash in "fire paint" or provincial (bronze) coins, or 1,200 cash in (bronze) coins cast before the Jiajing reign.[30] As a result, provincial coins had the same value in Beijing as in the provinces, and merchants could no longer profit by using them to pay their shop and transit fees.

The new policy halted the flow of provincial bronze coins to the inner treasury. Provincial mints continued to cast the coins, but now that merchants no longer brought them to Beijing, all these new coins remained in the provinces, leading to a sudden crash in their market value. Yunnan, the first province to open a mint, became the first to request its closure. In 1580, the governor of Yunnan sent a memorial to the imperial court in which he stated that he had not yet fulfilled the quota (490,000 cash annually), and as people in Yunnan still used only cowrie shells as money, he had no way to spend the coins already made. Zhang Xueyan agreed that Yunnan could stop making coins, and the Wanli emperor endorsed this course of action.

Closing the Yunnan mint initiated a discussion of the existing policy, especially whether the state should give all copper coins the same value. In 1580, a Nanjing scholar named Tang Yi, in a petition to the imperial court, criticized the practice of discriminating against the bronze coins made in the provinces and all the bronze coins produced before the Jiajing period. "The more coins one holds, the more loss he suffers." Tang Yi proposed the invention of a standardized coin for the entire empire. He also suggested that, the price remained stable after being set, in terms of a coin's conversion rate to silver.[31] The imperial court did not reply to Tang Yi. Shortly thereafter, a junior official in Beijing named Wan Xiangchun reiterated Tang's proposal and went further, suggesting that the state stop making and accepting diverse types of coins. Instead, it should cast a new standardized coin. If Tang and Wan's suggestions were accepted, there would be no difference between Beijing coins and provincial coins, and the provincial coins could be used in Beijing again.

30 *Qinding xu wenxian tongkao*, 626:257.

31 *WangMing liutai zouyi*, in *Siku quanmu congshu*, 74:749. Tang Yi was a native of Wuxi County in Changzhou Prefecture. He obtained a *jinshi* degree in 1568.

Far from accepting these suggestions, the Wanli emperor replied that not a single province had taken coin manufacture seriously, that Wan Xiangchun's proposal would achieve nothing but stir up trouble for people in Beijing, and that, because the practice of differentiating between three types of coins had been successful in Beijing for years, there was no need to make all coins look the same and have the same value. He vented his spleen by admonishing the Ministry of Works to investigate the effectiveness of any proposal more carefully before presenting it to him.[32] The emperor considered this a provincial problem and did not want the capital to be affected by it.

Having lost the Beijing market, merchants refused to buy the provincial coins. Provincial governments now found it hard to use the coins that they had made. In 1582, Wu Shanyan, the governor of Zhejiang, tried to pay soldiers at a garrison in Hangzhou in coins. Their monthly salary had been 0.9 tael of silver, but in the third month of the year, Wu Shanyan reduced their salaries by a third and then paid the remaining two-thirds half in silver and half in copper cash, at a rate of 800 per tael. Thus, a soldier would receive only 0.3 tael of silver plus 240 copper cash instead of 0.9 tael of silver. This was a severe cut, as a soldier needed 2,000 cash to obtain 1 tael of silver in Hangzhou markets. In other words, 240 copper cash equaled only 0.12 tael, which meant a soldier's salary was actually reduced by a little more than half, from 0.9 tael to the equivalent of 0.42 tael. The soldiers protested this large salary cut. But Wu Shanyan was obdurate; he not only refused to change his policy but also told the soldiers that if they were dissatisfied with their new salary and the form in which it was dispensed, they could quit their posts, return to their villages, and go back to farming. The soldiers angrily stormed his office. In the ensuing chaos, a group of soldiers dragged Wu Shanyan outside, tied him up, and beat him severely. When the protest became a mutiny, the entire city of Hangzhou shut down in fear. All the shops closed, and the streets were empty and silent. Finally, Zhejiang's provincial commissioner persuaded the soldiers to disperse by giving them silver from the provincial treasury.[33] Wu Shanyan was ordered to resign for incompetence.

The Hangzhou mutiny was a result of a major salary cut combined with low-value coins. Meanwhile, Grand Secretariat Zhang Juzheng, who had proposed their manufacture, was dying. He died three months after the mutiny; three months later, the Wanli emperor decreed that provincial governments could close their mints if they wanted to.[34] Most of them did.

---

32 *Wanli kuaiji lu*, 833:148.

33 For a detailed report of the Hangzhou mutiny, see Yao Shilin, *Jianzhi bian*, 5–7.

34 *Ming shilu*, Shenzong, 2378.

1.3 *"Golden Backs" for the Taicang Treasury*

Although provincial mints closed in 1582, the Beijing Ministry of Revenue still tried to raise money for its Taicang Treasury by making coins. The Taicang Treasury had begun to store coins from the Baoyuan Mint after Zhang Juzheng's reform, to add to its silver from the land tax. The Ministry of Revenue enacted two measures to strengthen the Taicang Treasury. First, it tried to hold on to its silver by paying officials in less silver and more copper cash. In 1585, with the emperor's permission, the ministry raised the percentage of copper cash in official salaries in Beijing from 10 percent to 20 percent.[35] Second, the ministry increased the manufacturing quota of copper coins from 100 million to 750 million cash a year, with the Beijing mint casting 450 million cash and the Nanjing mint 300 million cash. All the coins were "golden back," and each mint handed over only one-sixth of them to its respective Siyao Treasury; the remaining five-sixths from both mints went to the Taicang Treasury in Beijing.[36] In other words, the Taicang Treasury could collect a total of 625 million "golden back" coins every year.

The new policy was successful. After the 1578 reform, the Beijing market had preferred "golden back" coins, because they were worth more for tax payment. In 1585 the minister of revenue reported that, whereas the official price for a "golden back" coin was 800 per tael, the market price was 500.[37] Thus the new monetary policies, which increased the manufacturing quota and the percentage of "golden back" coins in salaries, were welcomed by merchants and capital officials. The Wanli emperor was probably pleased, too. When the manufacturing quota increased, his Siyao Treasury took in more "golden back" coins, making it easier to run the palace. Everyone was happy except the Nanjing Ministries of Revenue and Works. These ministries bore all the costs without receiving a single coin in return. Every year, the Baoyuan Mint in Nanjing was required to cast 450 million cash, of which five-sixths (375 million) was slated for the Taicang Treasury in Beijing and controlled by the Ministry of Revenue there, leaving one-sixth (75 million) for the Siyao Treasury in Nanjing, which was also the emperor's personal treasury, and financed the imperial palace in Nanjing.

Not surprisingly, the Nanjing mint began to produce low-quality coins. In 1589 Beijing's Ministry of Works complained that the "golden back" coins from the Nanjing mint were substandard and unacceptable. It suggested that the

35 *Ming shilu*, Shenzong, 2994–95. For example, an official with the rank 1A who used to receive 193.96 taels and 17,241 cash a year now received only 172.41 taels and 34,482 cash.

36 *Ming shilu*, Shenzong, 2998, 4024, 4721; *Qinding xu wenxian tongkao*, 626:253.

37 *Ming shilu*, Shenzong, 2994–95.

Beijing mint take over production for the 375 million cash if the Nanjing Ministries of Revenue and Works provided the corresponding manufacturing cost (in silver) for it. The Wanli emperor accepted and ordered the Beijing mint to cast the entire the Nanjing quota of 450 million cash from then on, for which the Nanjing Ministries of Revenue and Works had to pay Beijing.[38] This ushered in the golden age of the Baoyuan Mint in Beijing. It cast 750 million coins a year.

Coin making became a new source of revenue for the Taicang Treasury. The Ministries of Revenue in Beijing and Nanjing paid the Baoyuan Mint to buy metal at the rate of 14.89 taels of silver for every 10,000 coins cast (so the quota of 450 million coins cost about 670,000 taels). Although the silver payment was large, the Ministry of Revenue earned profit of 625 million cash in return (five-sixths of 750 million). Because they had paid the official salaries at the rate of 800 cash per tael, for a total of about 780,000 taels of silver, they made a profit of 110,000 taels.

To realize this profit, the Ministry of Revenue had to keep an eye on the emperor. In 1592, for instance, the emperor demanded an additional 25 million cash every year. Fortunately, a court official from the Ministry of Works ended the need to satisfy this demand.[39] At this point, the Ministry of Revenue and the Ministry of Works cooperated with each other, to their mutual benefit.

Then, in 1598, the Ministry of Revenue succumbed to greed. To make more money from minting coins without increasing the manufacturing quota, it turned to the exchange rate between copper coins and silver. Every year, it had to pay merchants large amounts of silver for various goods, including brass for the coins. Under the current regulation, the ministry could make 20 percent of these silver payments in copper coins, at the exchange rate of 800 per tael of silver. But in 1598 the Ministry of Revenue proposed an aggressive revision of the policy: when paying merchants, the ministry could pay 30 percent in copper cash, rather than 20 percent, and at the rate of only 500, instead of 800, per tael of silver. The Wanli emperor approved this proposal in the fourth month of 1599.[40]

As well as shortchanging merchants, the new policy reduced the amount of silver that the Ministry of Revenue paid to the Ministry of Works to buy metal for the mint and thereby ruined the relationship between the two ministries. The Ministry of Revenue had been paying the Ministry of Works 670,000 taels, in the form of 536,000 taels of silver plus 107.2 million copper cash, to

38 *Ming shilu*, Shenzong, 4024.

39 *Ming shilu*, Shenzong, 4721.

40 *Qinding xu wenxian tongkao*, 762:143.

buy metal. Under the new policy, these amounts dropped to 469,000 taels plus 100.5 million cash.

The Baoyuan Mint immediately halted operations. In the ninth month of 1599, the Ministry of Revenue reported to the throne that it had not received new coins for a long time and requested that the emperor urge the Ministry of Works to hand over the coin quota.[41] The Ministry of Works refused. In the first month of 1601, in a letter to the Ministry of Revenue, the Ministry of Works stated that the merchants who sold them metal found it impossible to conduct business at these prices and suggested that, instead of giving them the money to buy copper, the Ministry of Revenue give them the copper to make coins.[42]

Starting in 1601, the Ministry of Revenue had to buy the brass itself. It set a yearly quota of 600,000 catties a year. This was a modest goal because, for every 10,000 "golden back" coins, the mint needed 85.86 catties of brass.[43] In other words, 600,000 catties of copper would produce only about 70 million copper cash, even if all the coins were made of brass—far below the previous quota of 450 million. The Ministry of Revenue still found the task more difficult than expected. Merchants were reluctant to sell brass at the new conversion rate. Finally, after a three-month search, the ministry found three local merchants who accepted their sales contract. Under this contract, the merchants had to buy 600,000 catties of brass for the ministry, for which they would receive 60,000 taels of silver, of which 70 percent would be paid in silver and 30 percent in copper coins. For startup money, the merchants received the equivalent of 24,000 taels at the same proportions.

The merchants' progress was slow. They reported that they found little brass in the Beijing market and demanded that the ministry cover their cost of travel to Wuhu County in the Yangzi River valley in order to buy brass there. The ministry refused this request, but agreed to pay them the remainder of their 36,000 taels (60,000 taels–24,000 taels). Nevertheless, throughout 1601, the merchants were able to buy only 500,000 catties, which left them owing 100,000 catties. In 1602, the Ministry of Revenue stopped trying to work through the merchants and, instead, paid local officials in Wuhu County to buy brass. Although no purchase reports from Wuhu officials are available, it is unlikely that the ministry succeeded in this venture. Although the Ministry of Revenue agreed to pay the merchants a percentage in "golden back" coins at the conversion rate

41 *Ming shilu*, Shenzong, 6298–99.

42 See Zhao Shiqing, "Guokui minqiong xiuju qianfa yi kai caiyuan yi kuang minli shu," in Wu Liang, *Wanli shuchao*, in *Xuxiu siku quanshu*, 469:167.

43 Sun Chengze, *Guxiang zhai jianshang xjiuzhen Chunming mengyu lu*, 1881, chap. 47, 6a-15a (Waseda University Library).

of 500 per tael of silver, in 1602 the market rate of those coins had dropped to 600 per tael.[44]

To summarize, coin making in Beijing increased from 1585 to 1597, but in 1598, when the Ministry of Revenue changed the exchange rate, metal merchants canceled their contracts with the government. Production at the Baoyuan Mint was paralyzed by its inability to obtain brass in the market.

1.4 *Renting Furnaces at the Nanjing Mint*

Whereas production at the Beijing mint ground to a halt, the Baoyuan Mint in Nanjing was thriving. By producing substandard "golden back" coins, the Nanjing mint had been able to stop making coins for the Taicang Treasury by 1591.[45] Freed of this obligation, rather than closing down, the mint built more furnaces. From 1592 to 1600, the number of furnaces increased from 60 to 150, and, in 1601, 100 more furnaces were opened, for a total of 250.[46] At full working capacity, each furnace could produce 10,000 coins a day.[47] In other words, these 250 furnaces could produce 2.5 million cash a day.

The Nanjing mint had no trouble obtaining raw copper for coins. The merchants who had declined the contract offered by the Beijing Ministry of Revenue seem to have shifted their business to Nanjing. Jointly self-financed by the Nanjing Ministries of Revenue and Works, the Nanjing mint did not need to follow the rule of purchase (making 30 percent of a silver payment in copper cash at the ratio of 1:500) set up by the Beijing Ministry of Revenue. Without this limitation, it was relatively easy to buy metal in the market and expand production. The question was how those tons of newly minted copper coins had entered the market. For decades, the Nanjing mint needed only sixty furnaces to produce enough coins to pay its court officials. If sixty furnaces sufficed, why did the mint more than quadruple the number of furnaces?

The answer was that the Nanjing Ministry of Works had found a new income stream. As Grand Secretariat Ye Xianggao revealed later, the mint contracted out at least 100 furnaces to merchants who wanted to cast private coins legally.

44 Zhao Shiqing, "Guokui minqiong xiuju qianfa," 469:167.

45 The policy was implemented in 1591. See a memorial by Liu Yuanlin, an official at the Ministry of Works, in 1611 compiled in Dong Qichang, ed., *Shenmiao liuzhong zouzhu huiyao*, ca. 1622, in *Xuxiu siku quanshu*, 471:235.

46 A description by a Nanjing official called Wang Wanzuo in his memorial submitted in around 1611. See Hu Wokun, *Qiantong*, 1778, repr. *Qinding siku quanshu*, 662:394.

47 This information was from the 1611 memorial by Liu Yuanlin. See Dong Qichang, *Shenmiao liuzhong zouzhu huiyao*, 471: 234–35.

For this, it paid a fee called "work charges" of 50 taels a year.[48] By renting out 100 furnaces, the ministry earned 5,000 taels a year and spent nothing on management. In addition to the 250 furnaces owned by the Nanjing Ministry of Works, in 1602 the Nanjing Ministry of Revenue built 250 more furnaces to pay the troops stationed in Nanjing. In that same year, the Ministry of Works built a further 100 furnaces,[49] totaling an unprecedented 600 furnaces in Nanjing, of which 350 belonged to the Ministry of Works.

The 600 furnaces could produce 6 million cash a day—a considerable increase in copper cash in Nanjing. The resulting inflation was due not only to the increased supply but also to the low quality of the new coins. To maximize their profit, some furnace merchants cast their coins from lower-grade brass.[50] By 1605 inflation had risen to the point that Nanjing officials became concerned. That year, Censor Li Yunhu sent a memorial to the Wanli emperor, asking to reduce the number of furnaces in Nanjing. He stated that the exchange rate for a tael of silver was now more than 1,300 copper cash, which hurt both merchants and civilians. Moreover, many neighboring districts had refused to accept Nanjing coins. But the emperor did not reply.[51]

Then, in 1607, the Ministry of Works in Nanjing, which was operating 350 furnaces, asked to reduce this number, and this time the Wanli emperor approved the request. The ministry could reduce the number to 120 and run them in shifts, so that only 60 were operating at once.[52] (The decree did not mention the furnaces owned by the Ministry of Revenue. It is likely that they had already shut down.) By 1610, the market value of copper cash was still low, but Nanjing officials could do nothing to address the problem except try to eliminate counterfeiting. Liu Yuanlin, the vice minister of works in Nanjing, proposed rewarding people who reported counterfeits, punishing the relatives of criminals and assessing officials at least partly on their success in combating counterfeiting. The emperor endorsed his proposal.[53]

---

48 Ye Xianggao served as the Grand Secretariat from 1607 to 1614 and from 1621 to 1624. This information was in a personal note that he wrote in 1612 and recorded in his book of collected essays called *Qu bian*. See Ye Xianggao, *Qu bian*, in *Zhongguo yeshi jicheng xubian* (repr. Chengdu: Bashu shushe, 2000), 20:616.

49 A description by a Nanjing official named Wang Wanzuo. See Hu Wokun, *Qiantong*, 662:394.

50 See Ye Xianggao, *Qu bian*, 20:616.

51 Li Yunhu, "Yi ge xuanqian jian qianlu shu," in *HuangMing liutai zouyi*, repr. *Siku quanshu cunmu congshu, shibu*, 74:610.

52 This information was from Wang Wanzuo in a memorial submitted around 1611. See Hu Wokun, *Qiantong*, 662:397.

53 *Ming shilu*, Shenzong, 8999.

Even high inflation did not entirely extinguish hope that the government could make money by minting copper coins. In late 1610 the Wanli emperor ordered the Yingtian prefect to repair Pucheng, strategically located on the northern bank of the Yangzi River to provide defense of Nanjing on the southern bank. The emperor decreed that repair costs be shared equally among the Nanjing Ministries of Revenue, War, and Works. The cost was estimated at a total of 56,000 taels. But, a few months later, the estimate was revised to about 100,000 taels,[54] more than the ministries thought that they could afford.

In a memorial to the emperor, a Nanjing censor named Wang Wanzuo proposed that Yingtian Prefecture cast coins to cover the cost of repairing Pucheng. Wang stressed that the emperor had already given permission for this when he first decreed the casting of Wanli coins in 1576, which allowed Shuntian and Yingtian Prefectures, where the capitals were located, to cast coins in order to cover expenses.[55] The Wanli emperor referred Wang's proposal to the Ministry of Works in Beijing. In reply, Liu Yuanlin, the vice minister of works, stated that he supported the idea because copper coins were like water; the supply of them was unlimited. He only cautioned Yingtian Prefecture to calculate carefully how many furnaces it actually needed to build, so as to avoid the excess a few years earlier.[56] The emperor did not respond to the proposal, but at least he did not oppose it.

In the eighth month of 1611, Lu Changgeng, the prefect of Yingtian, met with Ding Bin, the supervisor of river defense, and the two agreed to start manufacturing copper coins to pay for the repairs in Pucheng. The Yingtian prefect governed a vast district, and tax collecting was part of his job. He could decide which coins to accept, giving him the perfect opportunity to sell the coins that he produced. Money changers in each city, who facilitated market exchanges as well tax payments, would buy the new coins in large amounts. On the twenty-eighth day of the month, the Yingtian prefect issued an official proclamation, reiterating the prohibition against private counterfeit coins and inviting the Nanjing money changers to exchange all their coins for the new copper coins. This implied, at least to the local population, that the Yingtian prefectural government was going to accept only its own coins for tax payments. As a result, the value of all other coins went into freefall. On the second day of the ninth month, what began as a fierce haggle over coin prices

54 This information was from a memorial presented by Fu Zonggao, a censor in Nanjing, in 1611. See Dong Qichang, *Shenmiao liuzhong zouzhu huiyao*, 471: 239–40.

55 Wang's memorial was compiled by Hu Wokun in his *Qiantong*, 662: 394–99.

56 In a memorial by Liu Yuanlin; see Dong Qichang, *Shenmiao liuzhong zouzhu huiyao*, 471: 233–39.

between a money changer and his customers escalated into a riot. An angry crowd marched to the offices of Lu Changgeng and Ding Bin. Saying he had to visit a friend, Lu fled and hid in the house of another official, but Ding Bin, according to his own account, went out on the street to quell the riot. In any case, after Lu issued a proclamation that he would accept all kinds of coins for tax payment, the rioters dispersed.[57]

In the wake of the Nanjing riot, the imperial court in Beijing determined that neither Lu nor Ding could be held responsible for the riot, but Yingtian Prefecture no longer had the right to cast coins. In his letter to the censors-in-chief, Grand Secretariat Ye Xianggao stated that the Ministries of Works should have the monopoly on casting coins, that giving this right to others would only cause problems, and that the administrative systems of "the southern capital and northern capital should be the same. As the manufacture of coins is a right reserved for the Baoyuan Mint, it should be no different in the southern capital."[58] Once again, the Baoyuan Mint became the single institution to cast coins in Nanjing, but it lacked the resources to do so.

After the riot, the imperial court in Beijing decided that the Baoyuan Mint in Nanjing should receive the profit from coin making to pay for the repairs in Pucheng and that it should first take out a loan for the precise amount necessary to do so from the ministries responsible for completing the repairs.[59] From what we can tell, Pucheng was repaired, but the absence of records makes it unclear in the end who paid for it.

2 Back into the Emperor's Wallet

In Beijing, coin production continued to lag behind the quota. Because the official exchange rate between taels of silver and copper coins was fixed at 1:500,

57 Ding Bin, "Liudu qianfa dahuai shu," 1611, in his *Ding Qinghuigong yiji*, repr. *Siku jihuishu congkan, jibu* (Beijing: Beijing chubanshe, 2000), 44: 60–61.

58 In a letter from Ye Xianggao to Shi Lianyue, the censors-in-chief, after the Nanjing riot. See Ye Xianggao, *Cangxia xucao*, n.d., repr. *Siku jihuishu congkan, jibu*, 125:314. Huang Aming gave a good account of the discussion between Ye Xianggao and different officials concerning the riot and the new arrangement for coin manufacture in Nanjing. See Huang Aming, "Wanli sanshijiu nian liudu zhuqian shijian ji liangjing yingdui," *Suzhou keji xueyuan xuebao (shehui kexue ban)* 44, no. 5 (2011): 59–66.

59 This meant that each of the Nanjing ministries (revenue, war, works) was to lend the mint 30,000 taels, and the Office of River Defense would lend the remaining 10,000 taels. This information is from the 1611 memorial by Censor Fu Zonggao. See Dong Qichang, *Shenmiao liuzhong zouzhu huiyao*, 471:240.

selling copper to the government was a losing proposition, one that metal merchants preferred to avoid. In 1611, a merchant wrote a petition to Censor Zhou Yongchun in Beijing to complain that the state's current conversion rate of 30 percent of its silver payments to merchants into copper cash was unfair; at the official rate at 500 cash per tael but a market rate of 660 per tael, merchants lost the equivalent of 160 cash (or 0.24 tael) for every tael of silver that the state paid them for their goods. Referring to the merchant's petition, the censor proposed that the state either make its payments entirely in silver or match the market rate for copper cash.

The Wanli emperor did not reply to the censor's proposal.[60] Some officials still considered the state policy workable. In 1615 another censor, Jiang Xing, argued that, for every tael of silver that the state invested in coin production, it could make a profit of 710 cash. When it paid merchants this 710 cash at the rate of 1:500, the state made a further profit of 210 cash (or 0.42 tael). Jiang suggested that, because metal merchants were being uncooperative, the state buy less costly copper in the mining districts, giving the contract for metal purchases to wealthy and honest people there.[61]

Then, in 1616, because the Baoyuan Mint in Beijing was still stymied by a lack of copper, military costs spiked due to a threat on the northeast border. That year, the Jurchen warlord Nurhaci, backed by his soldiers in the "Eight Banners," declared his imperial ambitions by proclaiming himself the "bright khan" of Jin dynasty, implying that he was the legitimate heir of the Jin dynasty that had ruled northern China in the twelfth century.[62] The Ming state had to rush to the defense of the Liaodong Peninsula against a possible invasion.

The 95,000 soldiers stationed in Liaodong were paid from the Taicang Treasury. In 1617 their salaries totaled 3.81 million taels, which were barely covered by the Treasury's yearly income of 3.89 million taels.[63] At the same time, Li Ruhua, the minister of revenue, needed money for many more soldiers and for military provisions such as grain, horses, and weapons. The Beijing mint had to find a way to accelerate production and supplement the silver in the treasury.

In 1618, with the emperor's approval, Li Ruhua adjusted the exchange rate for state purchases from 500 coins per tael to 600. This was closer to the market rate (660) for copper cash, and metal merchants became more willing to sell to the ministry. In addition to implementing this new rate, Li allotted 105,000

60 *Qinding xu wenxian tongkao*, 626:257.

61 *Ming shilu*, Shenzong, 10267–68.

62 Mark Elliot, *The Manchu Way: The Eight Banners and Ethnic Identity in Late Imperial China* (Stanford: Stanford University Press, 2001), 56.

63 *Ming shilu*, Shenzong, 10775.

taels of silver (a third of it in copper coins) from the Taicang Treasury to merchants, so that they could buy 1 million catties of high-grade brass for the Baoyuan Mint to make "golden back" coins. The new coins would be delivered to the Taicang Treasury and used in future payments (a third of it in silver) to merchants, at the new rate of 1:600.[64]

In this way, the Wanli coins put money into the Taicang treasury but played a minor role in the campaign against the Jurchens, because the military was paid in silver.[65] To pay for soldiers' salaries and military supplies to defend against invasion, the Ming government levied new taxes, payable in silver. In 1618, at Li Ruhua's recommendation, the Ming state added a 3.5 percent military surcharge on the land tax to be paid in silver for the benefit of the Liaodong military, totaling 2 million taels, which went to the Taicang Treasury to prepare for war.[66] In the first month of 1619, in addition to 95,000 soldiers in Liaodong, the Ming state sent an additional 11,000 soldiers there,[67] assuming that it would be well prepared. But, to its surprise, Nurhaci defeated the imperial forces at Sarhu in Liaodong two months later and took the peninsula. When news of the defeat reached Beijing, food prices in the capital soared, as residents feared a siege.[68] To send more soldiers to Liaodong, the government increased the Liaodong military surcharge to 7 percent in 1619 for the Taicang Treasury and in 1620 raised it a further two percentage points, which was for the Ministries of War and Works.[69]

In the seventh lunar month of 1620, the Wanli emperor died of illness at age fifty-seven, and his eldest son, Zhu Changluo, age thirty-eight, took the throne as the Taichang emperor. But the new emperor died only thirty days later, after ingesting a "miracle" remedy for an illness.[70] In the middle of the eighth month of 1620, his fourteen-year-old son Zhu Youxiao ascended the throne, taking Tianqi as his reign title in 1621. Even before Zhu Youxiao could formally take

---

64 *Ming shilu*, Shenzong, 10887.

65 Soldiers received such low salaries that they actually were paid the value of the silver in copper coins, but the Ministry of Revenue paid the garrison a lump sum in silver.

66 Li Xun, *Mingshi shihuo zhi*, 82.

67 *Ming shilu,* Shenzong, 10945.

68 Ray Huang, "The Lung-ch'ing and Wan-li Reigns, 2567–1620," in Mote and Twitchett, *Cambridge History of China,* 583.

69 Li Xun, *Mingshi shihuo zhi*, 82.

70 In the eighth lunar month, the thirty-year-old Taichang emperor, who had fallen seriously ill, ordered a minor official who claimed to possess a miracle drug to be brought to his chambers. Despite warnings from his ministers and court physicians that the medicine was of dubious value, the emperor took two red pills prepared by this official. He died at about dawn the following morning. See William Atwell, "The Tai-ch'ang, T'ien-ch'i, and Ch'ung-chen Reigns, 1620–1644," in Mote and Twitchett, *Cambridge History of China,* 593.

the throne, he had to organize and pay for the funerals of two emperors, his grandfather and his father, and build a tomb for his father. (The Wanli emperor had built his own tomb during his long reign.) The boy emperor had neither the money nor the time to this tomb. Fortunately, a tomb had been left vacant by the Jingtai emperor (r. 1449–1457), who had been denied his rightful burial as an emperor when his brother Zhu Qizhen usurped the throne to become the Tianshun emperor.[71]

After some renovations in the ninth month of 1621, the Taichang emperor and his two wives, who had predeceased him, were entombed.[72] The tomb's outer gardens and sculptures still needed a few millions of taels' worth of construction, but the Tianqi emperor could afford only 1 million taels from his Inner Chengyun Treasury for that purpose.[73]

To pay for the tombs, the Tianqi emperor needed not only enough silver to buy and transport the timber but copper cash to pay construction workers. After the Jiajing reign, when palace food expenses and soldiers were paid in silver, the role of copper cash in palace administration was limited. But laborers still received their salaries in copper cash.[74] If the emperor had had enough silver in his Inner Chengyun Treasury, he could exchange it for copper cash to pay them, but his silver had been spent on timber for the tombs. He decided to use the copper coins in his Siyao Treasury and then to expand coin manufacture. Because the Ministry of Works was on the brink of bankruptcy, he allowed the Ministry of Revenue to build its own mint. In the tenth month of 1621, the new emperor ordered it to cast Tianqi coins that would match the quality of the Wanli coins.[75]

Intending to expand his income from copper cash, he allowed the Ministries of Revenue in both capitals to build their own mints, extending the monopoly right of coin manufacture and increasing the number of imperial mints to four. The Tianqi emperor demanded a total of 5 million cash a season from these mints, with 1.5 million each from Beijing's Ministry of Works and Ministry of Revenue and 1 million each from the Nanjing Ministry of Works and Ministry

71 The Wanli emperor's tomb was of such grandeur that it had cost 8 million taels to build. A less impressive tomb would have cost half this amount. Xu Wenji and Chen Shilong, *Zhengshuo Mingchao shiliu di*, 249.

72 The Taichang emperor died before he had a chance to choose an empress. Therefore, his princess Lady Guo, who died in 1613, and his concubine Lady Wang, mother of the Tianqi emperor, who died in 1619, shared his tomb. See Hu Hansheng, *Ming shisan ling* (Beijing: Beijing chubanshe, 2018), 167–70.

73 See Hu Hansheng, *Ming shisan ling*, 170, 181.

74 The tomb builders were paid copper cash daily. See *Ming shilu*, Xizong, 3666.

75 *Ming shilu*, Xizong, 760.

of Revenue. These four institutions agreed that, to save on the cost of transportation, the Beijing ministries would produce 2.5 million each and collect silver for this service from their parallel institutions in Nanjing.[76] The Nanjing ministries would not be responsible for casting the new coins.

The Beijing Ministry of Revenue built a new mint in the capital. The Tianqi emperor named it Baoquan (Fount of Treasure Bureau), implying that the mint would be like a fountain that produces a never-ending flow of water.[77] This was either wishful thinking or evidence of the resilience of the idea that coin manufacture was an inexhaustible source of wealth. Unlike in the Wanli era, there was no longer even a pretense that this wealth was for the people. Once again, it went to the throne, to support palace expenses for construction projects.

But although the Nanjing Ministry of Revenue had agreed to pay 1,700 taels a season to Beijing's Ministry of Revenue to cast coins on its behalf, Nanjing never did so.[78] Worse still, the new Baoquan Mint turned the Beijing Ministry of Revenue into a formidable competitor for copper with the Ministry of Works. The Ministry of Revenue had provided the Baoyuan Mint with copper but ceased doing so. When the Ministry of Works asked to borrow copper from the Ministry of Revenue and pay for it with silver later, Chen Yuting, the revenue official in charge of the Baoquan Mint, refused, saying: "Silver is silver, and copper is copper. They cannot be lumped together."[79]

With what seems like short-sighted competitive zeal, Chen Yuting then implemented two measures that later drove the Baoyuan Mint out of business. First, he raised the price of zinc, the other metal in brass coins, to be charged to the Ministry of Revenue. He was not allowed to alter the purchase price for raw copper, which had been officially fixed at 0.14 tael per catty, but he raised the price of zinc 0.002 tael per catty higher than the market price and guaranteed that he would buy 2 catties of zinc at this price for every 8-catty purchase of raw copper.[80] This measure meant that the Ministry of Works, already financially constrained, had even greater difficulty finding copper in the market. Even if the Ministry of Works had been able to engage in a price war, Chen Yuting's second measure blocked the Ministry of Works from obtaining copper at the Chongwen Gate, which was staffed by tax-collecting officials from the Ministry of Revenue. In 1623, for example, when a metal merchant called Han Dechun, who had been under contract to the Ministry of Works, passed the Chongwen

76 Chen Yuting, *Baoquan xindu*, 1624, repr. *Xuxiu siku quanshu*, 838:496.
77 Chen Yuting, *Baoquan xindu*, 471.
78 Chen Yuting, *Baoquan xindu*, 496.
79 Chen Yuting, *Baoquan xindu*, 486.
80 Chen Yuting, *Baoquan xindu*, 507.

Gate with dozens of donkeys, officials demanded that he pay a tax because his Ministry of Works license had expired. In an effort to avoid paying this tax, Han agreed to sell all his copper directly to the Ministry of Revenue. When the news reached the Ministry of Works, which had been waiting for this shipment to keep its own mint operating, the official from the Ministry of Works who took charge of the Baoyuan Mint became so angry that he complained to the emperor. The Tianqi emperor then ordered the Ministry of Revenue, for the sake of the tomb construction, to share some of the copper that it had bought. In response, Chen Yuting agreed that, in the future, 40 percent of the copper that went through the Chongwen Gate would go to the Ministry of Works.[81] But it seems doubtful that the Ministry of Works ever obtained copper from this agreement. Because it had no official of its own at the Chongwen Gate, it had not way to determine the actual amount of copper that passed through it.

In 1625, the Ministry of Works obtained 20,000 catties of scrap copper that had been stored in the inner treasuries.[82] This copper enabled the Baoyuan Mint to hand over its full seasonal quota of 2.5 million cash to the emperor,[83] in its last large casting. Later the same month, the Ministry of Works told the emperor that its furnaces had mostly ceased operating and could not restart without a new supply of copper, though it would try to buy more copper through its officials and merchants in Jingzhou, Hubei Province, where the major copper market was.[84] By the following year, only 36 of the mint's 120 furnaces were operating.[85] Instead of increasing coinage, the Ministry of Works had effectively shut down the Baoyuan Mint. (The Baoyuan Mint continued to operate, but at a reduced and decreasing scale.) The Ministry of Revenue took over the task of coin manufacture and was able to keep 120 furnaces in operation.

The Taichang emperor's tomb was finally completed in 1626.[86] The prior year, the Tianqi emperor had begun an even larger construction project, repairing

81 Chen Yuting, *Baoquan xindu*, 498–99.

82 *Ming shilu*, Xizong, 2757–58.

83 *Ming shilu*, Xizong, 3110–11.

84 *Ming shilu*, Xizong, 3160–61.

85 *Ming shilu*, Xizong, 3464, 3675. By 1644, the last year of the Ming dynasty, the Baoyuan Mint in Beijing had only 10 furnaces. See *Chongzhen changbian* (*Tongshi* ed.) (1911, repr. Shanghai: Shenzhou guoguangshe, 1946), 72.

86 Construction on the Taichang emperor's tomb began in 1621 and was completed in the sixth month of 1626. There is no record of how much money it cost, but according to an official report, the government had spent 700,000 taels of silver by the first month in 1623. See Hu Hansheng, *Ming shisan ling*, 170.

three main halls in the Forbidden City that had burned down in 1597.[87] Because the repairs were costly, the Wanli emperor had not begun these repairs until 1615, and progress had been slow. When the Tianqi emperor was enthroned in 1621, an additional 8,000 pieces of timber were needed to complete the repair.[88] But repair work was suspended until 1625 in order to focus resources on his father's tomb. Coin manufacture had to continue so as to pay the construction workers on all these projects.

Repairs for the three main halls cost about 6 million taels.[89] The Tianqi emperor tried to come up with the money in various ways—encouraging officials to make donations, levying county surcharges, selling official positions, increasing the salt tax, and so on.[90] In 1626, Li Qiyuan, the minister of revenue, tried to help by ordering each province to build a new mint. Instead of coin manufacture "for the people," this time around Li set a profit quota in silver taels that each provincial mint would hand over to the Taicang Treasury.[91] In other words, the revenue from these mints would go directly to the imperial treasury.

The provincial mints did not live up to expectations, and Li retired two months after submitting his proposal. Guo Yunhou, the new minister of revenue, reported to the emperor that none of these local mints had been able to fulfill the silver quota.[92] Then, Yan Mingtai, the governor-general of Jizhou and Liaodong, petitioned the emperor to say that the Jizhou mint had produced such a meager profit from its mint in the prior year (about 7,000 taels) that he asked to keep the money to meet local needs. In reply, the Tianqi emperor ordered the Jizhou mint to shut down; not only was its profit small, but its coins were thin and poorly made.[93]

Relying on these several unstable resources, the three main halls were finally repaired early in the eighth month of 1627. The Tianqi emperor did not live to see his achievement. His health had declined since his tumble into a lake during a water game two years earlier. A month before the repairs were completed, he died at the age of twenty-two. As both of his children had died

---

87 The three main halls were the Huangji hall, the Zhongji hall, and the Jianji hall.

88 *Ming shilu*, Guangzong, 137.

89 According to a report from the Ministry of Works, the repair cost of the three main halls from 1625 to 1627 totaled 5.96 million taels. See *Ming shilu*, Xizong, 4236.

90 See Hu Hansheng, *Ming shisan ling*, 171.

91 *Ming shilu*, Xizong, 3345.

92 The ministry received about 10,000 taels each from Shaanxi and Henan, 7,000 taels from the Miyun garrison, 1,000 taels from Zhejiang, Jiangsu, and Shanxi, 100 taels from Fujian, and not a single tael from Huguang. *Ming shilu*, Xizong, 3741.

93 *Ming shilu*, Xizong, 3724.

in infancy, the throne passed to his eldest surviving brother, Zhu Youjian, who became the Chongzhen emperor,[94] the last emperor in the Ming dynasty.

Zhu Youjian ascended the throne in the eighth month of 1627. A month later, he consulted the Ministry of Works about a tomb for his late brother, the Tianqi emperor. The minister of works suggested building a small tomb resembling their father's tomb, which would cost the government only 2 million to 3 million taels. The Chongzhen emperor agreed, but unlike his late brother, who had donated 1 million taels for the Taichang emperor's tomb, he was able to contribute only half that amount. To obtain the other half, the minister of works proposed that every official donate as much as 100 taels of silver according to his rank, that each county donate 100 to 220 taels according to its size, and that the government sell official positions to acquire more money. The Chongzhen emperor endorsed all these proposals.[95] To supplement them, an official from the Ministry of Works proposed tearing down the "living shrines" that various provincial officials had built for Wei Zhongxian, the most infamous eunuch in the Tianqi reign,[96] in order to reuse the stone for the emperor's tomb. The Chongzhen emperor agreed at first, ordering Wei's arrest; the eunuch responded by committing suicide.[97] But high officials argued that he should not allow his late brother to be associated in yet another way with this notorious eunuch.[98]

Xue Fengxiang, the minister of works, reported to the emperor that he was having difficulty finding strong and able construction workers for the tomb, because the best workers could make more money working for wealthy families. He suggested using garrison soldiers instead, as had happened before, when 1,500 soldiers and their commander had joined the civilian workers in building the Taichang emperor's tomb, and each soldier had received 0.03 tael of silver per day as a food allowance. Although Xue preferred civilian workers to soldiers, who were less amenable, he agreed to pay the Ministry of War

---

94 Atwell, "The Tai-ch'ang, T'ien-ch'i, and Ch'ung-chen Reigns," 611.

95 Hu Hansheng, *Ming shisan ling*, 181.

96 Wei Zhongxian was also the most powerful eunuch in the Tianqi period. To please Wei, several provincial officials, starting with the governor of Zhejiang, built "living shrines" in their jurisdictions, to glorify his contributions and achievements. See Atwell, "The Tai-ch'ang, T'ien-ch'i, and Ch'ung-chen Reigns," 608–9.

97 As soon as he ascended the throne, the Chongzhen emperor ordered Wei Zhongxian's arrest for the crimes listed in the memorials that were pouring into the palace. Fearing the worst, Wei and a close eunuch associate hanged themselves. But even then the new emperor did not permit Wei to have an honorable death. Wei's corpse was dismembered, and his head publicly displayed, as a warning to those who might wish to follow in his footsteps. See Atwell, "The Tai-ch'ang, T'ien-ch'i, and Ch'ung-chen Reigns," 612–13.

98 Hu Hansheng, *Ming shisan ling*, 182.

for additional laborers from local garrisons.[99] Thus, along with the cost of the civilian workers, the estimated labor cost for the tomb was about 16 million cash for a year's work.[100] To build the new tomb, the Ministry of Works needed more copper coins from the imperial mints—its own Baoyuan Mint, which had been operating at a small scale, and the Ministry of Revenue's Baoquan Mint.

In the twelfth month of 1627, the emperor ordered the casting of Chongzhen coins.[101] To pay for new coins, the Ministry of Revenue made the emperor a splendid proposal: he would spend 100,000 taels a year to cast coins in the Baoquan Mint for the next four years.[102] Assuming that 1 tael of silver paid for casting 550 copper cash, 400,000 taels would produce 220 million cash, enough to pay 1,500 civilian laborers to work on the tomb for more than thirteen years. The question was: where would the Ministry of Revenue find this amount of silver? Its Taicang Treasury had been emptied to pay for soldiers and military supplies in resisting the Jurchen invasion.

Beijing's Ministry of Revenue proposed that Nanjing's Ministry of Revenue, along with some inland customhouses pay the 400,000 taels. This was a substantial increase in its tax quotas, as, for instance, taxes from the Hushu customhouse rose from 22,500 taels to 65,000 taels and from the Jiujiang customhouse the increase was from 12,500 to 46,000 taels.[103] They were required to send their silver to the Ministry of Revenue in Beijing every season for four years, at which time they would resume their old quotas.[104]

In this way, the Baoquan Mint took most of the responsibility for paying the workers on the Tianqi emperor's tomb. Although it must have been difficult for

99 In this report, probably because civilian laborers were paid in copper coins, Xue Fengxiang did not give their exact salary, but he emphasized that 0.03 tael a day was enough to hire a civilian worker. *MingQing shiliao* (Nanjing: Guoli zhongyang yanjiuyuan lishi yuyan yanjiu suo, 1930), vol. 2, no. 1, 36a–37b.

100 Assuming a generous exchange rate of 1:1,000 for the 0.03 tael, the daily salary of a civilian laborer would have been 30 copper cash. If the Ministry of Works hired 1,500 civilian laborers as well as 1,500 soldiers, it would have paid out 45,000 copper cash for one day's work, 1.35 million cash for one month's work, or 16 million cash for a year's work.

101 See Li Xun, *Mingshi shihuozhi jiaozhu*, 223.

102 *Chongzhen Changbian*, in *Ming shilu fulu* (repr. Taipei: Zhongyang yanjiuyuan lishi yuyan yanjiusuo, 1984), 13–14.

103 The budget was as follows: Nanjing's Ministry of Revenue: 100,000 taels; Hushu customs: 65,500 taels; Jiujing customs: 46,000 taels; Linqing customs: 43,300 taels; Hexiwu customs: 23,000 taels; Beixing customs: 60,000 taels; Yangzhou customs: 18,600 taels; and Chongwen Gate (of Beijing) customs: 10,000 taels.

104 *Chongzhen changbian*, in *Ming shilu fulu*, 15–16.

customhouses to raise the tax and send so much silver to Beijing, the Baoquan Mint produced 130 million coins in less than nine months in 1628.

As a result of the competition with the Ministry of Revenue's Baoquan Mint, the Baoyuan Mint in Beijing, run by the Ministry of Works, was operating at such a reduced scale that it was basically shut down. The Ministry of Revenue controlled the Chongwen Gate customs in Beijing as well as all the customhouses along the Grand Canal, preventing the Baoyuan Mint there from acquiring sufficient copper (or brass) for its normal operation, therefore, Beijing's Ministry of Works had to shift operations of its mint to Nanjing. It sent silver to the Nanjing mint for casting and then sent the coins to Beijing. This method of operations was costly and sluggish; in 1628, when the Baoquan Mint transferred 130 million copper coins to the Siyao Treasury, the Baoyuan Mint only handed over 60 million.

The Ministry of Works also set up a provincial mint in Jingzhou in 1630. Jingzhou had a big market for copper, and, more importantly, it had the only customhouse where the official in charge was from the Ministry of Works. But the Jingzhou mint only made provincial coins for local markets. Instead of giving its coins to Beijing's Ministry of Works, the provincial mint paid 5,000 taels a year for the privilege of making legal coins for local use.[105]

In 1628, northern and central China suffered a devastating drought. The resulting famine lasted more than a decade. When the government could not provide food to withstand the famine, violence erupted in northern Shaanxi, the center of the drought, and then spread to other parts of northern China.

In normal years, the Ming government could easily suppress rebels with troops paid in silver from the Taicang Treasury. But the drought had affected agriculture from northern to central China, diminishing the land tax revenue collected in silver by the Taicang Treasury. The Chongzhen emperor preferred to use his dwindling silver income to pay the soldiers guarding his northeastern frontier against the Jurchens, who seemed more formidable than starving rebels.

The Tianqi tomb had finally been completed in 1632, but in 1635 it was looted and damaged by Manchu invaders—Jurchens who took a new name under their new leader Hong Taiji, who was Nurhaci's son. After the Manchus retreated, the Ming government recruited workers to repair the tomb.[106]

Because of the breakdown in household registration and the loss of labor services, the emperor needed copper coins to pay construction workers in the capital and obtained them from imperial mints. But the Baoyuan Mint could

105 *Chongzhen changbian*, in *Ming shilu fulu*, 2383, 2868, 3169, 3189–90.

106 Hu Hansheng, *Ming shisan ling*, 183.

no longer afford the copper and laborers to make coins. In the final years of the dynasty, to conserve metal and labor, the Chongzhen emperor ordered the two imperial mints to cast five-cash coins. In the first month of 1644, the emperor asked the Ministry of Works why he had seen no five-cash coins from their Baoyuan Mint. The ministry replied that the Baoyuan Mint lacked the capital and was operating with only ten furnaces. The emperor instructed the mint to build more furnaces and hire more laborers.[107]

That same month, peasant rebels under the leadership of Li Zicheng had seized Chang'an, the provincial capital of Shaanxi. From there, they advanced rapidly through garrison cities such as Taiyuan, Datong, and Xuanfu, meeting little resistance as they headed to Beijing. Their sudden presence in Beijing on the eighteenth day of the third month of 1644 came as a shock to the populace. Some court officials fled, but by the time many of them understood the situation, the entire capital, including the palace, was in flames. It was too late for the Chongzhen emperor to escape, but he could still die with dignity. Early the next morning, accompanied by a loyal eunuch, the last Ming emperor climbed a small hill outside the northern gate of the palace and hanged himself from a tree.[108] The Ming dynasty had ended.

3 Conclusion

Although minting coins was seen as a way to wealth, the Ming coinage system never functioned well. But the downfall of the dynasty cannot be attributed to the coinage system, because copper coins never played a major role in Ming government finance. The government was supported first by the household registration system of in-kind taxes and labor services and, then, by silver.

Initially, the Ming emperors cast copper coins to pay for the less expensive, miscellaneous items that the deteriorating household system no longer supplied. As noted in the Chapter 3, the production of copper coins provisioned the emperor's table, but when most food merchants demanded payment in silver, copper coins lost even this function. This chapter shows that several government institutions attempted to assign copper cash a new role in government finance: providing additional revenue to supplement its silver income. But all these attempts ended in failure. In the last few decades of the Ming

107 *Chongzhen changbian* (*Tongshi* ed.), 72.

108 For a detailed introduction to the transition of dynasties, see Atwell, "The Tai-ch'ang, T'ien-ch'i, and Ch'ung-chen Reigns," 632–40.

dynasty, copper cash was used by the emperor mainly to pay construction workers building and repairing palace buildings in the capital.

The Ming emperor and officials understood that silver played the principal role in government finances. Why they did not simply abolish the coinage system is a mystery . Perhaps it was because the common people used copper coins for small transactions, regardless of whether the coins were legal or cast by the current government, and the state wanted to reap the profit for themselves from minting coins.

In ancient China, the term "chicken ribs" was used to describe something without meat or taste, as a metaphor for something that had dubious value but was not bad enough to give up. For the Ming government, copper coins were "chicken ribs."

CHAPTER 5

Conclusion: Small Change and State Administration in Ming China

Why did Ming emperors and statesmen bother with the "chicken ribs" of copper coin manufacture? Why go to the trouble of minting such small change, when plenty of coins from earlier dynasties were still in circulation? Why did copper coins become the state currency, at a time when, in Europe, copper coins were rarely used at all?

To address the last question first: at the time in Europe, low-value, full-bodied coins[1] were in short supply because of how they were made: they were struck, rather than poured into molds. Because the amount of effort required to strike a coin of any size or metal was the same, small coins cost more to make than larger ones, and copper coins cost more than gold or silver coins.[2] As a result, Europe had chronic shortages of small gold and silver coins, and neither rulers nor mint workers wanted to mint copper coins.[3] However, Chinese copper coins were cast in multiple molds before achieving their final form, and making them had been perceived as a way to generate infinite wealth for centuries. The choice of copper coins as a state currency was probably due to the greater accessibility of copper than silver at the time. Although the Ming state lacked a good supply route to its copper mines, officials could always buy copper on the market or even melt down coins made by previous dynasties to obtain raw materials for their mints.

When Zhu Yuanzhang founded the Ming empire, he issued copper coins for additional income, but then, after reorganizing state administration to diminish its reliance on money, he curtailed their use. He paid administrative

1 In France, until the mid-sixteenth century, many small "silver" coins were actually made from a mixture of silver and copper. See Thomas J. Sargent and Francois R. Velde, *The Big Problem of Small Change* (Princeton: Princeton University Press, 2001), 47.

2 Economic historian Carlo Cipolla showed that, in premodern Europe, minting gold or silver coins usually led to a shortage of full-bodied petty coins (copper or low-value silver or gold coins), because the profit margin for the latter was lower than that of higher-value coins made of gold or "good silver;" in his *Money, Prices, and Civilization in the Mediterranean World: Fifth to Seventeenth Century* (1956, repr., New York: Gordian Press, 1967), 28.

3 With the introduction of steam power to the minting press in the nineteenth century, mints finally could produce metal coins, whether in gold, silver, or copper, in large amounts at low cost.

 | DOI:10.1163/9789004687530_007

expenses with in-kind taxes and labor services from household registration. Ming soldiers and officials were paid out of the rice tribute (land tax); the capital was supplied with food from local and provincial farm households; construction projects were built with labor services and building materials from in-kind taxes; and so on. The Hongwu emperor's state currency, in the form of copper coins and, later, paper money, at first was only a give gifts to a guest. Neither currency was accepted as payment for taxes or used to pay officials' or military salaries. In its early years, the Ming empire did not run on money.

Meanwhile, copper coins and silver continued to circulate as they had for centuries, with copper cash used for small exchanges and silver ingots for larger purchases. Although, at first, the precious note was rarely used in the market, the Hongwu emperor set its value in terms of copper coins, with 1 *guan* equal to 1,000 cash. Subsequent emperors, adding copper and silver to the precious note as official currencies, set conversion rates among the three of them so that they could be used interchangeably. The many varieties of copper coins in circulation complicated this task, and a coin's market rate fluctuated, based in part on which ones were accepted in payment for taxes and government fees. But throughout the Ming, market conversion rates never matched official rates, which could cause problems—such as the loss of value for precious notes at a time when they were being used to pay official salaries or when the palace treasury was filled with low-grade copper coins. The economist Chen Chaunan, noting the difficulty that Ming officials had in fixing an official conversion rate between the two metal currencies (the bimetallic ratio) to approximate the market rate, wondered why the Ming state did not simply abandon the dual monetary system and shift to a single silver-based standard, to simplify fiscal administration.

In fact, the Ming state *did* fix the conversion rates (and the bimetallic ratio) *administratively*, several times. The state set conversion rates between all the different forms of payment, beginning with ratios between rice salaries and precious notes, later including rates for all three currencies—precious notes, copper coins, and silver. Using these conversion rates, the state paid its officials and soldiers and, later, the palace food suppliers.

But, as Chen pointed out, the Ming government could never make the market rate match the official ratio. Although the government might stipulate that 1 tael of silver equaled 700 copper cash, the market rate followed its own logic when determining the value of a coin. Modern governments try to converge the two rates by buying and selling currency in the market. In Ming China, the emperor simply decreed the official rate. When the market price diverged from the official rate, the emperors and the government blamed the discrepancy on merchants who were hoarding and speculating on different kinds of money or buyers spending the wrong kind of currency, leading to further decrees or penalties, usually with little effect.

Unlike modern economic historians, Ming emperors were not concerned about "the economy." When they began to print paper money in large quantities, their goal was to pay administrative expenses, mostly officials' salaries. When Ming emperors tried to reduce inflation in paper money, they did so only to ensure its worth in official salaries, not in the economy. In their defense, when they printed too much paper money, the resulting inflation only affected that currency. If paper money depreciated to the point that officials rejected it, the bureaucratic system was ruined, but the market was not affected much. Depreciated precious notes did not affect the price of silver or copper cash in the market; their price levels remained stable. The Hongwu emperor was not affected either, because he could still supply the palace and the capital through the household registration system.

Although Ming officials did not focus on the economy as such, they probably did have a basic understanding of how it worked: that agricultural products needed to be cheap enough to that people could afford to feed themselves, but without bankrupting farmers, and that merchants should maintain constant prices across locations and should not hoard goods in order to make excessive profits. But when officials talked about issuing money, it is not clear whether their objective was to strengthen the *economy* or simply to strengthen their own financial conditions. The emperors minted coins to improve their income, not the economy. When the provincial mints and the Ministry of Revenue began to cast coins, they did so for the same reason: to pay administrative expenses by creating another income stream.

It was traditional to turn to coin making for additional income and the Ming emperors, as we have seen, were in constant need of money for a variety of reasons. At first, the early Ming emperors (from Hongwu to Yongle) considered the entire capital as their domain, thus it was up to them to support all public expenditure (for soldiers, officials, foreign emissaries, princes, monks, construction, food, festivals, etc.) as well as palace expenses, and this was a costly undertaking. Over time, especially after the household registration system broke down, the throne had difficulty not only in paying the officials and soldiers stationed there, building tombs, and hosting state banquets but also with buying food for daily meals and offerings. The emperor then increasingly relied on the Ministry of Revenue to do so on behalf of the empire.

Also, as Ray Huang pointed out, even though the Ming state gradually converted payment accepted for taxes from in-kind and services into silver, it still followed its initial rule that each of the six ministries collected its own taxes and kept its own accounts. The emperor did not have a central institution, such as a single finance department, to keep track of how much silver he had to spend. To complicate fiscal matters further, the emperor's private money and state funds were not separated (e.g., when the emperor paid the military from his private treasuries or "borrowed" silver from the Taicang treasury to feed the palace), and the imperial accounting system was chaotic at best and non-existent at worst. Huang noted: "One of the basic characteristics of the Ming system was that it derived numerous small incomes from very diverse sources. These accounts were never integrated and a number of revenues were actually disbursed before auditing."[4] Because finance was decentralized, whenever an emperor needed money (e.g., to defend the borders or build a tomb for his father), he had to meet with two or more ministers to try to find the money; but no ministry wanted to open its private accounting or pay for the majority of the emperor's projects.

One of the main themes in every chapter in this book is how impecunious the Ming emperors were in terms of palace finances. As Hongwu set up the dynasty, the Ming emperors were total autocrats, with even less of a check on their power by the nobility or government officials than was the case in previous dynasties. But they lacked the resources to run their own palace. Minting copper coins seemed like a way out of their financial woes.

At the same time, managing the minting of coins was difficult in Ming China, because coin manufacture required an abundance of metal, fuel, and labor.[5] But making copper coins would not have been a losing proposition if the imperial mint had been able to control and spend its product, because after the coins were made, they were worth more in silver than they had cost to mint. The problem was that the coins made by the Baoyuan Mint belonged to the throne; after being cast, they went directly to the Siyao Treasury in the palace. This not only left the Baoyuan Mint without a profit from its labors but meant it was responsible for covering all the expenses of running the mint without receiving anything back. In short, this setup doomed the mint to operate at a loss.

After the Wanli emperor turned over control of the coins minted to the Ministry of Revenue, it was able to show a profit by setting the exchange rate in terms of administrative payments. It paid 20 percent of official salaries and

4 Huang, *Taxation and Government Finance*, 225.

5 Getting copper without a supply line between the Yunnan copper mines and Beijing was part of the problem. The Ming state owned copper mines, but the government also allowed civilians to own and run the mines. Because the official mines were less successful, beginning in the early years of the dynasty, Ming officials relied on the market to buy copper as well as the other metals that they needed. See Bai Shouyi, "Mingdai kuangye de fazhan," in his *Xuebu ji* (1956, repr. Beijing: Sanlian shudian, 1962), 74, 89.

other silver payments (e.g., to merchants) in copper cash at the fixed rate of 800 per tael of silver. By using coins as the state currency and controlling the exchange rate to silver, the Ministry of Revenue earned a tidy profit even as it paid the bills. This policy worked until the ministry became greedy, raising the percentage of coins in the silver payment and lowering the exchange rate. This pleased no one except the officials at the Ministry of Revenue. As shown in Chapter 4, copper merchants did not want to sell to the ministry on these terms.[6] As a result, the production of copper coins waned until the end of the Ming dynasty.

Money was used by the Ming state as an administrative, not an economic, tool to pay for officials and soldiers, to pay for the emperor's table, and to pay for his projects. In the early years, an emperor could mobilize workers and resources through the household registration system. But as that system broke down, the emperor and the officials who ran the six bureaus had to use money. The question then became who should pay for what, and this affected the kind of money that would be used. If the emperor had to pay, as for most of the Ming, he controlled the copper mint, he tried to raise money by issuing more coins and thereby obtaining a profit. If the Ministry of Revenue paid, it might allot some of its silver from the land tax, which was stored in the Taicang Treasury (and also had to be used to pay the military). As shown here, the manufacture of copper coins failed to generate the hoped-for income, leading the Ming state to rely increasingly on silver from the Ministry of Revenue to solve its money problems. Silver and the Ministry of Revenue became increasingly important.

But unlike in Europe, where bimetallic currencies were "hostile brothers," in China silver and copper continued to coexist amicably, mostly in entirely different markets. The economic historian Richard von Glahn wrote about copper cash and silver ingots in Ming China in terms of "the ascendancy of silver over coin."[7] He argued that a "coin economy" had existed before the silver economy and that "the transition from the coin economy to a silver economy took place ... over the course of the fourteenth century, even though coin remained an indispensable component of the monetary system throughout the late Ming and Qing periods."[8] Von Glahn's theory echoed studies by historians such

6 The Ministry of Works could buy little copper under the new measures and shifted responsibility for the copper to the Ministry of Revenue, who had no success either.

7 Von Glahn, *Fountain of Fortune,* 257.

8 Von Glahn, *Fountain of Fortune,* 10.

as Katô Shigeru, Wang Wencheng, and Gao Congming, who showed that silver already had been used widely in markets as early as the Song dynasty.[9]

But if copper coins were an indispensable part of the monetary system all the way through the late imperial period, what was the "silver economy" that supposedly replaced it? And if silver had been used since the Song dynasty, what was the "coin economy" that preceded it?

As small cash, copper coins never dominated China's economy; even in the early Ming, silver was the currency used to buy expensive goods. From the early to the mid-Ming, when market activity flourished, the use of both currencies seems to have increased, and silver ingots did not *replace* copper cash. Von Glahn's reference to a thriving "silver economy" applies to the growth in long-distance trade, because copper coins were too heavy and cumbersome for long-distance transport.[10] Beginning in the thirteenth century, whenever long-distance trade developed, silver had a place as the means of exchange.

It is harder to grasp von Glahn's use of the term "coin economy." Copper coins, because they were bulky and of low value, circulated only in local markets, at which grain and vegetable farmers and local craftsmen sold their wares.[11] This market was separate from the ones where silver was the preferred currency of exchange. Because the two currencies circulated simultaneously, usually in distinct and separate markets, there was no need for a transition from a "coin economy" to a "silver economy." Even in the final years of the Ming dynasty, copper coins were used for ordinary transactions such as retail trade, whereas silver bullion was used instead in large transactions such as land sales,[12] wholesale trade, or long-distance trade.

---

9 Katô Shigeru, *Tô Sô jidai ni okeru kingin no kenkyû* (Tokyo: Tôyô bunko, 1965); Gao Congming, *Songdai huobi yu huobi liutong yanjiu* (Baoding: Hebei daxue chubanshe, 2000); Wang Wencheng, *Songdai baiyin huobihua yanjiu* (Kunming: Yunnan daxue chubanshe, 2011).

10 In the early Hongwu period, one *shi* of rice cost 500 to 1,000 coins (see Peng Xinwei, *Zhongguo huobi shi*, 677). Assuming that these coins were all Hongwu coins and that one Hongwu coin weighed 2.67 g. (using my collection as a standard; see Figure 5), then a person would need to carry between 1,335 g. (nearly 3 lbs.) and 2,670 g. (nearly 6 lbs.) to buy a single *shi* of rice.

11 Karl Polanyi, *The Great Transformation: The Political and Economic Origins of Our Time* (Boston: Beacon Press, 2001), 66.

12 Sometimes large amounts of coins were used instead of silver, as when buying land, but these transactions were local, so transporting heavy coins was less of a problem. Matsubara Kentaro studied the transfer of land in the precolonial New Territories, when they were still part of Xin'an County in Guangdong Province. He discovered that most transfers of land were in small communities, where vendors and purchasers knew each other. It was not until new land policies that clearly defined ownership reduced the risk of purchasing village land for outsiders that the land market expanded. See Matsubara Kentaro, "Credit Institutions and the Land Market in the New Territories of Hong Kong: Local

FIGURE 7 The weight of copper coins. The Ming dynasty ended in 1644, but copper coins continued to serve as petty cash in local markets into the early twentieth century. In 1917, the American sociologist and photographer Sidney D. Gamble was on his way to a farmers market in Shifochang, Sichuan Province, when he encountered this man, who was either a merchant or a money changer, carrying thousands of copper coins on strings around his shoulders.
CREDIT: SIDNEY D. GAMBLE PHOTOGRAPHS COLLECTION, DUKE LIBRARY

Social Structuring and Colonization," in *Colonial Administration and Land Reform in East Asia*, ed. Cheung Sui-Wai (London: Routledge, 2017), 103–14.

Alfred Mitchell-Innes, an early twentieth-century politician and economist, saw all forms of money as tokens and considered their weight or material unimportant. What was significant was the name or distinguishing mark of the issuer, which would never guarantee a metallic standard but did guarantee that the issuer would accept this particular token in payment of a tax debt.[13] As shown in Chapter 1, the Hongwu emperor had to accept his paper money for tax payments in order to give it a market value. But the issuer's mark on a copper coin was of little importance in Ming China. In the market, no one cared who had made a coin—only whether it was good or inferior in terms of its weight, condition, copper content, or minting expense (the "golden backs"). The face value of one cash for any kind of copper coin was only applicable to taxes and government charges, and only for a while, until the palace treasury filled up with inferior coins as Gresham's law took effect. At that point, the state decided which "good" coins to accept and judged their worth, as people in the markets did.

As the Sons of Heaven, Ming emperors expected their subjects to use the state currency even after it had become worthless and shopkeepers to comply with their decrees and accept inferior copper coins or depreciated precious notes even when they lost money on the transaction. But Ming subjects spent or saved their money based on its market value, and even severe penalties did not dissuade them. When Ming emperors and statesmen realized that they could not control the market with threats, they turned to other solutions: accepting precious notes in payment of taxes and fees, making copper and silver official currencies, changing conversion rates between copper and silver to reflect market rates more closely, paying for goods and services in copper and silver, allowing provincial governments to mint coins, giving control of the mints and their product to the ministries, and so on. They were not modern economists acting in accordance with a theory; they were discovering what worked as they went along, sometimes relying on ancient traditional concepts—as in the case of minting copper coins to create a fountain of wealth—even when the results proved them wrong.

---

13 See Wray, *Credit and State Theories of Money*, 20, 42.

Works Cited

Arlington, L.C., and William Lewisohn. 1991. *In Search of Old Peking.* Hong Kong: Oxford University Press.

Atwell, William. 2002. "Time, Money, and the Weather: Ming China and the 'Great Depression' of the Mid-Fifteenth Century." *Journal of Asian Studies* 61, no. 1: 83–113.

Bai Shouyi 白壽彝. 1956/1962. "Mingdai kuangye de fazhan 明代礦業的發展." In *Xuebu ji* 學步集, edited by Bai Shouyi 白壽彝, 74–114. Repr. Beijing: Sanlian shudian.

Braudel, Fernand. 1992. *The Structures of Everyday Life: The Limits of the Possible.* Berkeley: University of California Press.

Brook, Timothy. 1998. *The Confusions of Pleasure: Commerce and Culture in Ming China.* Taipei: SMC.

Bu Shichang 卜世昌. 1605/1972. *HuangMing tongji shuyi* 皇明通紀述遺. Repr. Taipei: Guangwen shuju.

Campbell, Aurelia. 2020. *What the Emperor Built: Architecture and Empire in the Early Ming.* Seattle: University of Washington Press.

Cha Jizuo 查繼佐. 1672/1986. *Zuiwei lu* 罪惟録. Repr. Hangzhou: Zhejiang guji chubanshe.

Chan Hok-lam (Chen Xuelin) 陳學霖. 1997. "Xianluo gongshi 'Xie Wenbin' shijian pouxi 暹羅貢使謝文彬事件剖析." In *Mingdai renwu yu chuanshuo* 明代人物與傳說, edited by Chen Xuelin 陳學霖, 275–306. Hong Kong: Chinese University Press.

Chan, Hok-lam. 2008. *Legends of the Buildings of Old Peking.* Hong Kong: Chinese University Press.

Chan Hok-lam (Chen Xuelin) 陳學霖. 2008. *Liu Bowen yu Nazha cheng: Beijing jiancheng de chuanshuo* 劉伯溫與哪吒城:北京建城的傳說. Beijing: Sanlian shudian.

Chen, Chau-nan. 1972. "Bimetallism: Theory and Controversy in Perspective." *History of Political Economy* 4, no. 1: 89–112.

Chen, Chau-nan. 1975. "Flexible Bimetallic Rates in China, 1650–1850: A Historical Example of Optimum Currency Areas." *Journal of Money, Credit and Banking* 7, no. 3: 359–76.

Chen Yuting 陳于廷. 1624/2002. *Baoquan xindu* 寶泉新牘. Repr. *Xuxiu siku quanshu,* vol. 838: 471–523.

Chen Zilong 陳子龍, ed. 1638/1962. *Ming jingshi wenbian* 明經世文編. Repr. Beijing: Zhonghua shuju.

Chongzhen changbian (*Tongshi* ed.) 崇禎長編 (痛史本). 1911/1946. Repr. Shanghai: Shenzhou guoguangshe.

Chongzhen changbian 崇禎長編. n.d./1984. In *Ming shilu fulu* 明實錄附錄. Repr. Taipei: Zhongyang yanjiuyuan lishi yuyan yanjiusuo.

Cipolla, Carlo M. 1956/1967. *Money, Prices, and Civilization in the Mediterranean World: Fifth to Seventeenth Century.* Repr. New York: Gordian Press.

Dai Jin 戴金, ed. n.d./1994. *Huangming tiaofa shili leizuan* 皇明條法事類纂. Repr. *Zhongguo zhenxi falu dianji jicheng* 中國珍稀法律典籍集成, vols. 4–6. Beijing: Kexue chubanshe.

DaMing huidian 大明會典. 1587/2002. Repr. *Xuxiu siku quanshu*, vol. 792.

DaMing lu 大明律. n.d./1994. Repr. *Zhongguo zhenxi falu dianji jicheng* 中國珍稀法律典籍集成, series 2, 1: 278–394. Beijing: Kexue chubanshe.

Danjô Hiroshi 檀上寛. 1997. "Min hatsu no kaikin to chôkô: Minchô sensei shihai no rikai ni yosete 明初の海禁と朝貢—明朝專制支配の理解に寄せて." In *Min shin jidaishi no kihon mondai* 明清時代史の基本問題, edited by Mori Masao 森正夫 et al., 203–34. Tokyo: Kyûko shoin.

Ding Yi 丁易. 2011. *Mingdai tewu zhengzhi* 明代特務政治. Shanghai: Shanghai shudian.

Ding Bin 丁賓. 1611/2000. "Liudu qianfa dahuai shu 留都錢法大壞疏." In Ding Bin, 1638, *Ding Qinghuigong yiji* 丁惠清公遺集. Repr. *Siku jinhuishu congkan, jibu* 集部, vol. 44: 60–61.

Dong Qichang 董其昌, ed. c.1622/2002. *Shenmiao liuzhong zouzhu huiyao* 神廟留中奏疏彙要. Repr. *Xuxiu siku quanshu*, vols. 470, 471:1–260.

Dreyer, Edward L. 2007. *Zheng He: China and the Oceans in the Early Ming Dynasty, 1405–1433.* New York: Pearson Education.

Elliot, Mark. 2001. *The Manchu Way: The Eight Banners and Ethnic Identity in Late Imperial China.* Stanford: Stanford University Press.

Fairbank, John K., ed. 1968. *The Chinese World Order: Traditional China's Foreign Relations.* Cambridge: Harvard University Press.

Farmer, Edward L. 1976. *Early Ming Government: The Evolution of Dual Capitals.* Cambridge: Harvard University Press.

Fisher, Irving. 1962. *The Purchasing Power of Money: Its Determination and Relation to Credit Interest and Crises.* New York: Macmillan.

Fu Yiling 傅衣凌. 1980/1982. "Mingdai qianqi Huizhou tudi maimai qiyue zhong de tonghuo 明代前期徽州土地買賣契約中的通貨." Repr. *MingQing shehui jingji shi lunwen ji* 明清社會經濟史論文集, ed. Fu Yiling 傅衣凌, 241–51. Beijing: Renmin chubanshe.

Fujii Hiroshi 藤井宏. 1943. "Mingdai no toguchi shoshiohô ni tsuitnie 明代の戸口食鹽法に就いて." *Shakai keizai shigakkai* 社會經濟史學 13, no. 3: 213–42.

Gao Congming 高聰明. 2000. *Songdai huobi yu huobi liutong yanjiu* 宋代貨幣與貨幣流通研究. Baoding: Hebei daxue chubanshe.

Ge Zhenjia 葛振家. 2002. *Cuipu "Piaohai lu" pingzhu* 崔溥《漂海錄》評注. Beijing: Xianzhuang shuju.

Goetzmann, William N., and Elisabeth Koll. 2005. "Paying in Paper: A Government Voucher from the Southern Song." In *The Origins of Value*, edited by William N. Goetzmann and K. Geert Rouwenhorst, 91–103.

Goetzmann, William N., and K. Geert Rouwenhorst, ed. 2005. *The Origins of Value: The Financial Innovations That Created Modern Capital Markets*. New York: Oxford University Press.

Goodrich, L. Carrington, and Chaoying Fang, ed. 1976. *Dictionary of Ming Biography 1368–1644*. New York: Columbia University Press.

Goossaert, Vincent. 2007. *The Taoist of Peking, 1800–1949: A Social History of Urban Clerics*. Cambridge: Harvard University Asia Center.

Gu Qiyuan 顧起元. 1618/1987. *Kezuo zhuiyu* 客座贅語. Repr. Beijing: Zhonghua shuju.

Gujin tushu jicheng 古今圖書集成. 1726/1934. Repr. Shanghai: Zhonghua shuju.

Hamaguchi Fukuju 濱口福壽. 1972. "Ryûkei-Banreki no sempô no shin tenkai 隆慶萬曆期の錢法の新展開." *Tôyôshi kenkyû* 東洋史研究 31, no. 3: 381–400.

Han Dacheng 韓大成. 1991. *Mingdai chengshi yanjiu* 明代城市研究. Beijing: Zhongguo renmei daxue chubanshe.

Hongwu jingcheng tuzhi 洪武京城圖志. 1395/2006. Repr. Nanjing: Nanjing chubanshe.

Horii Kazuo 堀井一雄. 1940. "Kinkagin no senkai 金花銀の展開." *Tōyō shi kenkyō* 東洋史研究 5, no. 2: 128–40.

Hoshi Ayao 星斌夫. 1978. "Kinkajin kô 金花銀考." *Yamagata daigaku kiyô (Jinbun kagaku)* 山形大學紀要(人文科學) 9, no. 1: 123–55.

Hu Hansheng 胡漢生. 2018. *Ming shisan ling* 明十三陵. Beijing: Beijing chubanshe.

Hu Wokun 胡我琨. 1778/1986. *Qiantong* 錢通. Repr. *Qinding siku quanshu*, vol. 662: 365–816.

Huang Aming 黃阿明. 2011. "Wanli sanshijiu nian liudu zhuqian shijian ji liangjing yingdui 萬曆三十九年留都鑄錢事件與兩京應對." *Suzhou keji xueyuan xuebao (shehui kexue ban)* 蘇州科技學院學報（社會科學版）44, no. 5: 59–66.

HuangMing liutai zouyi 皇明留臺奏議. 1605/1996. In *Siku quanshu cunmu congshu*, 74: 455–767; 75: 1–157.

Huang, Ray. 1974. *Taxation and Government Finance in Sixteenth-Century Ming China*. Cambridge: Cambridge University Press.

Huang, Ray. 1981. *1587, A Year of No Significance: The Ming Dynasty in Decline*. New Haven: Yale University Press.

Huang, Ray. 1986. "The History of the Ming Dynasty and Today's World." *Chinese Studies in History* 19, no. 4: 3–36.

Huang, Shiu-Lan (Jully) Huang, and Wei-Chao Chang. 2016. *Along the River during the Qingming Festival*. Taipei: Cosmos Classics.

Hucker, Charles O. 1961. *The Traditional Chinese State in Ming Times (1368–1644)*. Tucson: University of Arizona Press.

Hucker, Charles O. 1985/1988. *A Dictionary of Official Titles in Imperial China*. Repr. Taipei: Southern Materials Center.

Katô Shigeru 加藤繁. 1965. *Tô Sô jidai ni okeru kingin no kenkyû* 唐宋時代に於ける金銀の研究. Tokyo: Tôyô bunko.

Kikuo Taniguchi 谷口規矩雄. 1993. "Minmatsu no Kinkajin nitsuite 明末の金花銀について." In *Chûgoku gendai no hô to shakai* 中国近世の法制と社会, edited by Kaoru Umehara 梅原郁, 485–510. Kyoto: Institute for Research in Humanities, Kyoto University.

Levathes, Louise. 1994. *When China Ruled the Seas: The Treasure Fleet of the Dragon Throne 1405–1433*. New York: Simon & Schuster.

Li, Chiao-ping. 1980. *Tien-kung-kai-wu: Exploitation of the Work of Nature: Chinese Agriculture and Technology in the XVII Century*. Taipei: China Academy.

Li Longqian 李龍潛. 2002. *MingQing jingji tanwei chubian* 明清經濟探微初編. Taipei: Daoxiang chubanshe.

Li Qingxin 李慶新. 2007. *Mingdai haiwai maoyi zhidu* 明代海外貿易制度. Beijing: Shehui kexue wenxian chubanshe.

Li Xun 李洵. 1982. *Mingshi shihuozhi jiaozhu* 明史食貨志校注. Beijing: Zhonghua shuju.

Li Yuanlong 李元龍. 1998. *Tiantan* 天壇. Beijing: Chaohua chubanshe.

Li Yunhu 李雲鵠. 1606/1996. "Yi ge xuanqian jian qianlu shu 議革錢爐疏萬曆." In *HuangMing liutai zouyi*. Repr. *Siku quanshu cunmu congshu, shibu* 史部 74: 610.

Liang Cai 梁材. *c.*1539/1962. "Yikan Guanglusi qianliang shu 議勘光祿寺錢糧疏." In Chen Zilong, ed. *Ming jinshi wenbian*. 909–15.

Liang, Fangzhong (Liang, Fang-chung). 1956. *The Single-Whip Method of Taxation in China*. Cambridge: Harvard East Asian Monographs.

Liang Fangzhong 梁方仲. 1939/2008. "Yunnan Yinkuang zhi shi de kaocha 雲南銀礦之史的考察." In Liang Fangzhong 梁方仲. *MingQing fushui yu shehui jingji*. 463–71.

Liang Fangzhong 梁方仲. 1957/2008. *Mingdai liangzhang zhidu* 明代糧長制度. Repr. Beijing: Zhonghua shuju.

Liang Fangzhong 梁方仲. 2008. *MingQing fushui yu shehui jingji* 明清賦稅與社會經濟. Beijing: Zhonghua shuju.

Liu Rouyu 劉若愚. nd/2000. *Zhuozhong zhi* 酌中志. Repr. *Siku jinhuishu congkan, shibu* 史部, vol. 71: 39–300.

Liu Yichen 劉怡辰. 2020. "Zhengtong yuannian (1436) zheyin ling chutai shimo zaitan 正統元年 (1436) 折銀令出臺始末再探." *Zhongguo shehui jingji shi yanjiu* 中國社會經濟史研究 5: 25–32.

Liu Zhiwei 劉志偉. 1997. *Zai guojia yu shehui zhijian: MingQing Guangdong lijia fuyi zhidu yanjiu* 在國家與社會之間：明清廣東里甲賦役制度研究. Guangzhou: Zhongshan daxue chubanshe.

Mancall, Mark. 1968. "The Ch'ing Tribute System: An Interpretive Essay." In John K. Fairbank, ed. *The Chinese World Order*. 63–89.

Matsubara, Kentaro. 2017. "Credit Institutions and the Land Market in the New Territories of Hong Kong: Local Social Structuring and Colonization." In *Colonial Administration and Land Reform in East Asia*, edited by Sui-Wai Cheung, 103–14. London: Routledge.

Meng Sen 孟森. 2002. *Mingshi jianyi* 明史講義. Shanghai: Shanghai guji chubanshe.

MingQing shiliao. 明清史料. 1930. Nanjing: Guoli zhongyang yanjiuyuan lishi yuyan yanjiu suo.

Mingshi 明史. 1739/1974. Repr. Beijing: Zhonghua shuju.

Ming shilu 明實錄. n.d./1962. Repr. Taipei: Academia Sinica.

Mitchell-Innes, Alfred. 1913/2004. "What Is Money?" Repr. Wary, ed. *Credit and State Theories of Money, 14–49.*

Mitchell-Innes, Alfred. 1913–14/2004. "The Credit Theory of Money." Repr. Wary, ed. *Credit and State Theories of Money, 50–78.*

Mote, Frederick W. 1977. "The Transformation of Nanking, 1350–1400." In *The City in Late Imperial China*, edited by G. William Skinner, 101–53. Taipei: Southern Materials Center.

Mote, Frederick W. 1977. "Yuan and Ming." In *Food in Chinese Culture: Anthropology and Historical Perspectives*, edited by Kwang-chih Chang, 193–257. New Haven: Yale University Press.

Mote, Frederick W., and Denis Twitchett, ed. 1998. *The Cambridge History of China,* vol. 7: *The Ming Dynasty, 1368–1644, Part 1.* New York: Cambridge University Press.

Peng Xinwei 彭信威. 1958/1988. *Zhongguo huobishi* 中國貨幣史. Repr. Shanghai: Shanghai renmin chubanshe.

Polanyi, Karl. 2001. *The Great Transformation: The Political and Economic Origins of Our Time.* Boston: Beacon Press.

Ptak, Roderich. 1991/1998. "China and Portugal at Sea: The Early Ming Trading System and the *Estado da India* Compared." In his *China and the Asian Seas: Trade, Travel, and Visions of the Other* (*1400–1700*), 21–38. Aldershot; Brookfield, Vt.: Ashgate.

Puk, Wing-kin. 2016. *The Rise and Fall of a Public Debt Market in 16th-Century China: The Story of the Ming Salt Certificate*. Leiden: Brill.

Qinding Siku quanshu 欽定四庫全書. 1787/1986. Repr. Taipei: Taiwan shangwu yinshuguan.

Qinding xu wenxian tongkao 欽定續文獻通考. 1784/1986. Repr. Qinding siku quanshu 欽定四庫全書, vols. 626–31.

Qiu Jun 丘濬. 1506. *Daxue yanyi bu* 大學衍義補.

Qiu Yongzhi 邱永志. 2017. "Zhanzheng, shichang yu guojia: Zhengtong Jingtai zhi ji tonghuo liutong tizhi de bianqian 戰爭、市場與國家：正統景泰之際通貨流通體制的變遷." *Zhongguo jingjishi yanjiu* 中國經濟史研究 6: 30–41.

Qiu Zhonglin 邱仲麟. 2004. "Huangdi de canzhuo: Mingdai de gongshan zhidu ji qi xiangguan wenti 皇帝的餐桌: 明代的宮膳制度及其相關問題." *Taida lishixi xuebao* 臺大歷史系學報 34: 1–42.

Sakuma Shigeo 佐久間重男. 1943. "Mingdai no shôzei seido 明代の商税制度." Shakai keizai shigakkai 社會經濟史學 13, no. 3: 243–72.

Sargent, Thomas J., and François R. Velde. 2001. *The Big Problem of Small Change.* Princeton: Princeton University Press.

Sen, Tansen. 2016. "The Impact of Zheng He's Expeditions on Indian Ocean Interactions." *Bulletin of SOAS* 79, no. 3: 609–36.

Shen Defu 沈德符. 1606/1959. *Wanli yehuo bian* 萬曆野獲編. Repr. Beijing: Zhonghua shuju.

Siku jinhuishu congkan 四庫禁燬書叢刊. 2000. Repr. Beijing: Beijing chubanshe.

Siku quanshu cunmu congshu 四庫全書存目叢書. 1996. Ji'nan: Qilu shushe.

Sima Qian 司馬遷. 104 BCE/1963. *Shiji* 史記. Repr. Beijing: Zhonghua shuju.

Skinner, G. William. 1985. "Presidential Address: The Structure of Chinese History." *Journal of Asian Studies* 44, no. 2: 271–92.

Su Xinhong 蘇新紅. 2015. "Mingdai Neiku de huangshi caizheng zhuangshuhua yanbian 明代內庫的皇室財政專屬化演變." *Mingdai yanjiu* 明代研究 24: 35–71.

Sun Chengze 孫承澤. 1881. *Guxiang zhai jianshang xjiuzhen Chunming mengyu lu* 古香齋鑒賞袖珍春明夢餘錄.

Tan Lun 譚綸. 1569/1962. "Lun licai shu 論理財疏." In *Ming jingshi wenbian*, edited by Chen Zilong. Repr. Beijing: Zhonghua shuju.

Tan Qian 談遷. 1636/2006. *Zaolin zazu* 棗林雜俎. Repr. Beijing: Zhonghua shuju.

The Travels of Marco Polo. 1986. Edited and with an introduction by Milton Rugoff. New York: New American Library.

Tsai, Shih-shan Henry. 1996. *The Eunuchs in the Ming Dynasty*. Albany: State University of New York.

von Glahn, Richard. 1996. *Fountain of Fortune: Money and Monetary Policy in China, 1000–1700*. Berkeley: University of California Press.

von Glahn, Richard. 2005. "The Origins of Paper Money." In *The Origins of Value*, edited by William N. Goetzmann and K. Geert Rouwenhorst, 65–89.

Wang Chunyu 王春瑜 and Du Wanyan 杜婉言. 2016. *Mingchao Huan'guan* 明朝宦官, Beijing: Shangwu yinshuguan.

Wang Liqi 王利器. 1992. *Yantie lun jiaozhu* 鹽鐵論校注. Beijing: Zhonghua shuju.

Wang Shu 王恕. 1491/1986. *Wangduanyi zouyi* 王端毅奏議. Repr. *Qinding Siku quanshu*, vol. 427: 453–704.

Wang Wencheng 王文成. 2011. *Songdai baiyin huobihua yanjiu* 宋代白銀貨幣化研究. Kunming: Yunnan daxue chubanshe.

Wang, Yi'e. 2004. *Daoism in China*. Translated by Zeng Chuanhui. Beijing: Wuzhou chuanbo chubanshe.

Wanli kuaiji lu 萬曆會計錄. 1581/2002. Repr. Xuxiu siku quanshu, vols. 831–33.

Wong, R. Bin. 2012. "Taxation and Good Governance in China, 1500–1914." In *The Rise of Fiscal States: A Global History, 1500–1914*, edited by Bartolomé Yun-Casalilla et al., 353–77. Cambridge: Cambridge University Press.

Wray, L. Randall, ed. 2004. *Credit and State Theories of Money: The Contributions of A. Mitchell Innes*. Cheltenham, UK: Edward Elgar.

Wu Han. 吳晗. 1965/2000. *Zhu Yuanzhang zhuan* 朱元璋傳. Repr. Tianjin: Baihua wenyi chubanshe.

Wu Han. 吳晗. 1936/1986. "Shiliu shiji qian zhi Zhongguo yu Nanyang 十六世紀前之中國與南洋." In Wu Han. *Wu Han Shixue lunzhu xuanji*, vol. 1: 604–45.

Wu Han. 吳晗. 1986. *Wu Han shixue lunzhu xuanji* 吳晗史學論著選集. Beijing: Renmin chubanshe.

Xu Daling 許大齡. 1959. "Mingdai Beijing de jingji shenghuo 明代北京的經濟生活." *Beijing daxue xuebao* 北京大學學報 4: 41–63.

Xu Jie 徐階. 1564/1997. "Qing tingzhi Baoyuanju zhuqian 請停止寶源局鑄錢." In *Shijing tangji* 世經堂集. *Siku quanshu cunmu congshu, jibu*, 79: 401–2.

Xu Wenji 徐文繼, and Chen Shilong 陳時龍. 2005. *Zhengshuo Mingchao shiliu di* 正說明朝十六帝. Beijing: Zhonghua shuju.

Xu Xueju 徐學敘. 1601/1993. *Guochao dianhui* 國朝典彙. Repr. Beijing: Beijing daxue chubanshe.

Xuxiu siku quanshu 續修四庫全書. 2002. Repr. Shanghai: Shanghai guji chubanshe.

Yang, Bin. 2019. *Cowrie Shells and Cowrie Money: A Global History*. London: Routledge.

Yang Qiqiao 楊啟樵. 2004. *MingQing huangshi yu fangshu* 明清皇室與方術. Shanghai: Shanghai shudian chubanshe.

Yao Shilin 姚士麟. n.d./1936. *Jianzhi bian* 見只編. Repr. Shanghai: Shangwu yinshugua.

Ye Xianggao 葉向高. n.d./2000. *Qu bian* 蘧編. In *Zhongguo yeshi jicheng xubian* 中國野史集成續編, 20: 587–725. Repr. Chengdu: Bashu shushe.

Ye Xianggao 葉向高. n.d./2000. *Cangxia xucao* 蒼霞續草. Repr. *Siku jinhuishu congkan, jibu* 集部, vol. 124: 587–700; 125:1–363.

Yang, Lien-sheng. 1952. *Money and Credit in China, a Short History.* Cambridge: Harvard University Press.

Young, Jason. 2013. *China's Hukou System: Markets, Migrants and Institutional Change.* London: Palgrave Macmillan.

Yu Zhijia 于志嘉. 1987. *Mingdai junhu shixi zhidu* 明代軍戶世襲制度. Taipei: Xuesheng shuju.

Yu Zhijia 于志嘉. 1993. "Mingdai liangjing jiandu yu weisuo junhu qianxi zhi guanxi 明代兩京建都與衛所軍戶遷徙之關係." *Zhongyang yanjiuyuan lishi yuyan yanjiusuo jikan* 中央研究院歷史語言研究所集刊 64, no. 1: 135–74.

Zhang Juzheng 張居正. 1577/1997. "Da Minfu Pang Xing'an 答閩撫龐惺庵." In *Zhang Juzheng ji* 張居正集, edited by Zhang Shunhui 張舜徽, 2: 701–2. Repr. Wuhan: Hubei renmin chubanshe.

Zhang Weihua 張維華. 1955. *Mingdai haiwai maoyi jianlun* 明代海外貿易簡論. Shanghai: Xuexi shenghuo chubanshe.

Zhao Lingyang 趙令揚. 1975. "Lun Mingdai zhi huanhuo 論明代的宦禍." In his *Mingshi lunji* 明史論集, 1–34. Hong Kong: Shixue yanjiu hui.

Zhao Shiqing 趙世卿, ed. *c.* 1602/2002. "Guokui minqiong xiuju qianfa yi kai caiyuan yi kuang minli shu 國匱民窮修舉錢法以開財源疏."In Wu Liang 吳亮, 1609. *Wanli shuchao* 萬曆疏鈔. Repr. *Xuxiu siku quanshu*, vols. 468–9.

Zhu Pengshou 朱彭壽. 1982. *Anle kangpingshi suibi* 安樂康平室隨筆. Beijing: Zhonghua shuju.

Zhu Xie 朱楔. 1956. *Zheng He* 鄭和. Beijing: Sanlian shujian.

Glossary

Anding 安定
Annam 安南
Ba (County) 巴
baochao 寶鈔
baochuan 寶船
Baoquan 寶泉
Baoyuan 寶源
Bei'an 北安
Beijing 北京
Beiping 北平
Bingzi 丙字
Bo 柏
Cai Yuji 蔡愈濟
Changmen 閶門
Changzhou 常州
chanshi 禪師
Chaoyang 朝陽
chaoguan 鈔關
Chaozhou 潮州
Chen Rui 陳瑞
Chen Ying 陳瑛
Chen Youliang 陳友諒
Chen Yuting 陳于廷
Chen Zuyi 陳祖義
Chenghua 成化
Chengtian 承天
Chengyun 承運
Chengzu 成祖
chi 尺
Choe Bu 崔溥
Chongwen 崇文
Chongyang 重陽
Chongzhen 崇禎
Chuzhou 處州
Da Ming 大明
Dadu 大都
Daizong 代宗

dan 擔
Daoyan 道衍
Datong 大同
Daxing 大興
Dayue Taihe shan 大岳太和山
Desheng 德勝
Ding Bin 丁賓
Dingzhou 汀州
Dingzi 丁字
Dong'an 東安
Dongbian 東便
Dongzhi 東直
Dongjiang mixiang 東江米巷
Dongjiao minxiang 東交民巷
Du Wenbin 杜文彬
Duanwu 端午
ducheng 都城
fang 坊
fengshui 風水
Fengtian dian 奉天殿
Fengyang 鳳陽
Fu Zonggao 傅宗皋
Fujian 福建
Gan Weilin 甘為霖
Gao Gong 高拱
Gao Wenjian 高文薦
Ge Shouli 葛守禮
Gobi 戈壁
Gu Qiyuan 顧起元
guan jiaozi 官交子
Guangdong 廣東
Guangxi 廣西
Guangzhou 廣州
Guangzong 光宗
guan 貫
Guo Tingwu 郭廷梧
Guo Yunhou 郭允厚
Guo 郭
Han Dechun 韓得春
Han Lin'er 韓林兒

Han Wen 韓文
Hanlin 翰林
Hangzhou 杭州
Han 漢
He Tong 何通
Henan 河南
Hengzhou 衡州
Hexiwu 河西務
Hong Taiji 皇太極
Hongwu *tongbao* 洪武通寶
Hongwu 洪武
Hongxi 洪熙
Hongzhi 弘治
Hu Weiyong 胡惟庸
Huagai dian 華蓋殿
Huai'an 淮安
Huai'rou 懷柔
Huai 淮
Huan Kuan 桓寬
huangcheng 皇城
Huangji 皇極
Huguang 湖廣
Huidi 惠帝
Huihui 回回
Huitong 會通
Huizhou 徽州
Hushu 湖墅
Ji'ning 濟寧
Jiajing 嘉靖
Jiang Xing 姜性
Jiangnan 江南
Jiangning 江寧
Jiangxi 江西
Jiang 蔣
Jianji 建極
Jianwen 建文
Jianyin 賤銀
jian 賤
Jiaotai dian 交泰殿
jiaozi 交子

Jiazi 甲字
jia 甲
Jiliao 薊遼
Jin Xueyan 靳學顏
Jingdi 景帝
Jingtai 景泰
Jingwu 金吾
Jingzhou 荊州
Jinhua yin 金花銀
Jinshazhou 金沙洲
Jinshen dian 謹身殿
jin (*catty*) 斤
Jin (dynasty) 金
jin (silk brocade) 錦
Jiqing *lu* 集慶路
Jiujiang 九江
Jizhou 薊州
Ji 紀
juan 絹
Kaifeng 開封
Kong Yi 孔顗
Kuang Ye 鄺埜
Kublai 忽必烈
Kunluqunxieti 坤祿羣謝提
Kunning gong 坤寧宮
Kuo (County) 漷
Laba 臘八
lama 喇嘛
Leizhou 雷州
Li Ruhua 李汝華
Li Yunhu 李元鵠
Li Zicheng 李自成
liangzhang 糧長
liang 兩
Liaodong 遼東
lijia 里甲
Lin Feng 林鳳
Linqing 臨清
Liu Jin 劉瑾
Liu Yuanlin 劉元霖

Liuqiu 琉球
li 里
Long Shou 龍綬
Longjiang 龍江
Longqing 隆慶
Lu Changeng 陸長庚
Lu'an 潞安
Lun licai shu 論理財疏
Ma Ang 馬昂
Ma Sanbao 馬三寶
mentan 門攤
Mingzhou 明州
Ming 明
min 民
Muzong 穆宗
mu 畝
Naiyingbimeiya 奈英必美亞
Nanchang 南昌
Nanjing 南京
Nei'ge 內閣
Neishutang 內書堂
Ningbo 寧波
Nurhaci 努爾哈赤
Pan Jixun 潘季馴
Pang Shangpeng 龐尚鵬
Pingyang 平陽
Pucheng 浦城
Qianqing gong 乾清宮
qian 錢
Qin'an dian 欽安殿
Qingming shanghe tu 清明上河圖
qing 頃
Qinhuai 秦淮
Qin 秦
Qiu Jun 丘濬
Qi 齊
Quanzhou 泉州
quan 泉
Renzong 仁宗
Sanhe 三河

Sarhu 薩爾滸
Shaanxi 陝西
Shandong 山東
Shang Lu 商輅
Shang Yang 商鞅
Shangxin 上新
Shangyuan 上元
Shanhai 山海
Shaoxing 紹興
Shen Defu 沈德符
Shenzong 神宗
Shi Jinqing 施進卿
Shi Lianyue 史蓮岳
Shibo si 市舶司
Shifochang 石佛場
Shizong 世宗
shi 石
Shuntian 順天
shuzui 贖罪
Siam 暹羅
Sichuan 四川
Sima Qian 司馬遷
Siyao 司鑰
Sizong 思宗
Song Yingxing 宋應星
Songjiang 松江
Taicang 太倉
Taichang 泰昌
Taijian 太監
Taiyuan 太原
Taizhou 台州
Taizong 太宗
Taizu 太祖
Tan Lun 譚綸
Tang He 湯和
Tang Yi 唐裔
Tiangong kaiwu 天工開物
Tianjin 天津
Tianqi 天啟
Tianshun 天順

Tongzhou 通州
Tumu 土木
Wan Xiangchun 萬象春
Wang Fu 王復
Wang Wanzuo 王萬祚
Wang Yuan 王原
Wang Zhi 汪直
Wang Zuo 王佐
Wang 王
Wanli 萬曆
Wanping 宛平
Wansui 萬歲
Wan 萬
Wei Zhongxian 魏忠賢
wenqi 文綺
Wenzhou 溫州
wen 文
Wu Shanyan 吳善言
Wuchang 武昌
Wudang 武當
Wudi 武帝
Wuhu 蕪湖
Wuzi 戊字
Wuzong 武宗
Wu 吳
Xia Yuanji 夏原吉
xiafan guanjun 下番官軍
Xianling 顯靈
Xianzong 憲宗
Xiaozong 孝宗
Xibian 西便
Xing 興
Xin 信
Xizhi 西直
Xizong 熹宗
Xu Jie 徐階
Xu Shouhui 徐壽輝
Xuande 宣德
Xuanfu 宣府
Xuanwu 玄武

Xuanzong 宣宗
Xue Fengxiang 薛鳳翔
Xuzhou 徐州
Yan Mingtai 閻鳴泰
Yang Jiaxiang 楊家相
Yang Shen 楊慎
Yangzhou 揚州
yang 陽
Yantie lun 鹽鐵論
Yanzhou 嚴州
Yan 燕
Ye Qi 葉淇
Ye Xianggao 葉向高
Yin Song 尹崧
Ying Zheng 嬴政
Yingtian 應天
Yingzong 英宗
yin (silver) 銀
yin 陰
Yizhou 益州
Yizi 乙字
Yongding 永定
Yongle 永樂
You'an 右安
Yuan 元
Yunnan 雲南
Zeng Bingzheng 曾秉正
Zhang Juzheng 張居正
Zhang Mao 張懋
Zhang Shicheng 張士誠
Zhang Wen 張文
Zhang Xiang 張祥
Zhang Xueyan 張學顏
Zhang Zeduan 張擇端
zhang 丈
Zhaodi 昭帝
Zhejiang 浙江
Zheng He 鄭和
Zhengde 正德
Zhengtong 正統

Zhengyang 正陽
Zhenjiang 鎮江
Zhenla 真臘
Zhenshan 鎮山
Zhenwu 真武
Zhili 直隸
Zhongji 中極
Zhongyuan 中元
Zhou Hongmo 周洪謨
Zhou Liangyin 周良寅
Zhou Side 周思德
Zhou Yongchun 周永春
Zhou Zhen 周珍
Zhu Biao 朱標
Zhu Changluo 朱常洛
Zhu Daoshan 朱道山
Zhu Di 朱棣
Zhu Gaochi 朱高熾
Zhu Houcong 朱厚熜
Zhu Houzhao 朱厚照
Zhu Jianshen 朱見深
Zhu Qiyu 朱祁鈺
Zhu Qizhen 朱祁鎮
Zhu Yijun 朱翊鈞
Zhu Youjian 朱由檢
Zhu Youtang 朱佑樘
Zhu Youxiao 朱由校
Zhu Youyuan 朱祐杬
Zhu Yuanzhang 朱元璋
Zhu Yunwen 朱允炆
Zhu Zaihou 朱載垕
Zhu Zhanji 朱瞻基
zhu 銖
Zou Wensheng 鄒文盛
Zuo'an 左安

Index

www.ingramcontent.com/pod-product-compliance
Lightning Source LLC
Chambersburg PA
CBHW071322230926
51849CB00002B/289
9789004687523